Understanding
Muslim Political Life
in America

In the series *Religious Engagement in Democratic Politics*, edited by Paul A. Djupe

Understanding Muslim Political Life in America

Contested Citizenship in the Twenty-First Century

EDITED BY BRIAN R. CALFANO AND
NAZITA LAJEVARDI

TEMPLE UNIVERSITY PRESS
Philadelphia • *Rome* • *Tokyo*

TEMPLE UNIVERSITY PRESS
Philadelphia, Pennsylvania 19122
tupress.temple.edu

Library of Congress Cataloging-in-Publication Data

Names: Calfano, Brian Robert, 1977– editor. | Lajevardi, Nazita, editor.
Title: Understanding Muslim political life in America : contested citizenship
 in the twenty-first century / edited by Brian R. Calfano and Nazita Lajevardi.
Description: Philadelphia : Temple University Press, 2019. | Series: Religious
 engagement in democratic politics | Includes bibliographical references and index.
Identifiers: LCCN 2018043421 (print) | LCCN 2018043874 (ebook) |
 ISBN 9781439917381 (E-book) | ISBN 9781439917367 (cloth) |
 ISBN 9781439917374 (pbk.)
Subjects: LCSH: Muslims—Political aspects—United States. | Muslims—United States—
 Social conditions—21st century. | Muslims—United States—Ethnic identity. | Islam—
 United States. | United States—Ethnic relations—21st century.
Classification: LCC E184.M88 (ebook) | LCC E184.M88 U53 2019 (print) |
 DDC 323.3/82970973—dc23
LC record available at https://lccn.loc.gov/2018043421

Contents

    and Intergroup Trust • *Brian R. Calfano, Oguzhan (Oz) Dincer,*
    Danielle M. McLaughlin, and Yusuf Sarfati   132

9 Performance Politics: Negotiating Muslim and American
    Identities • *Brian R. Calfano, Valerie Martinez-Ebers,*
    Tony E. Carey Jr., and Alejandro J. Beutel   154

10 Gauging Political Tolerance through a List Experiment: Findings
    from a Survey of Muslim Americans • *Youssef Chouhoud*   182

11 Best Practices for Gathering Public Opinion Data among
    Muslim Americans • *Matt A. Barreto and Karam Dana*   202

12 Conclusions and New Directions for the Study of
    American Muslims • *Brian R. Calfano and Nazita Lajevardi*   215

    Contributors   227

    Index   231

Figures and Tables

Figures

Tables

Preface and Acknowledgments

This book offers an update to and reappraisal of what we know about Muslims in American political life and what we have yet to learn. Contributors to this volume first came together at two meetings of the Muslim Americans Workshop. With support from the National Science Foundation, we brought together scholars from across the country and held two conferences, in December 2016 at Menlo College and in December 2017 at the University of California, Los Angeles. Participants discussed the state of political science scholarship on Muslim American political attitudes and behavior and explored how we might work together to generate and share more such scholarly work. In this book, contributors highlight topical areas of theoretical interest regarding Muslim identity, ethnic and racial diversity, relations with law enforcement, political attitudes and participation, and even reactions to commonly used survey measures of Muslim Americans. The chapters are inherently linked and even speak to future directions of research in Muslim American scholarship. The answers that these researchers provide to open questions of interest are the result of various elaborate research projects, academic exchanges, and meetings over the last two years that involved the contributors and others. The editors thank the contributors, Melissa Michelson, Matt Barreto, Gary Segura, Menlo College, and the University of California, Los Angeles, for providing the resources and opportunities for this collaborative project.

Understanding
Muslim Political Life
in America

Introduction

BRIAN R. CALFANO AND
NAZITA LAJEVARDI

M uslim Americans are at a political crossroads. On the one hand, many Muslims possess the economic and educational resources to realize the American dream. And, importantly, there is evidence that Muslims are coalescing into a voting bloc of consequence in some areas of the country where they constitute significant portions of the population (see Martin 2009). On the other hand, social and political pressures might keep the dream out of reach for American Muslims, particularly if anti-Muslim policies, attitudes, and rhetoric continue to gain momentum. Since the attacks on September 11, 2001, American politics has treated Muslims as singular. But is this appropriate? Do the social, political, economic, and gendered realities of Muslim life in America effectively sustain a pan-ethnic identity in the post-9/11 era, or do differences manifest despite the scrutiny directed at Muslims in contemporary America? To answer these questions, we need a social science of Muslims that recognizes their quotidian integration into American public life, just like other Americans. In developing this new area of research, we may also generate and test core social science theories in the context of this critical group. Our volume provides advancements on both fronts.

Both before and after the terrorist attacks of 9/11, Muslims have been routinely the subjects of numerous scholarly assessments intended to bring clarity to the social, religious, and political dynamics that this diverse religious community faces. In some cases, scholars have succeeded in fitting pieces of the empirical puzzles surrounding American Muslims together. In many other cases, however, initial analytical attempts have left interested observers uninterested; with many academic gatekeepers questioning the relevance of the American Muslim public in American politics. Yet it is apparent to any passive observer of American politics that Muslims are central. The time is therefore ripe for scholarship that unpacks the political experiences of American Muslims in the twenty-first century.

In fact, the trends that we assess in this volume have been years in the making. Muslim Americans have become increasingly "racialized" since 9/11, with external markers of dress, skin color, accent, and language functioning as heuristics for a religion constructed as a threat to American culture and national security (Jamal 2009; Selod 2015). This racialization process, however, did not develop in a vacuum. Considerable evidence demonstrates that Muslims have historically been linked to stereotypes of violence, intolerance, and extremism (Esposito 1999; Khan and Ecklund 2013; Said 1979; Shaheen 2003), and that the 9/11 attacks and subsequent events played an important role in shaping Americans' perceptions of Muslims (Dana et al. 2018).

Non-Muslims can fall into the trap of perceiving Muslims as a uniform collective or as part of a panethnic group. But this volume seeks to unpack the great deal of diversity in the socialization experiences of Muslim Americans (see Jackson 2005). Muslims in the United States vary in their national origin, languages spoken, religiosity, socioeconomic status, and partisanship. But these differences are accompanied by the reality that a subsuming Muslim identity in America has taken root, owing as much to the social identity pressures that Muslims deal with regularly as to the nature of Islamic teaching as a transcendent force (Haddad and Esposito 1998; Khan 1998). In fact, Muslims often appear unwilling to endorse differentiation along intrareligious and nationalistic lines, perhaps reflecting elements of a panethnic identity formation post-9/11 or reflecting the concept of *ummah*—the collective community of Muslims (see Project MAPS and Zogby International 2004; Barreto et al. 2007). This is not to say that subgroup identities are not important or recognized by Muslims, but aggregating up along the racialized lines as Amaney Jamal (2005b) recommends (i.e., focusing on South Asian, Arab, and African American Muslims) is a good idea. Finally, and in looking for links between Muslim religiosity and political behavior, Ba-Yunus and Kone (2004) remind us that, as with many Christians, there is variation (not uniformity) in Muslim religiosity (see also Barreto and Bozonelos 2009). Taking a cue from previous scholarship, our contributors focus on the inherent heterogeneities among the American Muslim population when exploring their political behavior.

The study of Muslims in American politics is often punctuated by events that continue to shape the public discourse and perceptions about the group.

The barbaric and well-publicized actions of ISIS militants in Syria and Iraq, isolated events such as the 2010 Fort Hood shooting, and the continued (and erroneous) perception articulated by some critics that U.S. Muslims have not gone on record often enough to denounce brutality waged in the name of their faith continually undermine how the public perceives Muslims. Events involving Muslims and Islam, which are often sensationalized by news media coverage, have offered scholars opportunities to produce studies on Muslim life in America that take several of these events as starting points for inquiry. But this kind of episodic approach to understanding Muslims has significant limitations. This may be due to the discipline's focus on advancing theoretically driven insights into phenomena rather than responding to each event in a more inductive manner.

While the episodic approach has served some scholars well, our reading of the extant social science literature on Muslim Americans is that it has reached a point where new insights into Muslim experiences can be achieved by coupling existing insights from the literature with new ideas for future empirical assessment through advances in research design, data collection, and the extension of existing questions and theories. In light of the period after 9/11 and especially now during the Trump presidency, it is especially crucial for scholars to think deeply about testing how existing social science theories pertain to Muslim Americans. How do they resemble other marginalized groups? Are their experiences distinct? Does their basis as a religious group allow conflict with their increasing racialization?

Our reading of the literature suggests several existing themes. The first is that Muslims in America are scrutinized by out-group non-Muslims because of their faith and the assumptions that many in government and the general public make about Islam and extremism. The second is that Muslims represent a diverse collection of ethnic, racial, national, and religious subgroups that have been packaged into a panethnic Muslim identity in the years since 9/11, in many instances, without their consent. Third, and most importantly, the literature contains a collection of findings about Muslim political beliefs and behavior that show them to hold a mix of political views, to both broach and shy away from political activity at various times, and to adopt many democratic norms, including tolerance of political and religious difference. But the literature has not yet congealed to predict with much certainty just how Muslims will behave as an identity group in American politics. While we have some insights from the literature discussed below, scholars are still in the beginning stages of identifying the types of questions they should ask about Muslims and the appropriate theoretical lenses to apply.

Our goal with this volume is to offer an update and reappraisal of what we know about Muslims in American political life and what we have yet to learn. In so doing, our contributors highlight topical areas of theoretical interest regarding Muslim identity, ethnic and racial diversity, relations with law enforcement, political attitudes and participation, and even reactions to commonly used survey measures of Muslim Americans. Of course, an understandable response might simply be to suggest that scholars get busy with extending their research agendas on American Muslims using similar methods used to study other marginalized groups. Another question, for instance, is whether U.S. Muslims are racialized. Some scholarship argues yes (see Dana et al. 2018; Lajevardi and Oskooii 2018; Jamal 2009; Selod 2015) and conducts its analysis through this lens; though more empirical evidence is required to test this claim. Yet part of the difficulty in conducting research on Muslim Americans is that it can be hard to collect data and isolate evidence of direct causality between outcomes and potential antecedents. The contributors then assess how the insights offered in their chapters fit into advancing the agenda of what is known (and what can be better understood) about Muslim Americans. The chapter topics represent a cross-section of the "state of the art" in quantitative research on American Muslims at present. In this way, the chapters serve as vignettes of what we know, do not know, and what we should learn to appropriately assess Muslim Americans and their political futures.

At the same time, and though not a book on analytical methods per se, we present diverse ideas and methodological approaches in research design as a way to illustrate how progress in studying Muslim Americans to this point might be extended. The good news is that we are not beginning from scratch with this effort. As we describe below, the Muslim American politics literature benefits from a decades-long tradition of scholarly inquiry—research that helped establish understanding basic questions surrounding Muslim experiences in the United States; particularly community building, identity, and gender-based experiences. But these studies are predominantly qualitative, which makes replication of their findings difficult. Pew (2007, 2011) and Gallup (2009, 2011) have released omnibus quantitative surveys of the U.S. Muslim population, but the observational data collected in those surveys are not suited for testing direct causal hypotheses. The same is true for the various studies conducted on behalf of the Council on American-Islamic Relations (2006; see also Bagby, Perl, and Froehle 2001). To be sure, these data can be used to advance avenues of inquiry not yet fully developed, which several chapters in this volume do. Importantly, some scholars have combined the use of randomized experiments in surveys of Muslim communities to gain leverage on casual mechanisms in large-N studies (see Djupe and Calfano 2013; Suhay, Calfano, and Dawe 2015; Calfano 2018), which can serve as a template for future research.

Contributors to this volume first came together at two Muslim American Workshops. With support from the National Science Foundation, we brought together scholars from across the country for two conferences in December 2016 and December 2017 to discuss the state of political science scholarship on Muslim American political attitudes and behavior, and how we might work together to generate and share more such scholarly work. Below and in the following chapters, we detail the scholarly gaps workshop participants identified and present their scholarship filling those gaps. The topics addressed are items that these scholars—many of whom have pioneered the study of Muslim American politics with some of the most persuasive empirical publications about Muslim Americans—identify as key starting points in honing the overall investigation of political puzzles relating to Muslim politics. Our aim is to link the methodologies, findings, and insights from the volume chapters to current realities of American politics, including some lingering thoughts about the effects from the Trump administration. We conclude with a set of suggestions on how to foster increased scholarly attention to overarching questions about this now perennially relevant group in American society.

Muslims and American Politics before and after 9/11

Understanding the current realities Muslims in America face means putting past experiences in the proper context. One of the most common misconceptions of Muslims in America is that their arrival to the nation is relatively recent. In reality, the origins of Muslim life in North America can be traced to the period before British settlers arrived in the early seventeenth century and to American slavery. It is, therefore, unsurprising that dozens of scholarly assessments of Muslims—including political realities confronting this group—stretch back decades, including well-received volumes from Yvonne Haddad (1991) and Jane Smith (1999). This work has done much to shape the literature on Muslim political experiences in America. In some ways, both Haddad and Smith presaged the dominant scholarly focus on topics regarding Islamic political thought, the role of Muslims in their local communities, the experiences of Muslims in different racial and gender subgroups (included and especially African American Muslims), Muslim perceptions of U.S. foreign policy in the Middle East, and the public's attitudes toward Muslim Americans. For its part, Smith's work provided a particular focus on struggles that Muslim women face in living out their identities in a culture that emphasizes materialism and individualism.

Other pre-2001 scholarship provided in-depth studies of Muslim history, perhaps best typified by Allan Austin's (1984) historical examination of

Muslim experiences in the Antebellum south and Yvonne Haddad and Adair Lummis's (1987) book detailing the localized community ecologies of Muslims throughout the United States. Meanwhile, Richard Wormser's (1994) focus on Muslim youth experiences and the community's racial and ethnic diversity (particularly as it pertains to African Americans and the Nation of Islam) is complemented by Aminah McCloud's (1995) work on African American Islam and, specifically, her contention that there is much greater diversity among "black Muslims" than typically assumed. Haddad and Smith (1994) explored the dynamics of developing an Islamic jurisprudence by American courts immigration trends, the effects of slavery and civil rights struggles, and Haddad and John Esposito (1997) offered a platform for scholars to advanced gendered interpretations of the Qur'an.[1]

Returning to the pre-9/11 literature on Muslims, the scholarship documents that many of the challenges Muslims face today—including government scrutiny and out-group-based discrimination—were present prior to the 9/11 attacks, though to a lesser extent. As noted earlier, a characteristic of these pre-9/11 academic works, however, is that they are primarily qualitative, which makes research replication more difficult. Importantly, some of the literature from this period could not agree on which group to study and instead focused on a wide range of identities, including Arab—and not Muslim—American mobility and discrimination. Articles by Nadine Naber (2000); Mona Faragallah, Walter Schumm, and Farrell Webb (1997); and Zeina Seikaly (2001) are but a few examples of influential works documenting Arab American identity, invisibility, discrimination, and inequality. Fu-

---

1. Concerning the Nation of Islam, we are conscious of the fact that many readers will have heard of the group and some of its leadership, including Louis Farrakhan. It bears mentioning, however, that while the group uses the term *Islam* in its name, the Nation of Islam does not practice an orthodox form of Islam. The main point of departure between the Nation of Islam and Islam as it is traditionally practiced is the Nation of Islam's belief that God incarnate was a man named W. F. Fard who brought a series of teachings to the Detroit area in the 1930s. The group also believes that Fard's protégée, Elijah Mohammad, was the Prophet. In assuming group leadership in 1934, Elijah Mohammad further articulated Nation of Islam beliefs, including that blacks are the master race and that a small percentage of people control the means of manipulating most of the human race in perpetuation of existing power structures (Lee 1996). The Nation of Islam may be best described as a culture of opposition established to counterbalance the substantial and negative effects of slavery and Jim Crow (Lipsitz 1988; Gardell 1996). Though the Nation of Islam has received substantial publicity at times and serves as a pathway to understanding perceptions and experiences of some African American Muslims in the United States, the group's teachings and political ideologies are substantially removed from the practices of most American Muslims. Thus, we do not spend considerable space in this volume on the group.

ture political science scholarship on Muslim Americans stands on the shoulders of these seminal pre-9/11 studies and must take into account that scholarship must incorporate a shifting panethnic identity.

Though not a book on Muslims and the Trump presidency, Trump's arrival on the political stage reminds us that this is the second time in two decades that major political forces have significantly affected Muslim life in America beyond what might be termed the baseline level of public suspicion or scrutiny of Muslims and Islam, which Jamal (2008) argues has existed in American politics for decades prior to 9/11. Before 9/11, Muslims were primarily identified by national origin and predominantly faced discrimination on this basis. Episodic events during this time were often connected to national-origin groups, and the conveyance of stereotypes was digested by the public as pertaining to specific national origin groups. For example, the Iranian hostage crisis during the Islamic Revolution of 1979 was related to Iranians in America, and the TWA hijacking in 1985 was related to Lebanese in America.

Following the 9/11 attacks and before the inflammatory rhetoric and policy implementation attempts from Trump and other Republicans, there was a pronounced spike in reported hate crimes against Muslims and Arabs that began in late 2001 and early 2002 (Human Rights Watch 2002). Before 9/11, only a few dozen anti-Muslim hate crimes per year were reported. The number reached five hundred by the end of 2001 and then stabilized in ensuing years, although an increase in incidents was detected after Trump's election in 2016 (see Ingraham 2015; Pitter 2017; South Asian American Leaders of Tomorrow 2001). Regardless of trend fluctuations in given years, it is clear that the post-9/11 period includes a generally higher level of public scrutiny directed at Muslim Americans (Cainkar 2007). And, as Jamal (2008) notes, maltreatment of Muslims (measured in reported hate crime incidents) increased exponentially from previous levels prior to 9/11.

There was a mix of positive and negative trends about the treatment of Muslims in the years after 9/11. On the one hand, through two audit studies on state legislators, Nazita Lajevardi (2018) finds that Muslim American individuals and their leaders are less able to access politics—either through an internship or through a legislative visit—compared to their white and Christian counterparts. On the other hand, Shane Martin (2009) finds evidence of legislator responsiveness to Muslims in their congressional districts and high-minded rhetoric from President George W. Bush in support of the Muslim community. These constructive government initiatives may have been encouraged by determination from American Muslims not to go into hiding following 9/11 but, instead, to work to ensure their civil liberties, while cooperating with law enforcement where appropriate (see Bakalian

and Bozorgmehr 2009). Despite their attempts to cooperate with law enforcement, there was still a great deal of evidence that the federal government was complicit in violating Muslim civil liberties in the months and
years following 9/11 (see Iftikhar 2007). For example, congressional officials
like Representative Peter King of New York pushed consistently for increased FBI surveillance of the Muslim community. And it did not take
long for political commentators at the time to introduce conflictual narratives about the nation's "new normal" patterned on Huntington's writings
about the need for democratic societies to be wary of Islamic teachings and
the Muslims who follow them (see Nacos and Torres-Reyna 2007). This
framing of Islam has contributed to lingering anti-Muslim sentiment in
media coverage (Dana, Barreto, and Oskooii 2011). Related work by Kimberly Powell (2011) and Nazita Lajevardi (2017) documents how the post-
9/11 framing of both foreign and domestic Muslims in media coverage is
voluminous and negative in sentiment. Muslim scholarship since 9/11 has
continued the themes articulated in the earlier research, but with a more
robust focus on discrimination against Muslims, Muslim political attachments and activity, and the dynamics of Muslim identity—mainly from the
vantage point of quantitative data. In this section, we discuss briefly opportunities for pushing our understanding of American Muslim politics
forward.

Compared to those of other faiths, less is known about Muslim American political engagement (Ayers and Hoffstetter 2008), although scholars
have made notable progress toward understanding both the social and psychological aspects of Muslim life in American society and politics. For example, John Ayers (2007), Ayers and C. Richard Hofstetter (2008), and Farida
Jalazai (2011) used a hybrid of social psychological explanations for Muslim
political behavior and engagement. Drawing on affective intelligence theory
(Marcus, Neuman, and MacKuen 2000), elements of social identity theory
(Tajfel and Turner 1979), and aspects of the personal religion indicators often
used in the study of American Christianity (e.g., Leege and Kellstedt 1993;
Djupe and Gilbert 2006), Ayers and Hofstetter (2008) and Jalazai (2009) assessed how reported anxiety levels as measured in a 2004 national Zogby
poll of American Muslims affect reported political participation across a
variety of Muslim ethnic subgroups. The authors report a robust and positive
relationship between reported anxiety and Muslim political engagement,
with racial and ethnic subgroup controls (African Americans excepted)
showing little impact on the outcome variables. Gendered perceptions of
community and economic interests have also been found to differentiate
engagement patterns between women and men (Jamal 2005a). Muslims also
increase stated levels of political tolerance when engaging in social network

discussion with other Muslims (Djupe and Calfano 2012). The clear effects from the religion variables in these studies suggest a variety of areas for follow-up, but new data and research design approaches are needed.

Taking a cue from Jamal's (2005b) landmark study, some scholars turned their attention to Muslim politics as meted through activity in mosques or Islamic centers. The best known of these projects is the Muslim American Public Opinion Survey (Barreto et al. 2007). Rather than attempting to generate a representative sample of U.S. Muslims—a challenge given the lack of religious affiliation data in the U.S. Census—Barreto et al. used a form of probability and cluster sampling that focused on sample generation from high-density Muslim population areas across the United States. The researchers then surveyed mosque attendees in six metropolitan areas: Seattle, Dearborn, San Diego, Irvine, Riverside, and Raleigh-Durham. A similar effort is the 2006 Mosque Survey of Muslims in the United States (Choi, Gasim, and Patterson 2011). A smaller such effort was conducted in 2013 in Southern California (Lajevardi, Marar, and Michelson 2014). These mosque-based studies provide numerous insights into Muslim partisanship, voting behavior, opinion, and political activity. They also reflect Jamal's oft-cited link between mosque involvement, group consciousness/identity, and political activity.

There thus exists already a body of work aimed at understanding various aspects of (Arab and) Muslim life in America. This older line of scholarship documents that many of the challenges faced by Muslims today, including scrutiny and discrimination, were present prior to the 9/11 attacks. However, the increasing association of Muslims with terrorism in the wake of the attacks, and emphasized during the 2016 presidential campaign, served to crystallize for many Muslims a newly salient identity as part of the Muslim American community and their role in American politics. Arguably, what 9/11 did for the Muslim politics literature was to draw attention from quantitatively oriented scholars who could leverage survey data to assess the American Muslim community. Less clear is that 9/11 changed essential questions scholars asked about Muslims prior to the event. If anything, 9/11 made Muslim scholarship more urgent to conduct, and the examples of non-Muslim and government scrutiny more obvious as quantitative data was collected. But, in reality, the scholarship generally has not coalesced around common theoretical frameworks or empirical approaches; nor has it fully unpacked the determinants of Muslim American political behavior. This volume looks to help pivot toward greater commonality.

Much of the non-Muslim public has been conditioned since 2001 to hold negative and scrutinizing views of Muslims living in their midst (Penning 2009), though the "otherization" and racialization of Muslims made them social targets at least as far back as the 1960s (Jamal 2008). The public's negative attitudes toward U.S. Muslims may help explain why, despite inclusive rhetoric from former presidents George W. Bush and Barack Obama, Muslim organizations have long claimed a systematic effort by law enforcement at all levels to profile, monitor, and harass community members (Johnson 2014). Yet it is not only Republicans who contribute to negative impressions of American Muslims and Islam. Democrats and other thought leaders are also responsible, particularly when these leaders hold local and state level office in the south and portions of the Midwest (Decker 2015).

The result is that Muslims in America have encountered imposed identity dynamics on a large and bipartisan scale, the intent of which has been to accentuate a national identity that preferences racial, ethnic, political, and religious identities that are decidedly non-Muslim. This boundary formation casts Muslims in the position of a subaltern group whose role in the social and political structure is that of outsiders, and perhaps dangerous ones at that (Haddad and Smith 1994; Reif 1995; Calfano 2018). To be sure, Muslims have some agency in creating social representations and shared identities according to sincerely held preferences (Hopkins and Kahani-Hopkins 2004), but Muslim efficacy in this process is limited in the U.S. context. Indeed, in the aftermath of their collective treatment since the 9/11 attacks, Muslims are among the most delegitimized groups from both a political and social standpoint (Reicher 2004; Pew Research Center 2017a).

Muslim Americans Workshop and This Volume

The studies referenced above have generated important insights into Muslim American politics, but much remains unknown and unexplored. As previewed above, we brought interested faculty and graduate students together for a full-day workshop in December 2016 at Menlo College as a first step in planning and conducting a large-N, in-depth, multilingual survey of this understudied community. Throughout the workshop, we discussed the extant literature, identified lingering questions, and planned how to ensure that the data collection is conducted so as to maximize usefulness and minimize overlap of effort by various scholars. We followed up with a second workshop at the University of California, Los Angeles, in December 2017.

Workshop participants identified several themes ripe to explore in the ongoing study of Muslim Americans, including identity, behavior, and policy preferences. Specific research topics included the racialized and panethnic formation of Muslim American identity in the years after the 9/11 attacks, predictors of Muslim American political participation and activism, the difference between religious identity and religiosity, the factors that strengthen Muslim American identity, testing respondents' knowledge of Islam, covert versus overt identity, and how negative and positive discrimination have affected identity.

While discussing the available samples and previous measures of Muslim American political behavior, participants expressed frustration. This is in part because Muslim Americans often report participating in politics at the same rate as whites. Scholars have strong reservations about this finding and question whether social desirability bias may be responsible for driving high reporting rates. Workshop attendees offered numerous alternative suggestions for measuring civic participation by Muslim Americans, including attending meetings addressing Muslim-specific issues, studying collective versus individual political participation, and searching for examples of political elites who visit mosques in an effort to recruit the community (see Calfano, Lajevardi, and Michelson 2017).

Increased recent attention to Muslim Americans has led to the emergence of a Muslim American political identity. Polls indicate that faith is important to Muslims in making their voting decisions (Wald and Calhoun-Brown 2014). And American foreign policy in the Middle East and U.S. relations with Muslim countries have been influential in solidifying Muslim American identity (Haddad and Harb 2014). Issues that were salient to American Muslims in the aftermath of 9/11 likely differed from those that were important prior, and may have since evolved with rising Islamophobia, increased terrorism, and the emergence of Trump as a presidential contender in the 2016 presidential election. Muslims have every reason to be concerned with policy given President Trump's repeated attempts to halt entry to the United States from many majority-Muslim countries. Other policies discussed during Trump's 2016 presidential campaign may yet find their way into an executive order or new legislation, such as increased surveillance of U.S. mosques, the policing of low-income Muslim neighborhoods, and the implementation of a Muslim registry. Researchers hope to explore Muslim American attitudes and reactions toward these policies that affect their communities, as well as how Muslim American identity is related to other political attitudes. These include policies relevant to the lesbian, gay, bisexual, and transgender (LGBT) community, economic policy, environmental policy, immigration policy, the secularization of religion in the United States, interventionist foreign policy stances, and the Israeli-Palestinian conflict.

To explore these themes, scholars must devise novel methodological and sampling techniques (some of which feature in the following chapters). Unfortunately, it is virtually impossible to field a nationally representative survey of American Muslims. The good news is that the Pew and Institute for Social Policy and Understanding studies provide templates for researchers in generating something close to a representative sample. The bad news is that developing these representative studies is costly. In addition, existing surveys tend to lag in their inclusion of African American Muslim respondents (compared to white, Asian, and Middle Eastern Muslims). Given the importance of intersecting religious and racial identities, working to improve the inclusion of African Americans in Muslim American survey samples should be a priority for researchers. Doing so will require building greater trust between members of the Muslim community and researchers, something that until now has been challenging given rational fears of surveillance by Muslim Americans generally and by African American Muslims in particular. Previous studies have been creative in how they identify and incorporate American Muslims into their surveys. Given that American Muslims are difficult to identify (e.g., no data collection on religion in the U.S. Census), scholars are challenged with respondent recruitment, and must often rely on convenience, unrepresentative, and small samples. Moreover, heightened anxiety stemming from political rhetoric and policy may make Muslim reluctance to participate in scholarly research an even greater challenge for scholars (Calfano, Lajevardi, and Michelson 2017).

Finally, we note the attention that researchers, policy makers, and advocacy groups must pay to any policy recommendations that stem from this research. Some empirical work (e.g., Hobbs and Lajevardi 2018; Oskooii 2016) has demonstrated that, in the face of discrimination, American Muslims have responded by retreating, feeling anxious, and censoring themselves. One recommendation that community and religious leaders have offered to American Muslims, as Karam Dana and colleagues (2018) point out, is to remove religious identifiers—such as the hijab and other religious garb—and become more invisible as a means of avoiding harassment. Moreover, there is ample anecdotal evidence that Muslim Americans report fearing the visibility they encounter in ordinary American society. These fears are predominantly rooted in anxieties over physical harm. We encourage readers to consider whether invisibility, even if temporary, is a realistic diagnosis in a pluralistic society.

Overview of the Book

In the following chapters, we present a number of studies covering a variety of topics assessing the Muslim American experience post-9/11 era and prior to the Trump era. If we are ever to truly understand how this community has come to fare so negatively in recent times, it is critical that researchers have a firm grasp of the Muslim American experience in the intervening fifteen years. The approach we take in each of the following chapters is to highlight an example of a contemporary political issue or topic facing Muslim Americans post-9/11. These chapters span interactions with law enforcement, reactions to identity labels used in Muslim surveys, the role of gender relations, and methodological suggestions for assessing Muslim Americans. As part of each chapter, we also explore where extensions of research on the questions and findings posed might go next. This is where we consider opportunities for innovation in political science methodology to build on insights the authors of each chapter present. We now present highlights from each of the following chapters.

Chapter 2 provides a historical overview and focuses on the variable relationships Muslims and the United States have had since the nation's founding. This relationship is sometimes positive, sometimes negative, and always dense in political and societal pressures and opinions. In examining this relationship, Matt Barreto and Karam Dana walk readers through a basic history and profile of Muslims in the United States. The authors then examine how discrimination and politics impact American Muslims, both native and foreign born. The functions of the mosque and the impacts of 9/11 are also highlighted, as they both play roles in the social and political development and stigmatization of Muslims.

Chapter 3 focuses on Islam and gender. The visibility of the hijab and the widespread discussions and now enactments of burqa bans throughout the world since 9/11 indicate that a focus on gender is necessary to understand an important facet of Muslim discrimination. Since dominant interpretations of Islam have developed outside the United States, it is instructive to briefly review the dynamics of gender rights within the wider Muslim world. While Islam is a global religion, much of the popular thought surrounding Islam, including gender relations between Muslims, comes from the Arab world. There is a complex history of gender status within Islamic societies. The articulation of alternative and more liberal/feminist constructs within Islam notwithstanding, the continuing controversy surrounding women's rights and Islam is spurred by traditionalist Islamism's influence across state borders—a reality even more pronounced in the social media age. Clearly there is a history of patriarchal interpretation in Islam that has caused immense difficulty for women, but what does this mean for American Muslim women? The authors offer a brief review of what scholars have said thus far about this question, as well as some initial thoughts for further scholarly reflection.

Chapter 4 focuses on Middle Eastern and Muslim Americans' battle for recognition and on how the preferred ethno-racial identities of members of this community help us understand Muslim political attitudes and behaviors. First, the authors review the history of the battle to be recognized as white by various U.S. subgroups, particularly by Middle Eastern and Muslim Americans. Second, they review how those identities have been highlighted and activated since 2015 as a result of the Trump election campaign and the actions and policies of the early Trump administration. Next, the authors describe their hypotheses about identity and describe findings from a unique data collection effort in California in 2013 and in an online sample of Muslim Americans in 2017 (after President Trump's election). Fourth, and finally, they discuss how their findings help predict what we expect to see from Muslim American and Middle Eastern Americans moving forward.

Chapter 5 considers the tenuous relationship between American Muslims and the law enforcement community post-9/11. Since 9/11, law enforcement agencies have enacted surveillance programs typified by the New York Police Department's surveillance program that extended to all mosques within a one-hundred-mile radius of New York City and President Obama's Countering Violent Extremism program. This chapter considers the nuanced challenges and opportunities for government and law enforcement agencies in serving a minority group like American Muslims in the post-9/11 context.

Chapter 6 builds on the law enforcement theme in Chapter 5 by focusing on how the post-9/11 scrutiny has affected American Muslims' relationship with U.S. law enforcement. Rachel Gillum examines whether individual Muslims believe that their religious identity will result in differential treatment by authorities. Using a randomized survey experiment, Gillum compares Muslims' attitudes toward police behavior when the suspect is Muslim American versus a different background. She explores the reasons for the variance in Muslims' levels of trust in the police and attitudes toward government, including the effect of immigrants' experiences with law enforcement in their country of origin. Her analysis suggests that citizenship and expectations for assimilation and equality matters for perceptions of this relationship. Specifically, U.S.-born Muslims have internalized negative views of government, and are more likely to anticipate that police behavior toward Muslims will be discriminatory. Foreign-born Muslims, however, do not appear to believe that the police treat Muslims differently than non-Muslims and, instead, base their judgments of American law enforcement on their experiences in their country of origin. Immigrant Muslims whose home country had corrupt institutions are more likely to expect bad behavior from American police forces.

Chapter 7 shifts the focus from American Muslims to the American public writ large and details how Islam has played a key role in the growing differences between Republicans and Democrats. The author argues that the conflict over the 9/11 Mosque was the "first shot" in a growing cultural divide between partisans over Islam. Partisan conflict over Islam had not fully developed by 2010. But a year later, Republicans were increasingly likely to see Islam negatively and to accept the false notion that Obama was not born in the United States, to believe that the president was himself a Muslim, and to see a "clash of civilizations" between Christianity and Islam. Republicans exploited fears of radical Islam by linking it to what had seemed to be an uncontroversial community center in Manhattan. By 2016 the conflict over identities had moved to the center of political debate. Utilizing survey data from several sources, the author offers an assessment of the dynamics behind the public's negative views of Muslims, which increasingly fall along partisan lines.

Chapter 8 continues with the focus on non-Muslim perceptions by exploring results from a survey experiment on non-Muslim residents in Chicago intended to spur intergroup trust. The authors find that, while priming religious identity among Christian subjects helps improve trust across the board, this effect does not extend to trust of Muslims. Only the priming of religion and superordinate group framing (in the form of asking about one's willingness to help out-group members) shows consistent statistically significant and positive effects on perceptions of the Muslim out-group.

Chapter 9 shifts to the question of American Muslim identity and assesses whether asking Muslims to identify "first" as Muslim or American (as the question has frequently been used in Pew surveys) affects how Muslims respond to political and policy-related survey questions. Using data from the 2007 Pew national survey of Muslims residing in the United States, the authors examine the relationship between group identification, gender, and race with opinions regarding Islam's treatment of women, evaluations of Al Qaeda, and the role Arabs played in the 9/11 attacks. Second, the authors use the theory of social identity performance to develop expectations as to how Muslims responses to questions about political motives and activities are influenced by priming questions that force respondents to acknowledge and prioritize their religious identity.

In Chapter 10, Youssef Chouhoud studies Muslim Americans' political tolerance, an indicator of assimilation. With anti-Muslim sentiment in the United States relatively high and periodically spiking in accordance with intermittent controversies (e.g., the so-called Ground Zero mosque), investigating the attitudes of American Muslims themselves could shed light on the factors influencing negative appraisals of this community. That is, animosity and intolerance toward this religious minority (which previous chapters in this volume have elaborated on) may be motivated in part by a belief that Muslims in America are particularly dogmatic and wish to impose their views rather than allow all views to be heard. The movement to ban sharia in several state legislatures across the country, for example, speaks to the perception that Islam promotes a legal and political system that seeks to supersede existing U.S. laws and government.

In Chapter 11, Karam Dana and Matt Barreto explore the different methodologies that can be used to gather public opinion survey data among Muslims in the United States and what the challenges and opportunities are with these different approaches. Ultimately, the authors conclude that social scientists can and should collect more public opinion data from American Muslims so that their viewpoints can be included in the national debate about diversity and democracy. To this end, the authors focus on large-*n* quantitative public opinion data as a methodological approach for understanding Muslim American social and political incorporation.

In Chapter 12, we tie the previous chapters together by considering future directions of research in Muslim American scholarship, including methodological ways of assessing the effects of Muslim American experiences through techniques such as random assignment in experiments. Although this is not a book on Trump, the 2016 election reminds students of identity politics and related subjects that the maltreatment of minority groups—even those that have seen some progress in their social status relative to the majority—is ripe for reoccurrence without much warning. Though it is impossible to predict exactly where the effects of Trump's anti-Muslim rhetoric (and attendant reaction by those sharing his worldview) will lead, it is safe to suggest that any earlier attempts by leaders of both major political parties to encourage Americans to discount negative stereotypes of Muslims have been stunted as a result of the president's posture toward Islam and its followers.

REFERENCES

Austin, A. D. 1984. *African Muslims in Antebellum America: A Sourcebook*. New York: Routledge.

Ayers, J. W. 2007. "Changing Sides: 9/11 and the American Muslim Voter." *Review of Religious Research* 49:187–198.

Ayers, J. W., and C. R. Hofstetter. 2008. "American Muslim Political Participation following 9/11: Religious Belief, Political Resources, Social Structures, and Political Awareness." *Politics and Religion* 1:3–26.

Bagby, I., P. M. Perl, and B. T. Froehle. 2001. "The Mosque in America: A National Portrait; A Report from the Mosque Study Project." Available at http://icnl.com/files/Masjid_Study_Project_2000_Report.pdf.

Bakalian, A., and M. Bozorgmehr. 2009. *Backlash 9/11: Middle Eastern and Muslim Americans Respond*. Berkeley: University of California Press.

Barreto, M. A., and D. Bozonelos. 2009. "Democrat, Republican, or None of the Above? The Role of Religiosity in Muslim American Party Identification." *Politics and Religion* 2:200–229.

Barreto, M. A., D. Bozonelos, K. Dana, N. Masuoka, and S. Ozyurt. 2007. *2007 Muslim American Public Opinion Survey*. Washington Institute for the Study of Ethnicity and Race. Available at http://mattbarreto.com/data/index.html.

Ba-Yunus, I., and K. Kone. 2004. "Muslim Americans: A Demographic Report." In *Muslims' Place in the American Public Square: Hopes, Fears, and Aspirations*, edited by Z. Bukhari, S. S. Anyang, M. Ahmad, and J. L. Esposito, 299–321. New York: Altamira.

Cainkar, L. 2007. "Thinking Outside the Box." In *From Invisible Citizens to Visible Subjects: Arab Americans and Race before and after 9/11*, edited by A. Jamal and N. Naber, 46–80. Syracuse, NY: Syracuse University Press.

Calfano, B. 2018. *Muslims, Identity, and American Politics*. New York: Routledge.

Calfano, B. R., N. Lajevardi, and M. Michelson. 2017. "Trumped Up Challenges: Limitations, Opportunities, and the Future of Political Research on Muslim Americans." *Politics, Groups, and Identities*, October 17. Available at https://www.tandfonline.com/doi/full/10.1080/21565503.2017.1386573.

Choi, J., G. Gasim, and D. Patterson. 2011. "Identity, Issues, and Religious Commitment and Participation: Explaining Turnout among Mosque-Attending Muslim Americans." *Studies in Ethnicity and Nationalism* 11:343–364.

Council on American-Islamic Relations. 2006. "American Muslim Voters: A Demographic Profile and Survey of Attitudes." Available at https://d3n8a8pro7vhmx.cloudfront.net/cairhq/pages/14738/attachments/original/1506340148/American_Muslim_Voter_Survey_2006.pdf?1506340148.

Dana, K., M. A. Barreto, and K.A.R. Oskooii. 2011. "Mosques as American Institutions: Mosque Attendance, Religiosity, and Integration into the Political System among American Muslims." *Religions* 2:504–524.

Dana, K., N. Lajevardi, K.A.R. Oskooii, and H. L. Walker. 2018. "Veiled Politics: Experiences with Discrimination among Muslim Americans." *Politics and Religion*, June 13. Available at https://doi.org/10.1017/S1755048318000287.

Decker, C. 2015. "Rep. Loretta Sanchez: 'I've Never Attacked Muslims.'" *Los Angeles Times*, December 14. Available at http://beta.latimes.com/politics/la-pol-ca-loretta-sanchez-muslims-comment-20151214-story.html.

Djupe, P. A., and B. R. Calfano. 2012. "American Muslim Investment in Civil Society: Political Discussion, Disagreement, and Tolerance." *Political Research Quarterly* 65:516–528.

———. 2013. *God Talk: Experimenting with the Religious Causes of Public Opinion*. Philadelphia: Temple University Press.

Djupe, P. A., and C. P. Gilbert. 2006. "The Resourceful Believer: Generating Civic Skills in Church." *Journal of Politics* 68:116–127.

Esposito, J. L. 1999. *The Islamic Threat: Myth or Reality?* New York: Oxford University Press.

Faragallah, M. H., W. R. Schumm, and F. J. Webb. 1997. "Acculturation of Arab-American Immigrants: An Exploratory Study." *Journal of Comparative Family Studies* 28:182–203.

Gallup. 2009. "Muslim Americans: A National Portrait; An In-Depth Analysis of America's Most Diverse Religious Community." Available at https://slideplayer.com/slide/6382533.

———. 2011. "Muslim Americans: Faith, Freedom, and the Future: Examining U.S. Muslims' Political, Social, and Spiritual Engagement 10 Years after September 11."

Available at https://news.gallup.com/poll/148931/presentation-muslim-americans-faith-freedom-future.aspx.

Gardell, M. 1996. *In the Name of Elijah Muhammad: Louis Farrakhan and the Nation of Islam.* Durham, NC: Duke University Press.

Haddad, Y. Y. 1991. "American Foreign Policy in the Middle East and Its Impact on the Identity of Arab Muslims in the United States." In *The Muslims of America*, edited by Y. Y. Haddad, 217–235. New York: Oxford University Press.

Haddad, Y. Y., and J. Esposito. 1998. *Muslims on the Americanization Path.* Atlanta: Scholars Press.

Haddad, Y. Y., and N. N. Harb. 2014. "Post-9/11: Making Islam an American Religion." *Religions* 5 (2): 477–501.

Haddad, Y. Y., and A. Lummis. 1987. *Islamic Values in the United States: A Comparative Study.* New York: Oxford University Press.

Haddad, Y. Y., and J. I. Smith. 1994. *Muslim Communities in North America.* New York: SUNY Press.

Hobbs, W., and N. Lajevardi. 2018. "Effects of Divisive Political Campaigns on the Day-to-Day Segregation of Arab and Muslim Americans." *American Political Science Review*, December 27. Available at https://doi.org/10.1017/S0003055418000801.

Hopkins, N., and V. Kahani-Hopkins. 2004. "Identity Construction and British Muslims' Political Activity: Beyond Rational Actor Theory." *British Journal of Social Psychology* 43:339–356.

Human Rights Watch. 2002. "World Report 2002: United States." Available at http://www.hrw.org/wr2k2/us.html#Hate%20Crimes.

Iftikhar, A. 2007. *The Status of Muslim Civil Rights in the United States—Presumption of Guilt.* Washington, DC: Council on American Islamic Relations.

Ingraham, C. 2015. "Anti-Muslim Hate Crimes Are Still Five Times More Common Today than before 9/11." *Washington Post*, February 11. Available at https://www.washingtonpost.com/news/wonk/wp/2015/02/11/anti-muslim-hate-crimes-are-still-five-times-more-common-today-than-before-911.

Jackson, S. A. 2005. *Islam and the Blackamerican: Looking to the Third Resurrection.* New York: Oxford University Press.

Jalazai, F. 2009. "The Politics of Muslims in America." *Politics and Religion* 2:163–199.

———. 2011. "Anxious and Active: Muslim Perception of Discrimination and Its Political Consequences in the Post–September 11th 2011 United States." *Politics and Religion* 4:71–107.

Jamal, A. 2005a. "Mosques, Collective Identity, and Gender Differences among Arab American Muslims." *Journal of Middle East Women's Studies* 1:53–78.

———. 2005b. "The Political Participation and Engagement of Muslim Americans." *American Politics Research* 33:521–544.

———. 2008. "Arab American Racialization." In *Race and Arab Americans after 9/11: From Invisible Citizens to Visible Subjects*, edited by A. Jamal and N. Naber, 318–326. Syracuse, NY: Syracuse University Press.

———. 2009. *Barriers to Democracy: The Other Side of Social Capital in Palestine and the Arab World.* Princeton, NJ: Princeton University Press.

Johnson, B. 2014. "CAIR: Holder Did 'Very Little' to Address 'Harassment of Muslim Communities' by Law Enforcement." *PJ Media*, September 29. Available at https://pjmedia.com/blog/cair-holder-did-very-little-to-address-harassment-of-muslim-communities-by-law-enforcement.

Khan, M.A.M. 1998. *Muslims on the Americanization Path.* Atlanta, GA: Scholars Press.

Khan, M., and K. Ecklund. 2012. "Attitudes toward Muslim Americans Post-9/11." *Journal of Muslim Mental Health* 7 (1). Available at https://quod.lib.umich.edu/j/jmmh/10381607.0007.101/--attitudes-toward-muslim-americans-post-911?rgn=main;view=fulltext.

Lajevardi, N. 2017. "A Comprehensive Study of Muslim American Discrimination by Legislators, the Media, and the Masses." Ph.D. diss., University of California, San Diego.

———. 2018. "Access Denied: Exploring Muslim American Representation and Exclusion by State Legislators." *Politics, Groups, and Identities*, November 8. Available at https://doi.org/10.1080/21565503.2018.1528161.

Lajevardi, N., M. Y. Marar, and M. Michelson. 2014. "The Unbearable Whiteness of Being Middle Eastern." Paper presented at the 37th meeting of the Politics of Race, Immigration, and Ethnicity Consortium (PRIEC), University of California, San Diego, May 23.

Lajevardi, N., and K.A.R. Oskooii. 2018. "Old-Fashioned Racism, Contemporary Islamophobia, and the Isolation of Muslim Americans in the Age of Trump." *Journal of Race, Ethnicity and Politics* 3 (1): 112–152.

Lee, M. 1996. *The Nation of Islam: An American Millenarian Movement*. Syracuse, NY: Syracuse University Press.

Leege, D. C., and L. A. Kellstedt. 1993. *Rediscovering the Religious Factor in American Politics*. New York: M. E. Sharpe.

Lipsitz, G. 1998. *A Life in the Struggle: Ivory and Perry and the Culture of Opposition*. Philadelphia: Temple University Press.

Marcus, G .E., W. R. Neuman, and M. MacKuen. 2000. *Affective Intelligence and Political Judgment*. Chicago: University of Chicago Press.

Martin, S. 2009. "The Congressional Representation of Muslim-American Constituents." *Politics and Religion* 2:230–246.

McCloud, A. B. 1995. *African American Islam*. New York: Routledge.

Naber, N. 2000. "Ambiguous Insiders: An Investigation of Arab American Invisibility." *Ethnic and Racial Studies* 23:37–61.

Nacos, B. L., and O. Torres-Reyna. 2007. *Fueling Our Fears: Stereotyping, Media Coverage, and Public Opinion on Muslim Americans*. Lanham, MD: Rowman and Littlefield.

Oskooii, K. A. 2016. "How Discrimination Impacts Sociopolitical Behavior: A Multidimensional Perspective." *Political Psychology* 37 (5): 613–640.

Penning, J. M. 2009. "Americans' Views of Muslims and Mormons: A Social Identity Approach." *Politics and Religion* 2:277–302.

Pew Research Center. 2007. "Muslim Americans: Middle Class and Mostly Mainstream." May 22. Available at http://www.pewresearch.org/2007/05/22/muslim-americans-middle-class-and-mostly-mainstream.

———. 2011. "Muslim Americans: No Signs of Growth in Alienation or Support for Extremism." Available at http://www.pewresearch.org/2007/05/22/muslim-americans-middle-class-and-mostly-mainstream.

———. 2017. "Americans Express Increasingly Warm Feelings toward Religious Groups." Available at http://www.pewforum.org/2017/02/15/americans-express-increasingly-warm-feelings-toward-religious-groups.

Pitter, L. 2017. "Hate Crimes against Muslims in US Continue to Rise in 2016." Human Rights Watch, May 11. Available at https://www.hrw.org/news/2017/05/11/hate-crimes-against-muslims-us-continue-rise-2016.

Powell, K. A. 2011. "Framing Islam: An Analysis of U.S. Media Coverage of Terrorism since 9/11." *Communication Studies* 62:90–112.

Project MAPS and Zogby International. 2004. "Muslims in the American Public Square: Shifting Political Winds and Fallout from 9/11, Afghanistan, and Iraq." Available at https://www.aclu.org/files/fbimappingfoia/20111110/ACLURM001733.pdf.

Reicher, S. 2004. "The Context of Social Identity: Domination, Resistance, and Change." *Political Psychology* 25:921–945.

Reif, D. 1995. *Slaughterhouse: Bosnia and the Failure of the West*. Colchester, UK: Vintage.

Said, E. 1979. *Orientalism*. New York: Vintage.

Seikaly, Z. A. 2001. "At Risk of Prejudice: The Arab American Community." *Social Education* 65:349–352.

Selod, S. 2015. "Citizenship Denied: The Racialization of Muslim American Men and Women Post-9/11." *Critical Sociology* 41 (1): 77–95.

Shaheen, J. G. 2003. "Reel Bad Arabs: How Hollywood Vilifies a People." *Annals of the American Academy of Political and Social Science* 588 (1): 171–193.

Smith, J. 1999. *Islam in America*. New York: Columbia University Press.

South Asian American Leaders of Tomorrow. 2001. "American Backlash: Terrorists Bring War Home in More Ways than One." Available at http://saalt.org/wp-content/uploads/2012/09/American-Backlash-Terrorist-Bring-War-Home-in-More-Ways-Than-One.pdf.

Suhay, E., B. Calfano, and R. Dawe. 2015. "Social Norms, Dual Identities, and National Attachment: How the Perceived Patriotism of Group Members Influences Muslim Americans." *Politics, Groups, and Identities* 4:63–83.

Tajfel, H., and J. C. Turner. 1979. "An Integrative Theory of Social Conflict." In *The Social Psychology of Intergroup Relations*, edited by S. Worchel and W. G. Austin, 56–65. Monterey, CA: Brooks-Cole.

Wald, K. D., and A. Calhoun-Brown. 2010. *Religion and Politics in the United States*. 6th ed. Lanham, MD: Rowman and Littlefield.

Wormser, R. 1994. *American Islam: Growing Up Muslim in America*. New York: Walker.

American Muslims and the State

Contexts and Contentions

KARAM DANA AND

MATT A. BARRETO

L ong before Donald Trump's 2017 executive order that banned visitors from seven Muslim-majority countries, Muslims and the United States have had a complex relationship. This relationship is sometimes positive, sometimes negative, and always dense in political and societal pressures and opinions. In order to examine this relationship, we provide a basic history and profile of Muslims in the United States. We then examine how discrimination and politics affect American Muslims, both native and foreign born. The functions of the mosque and the impacts of 9/11 are also highlighted, as they both play roles in the development and stigmatization of Muslims. Despite the U.S. media's depiction of Muslims as homogenous, the diversity within the Muslim community proves that there are myriad beliefs and practices that render homogeneity impossible. American Muslims are multifaceted, with different origins and experiences, views, and practices.

We argue that those looking to understand the American Muslim experience should do so through the paradox of diversity and cohesion. On the one hand, there is no such thing as a typical American Muslim. The Muslim community is more diverse and distinct than any other, given its linguistic, cultural, and racial differences. Muslims who are living in the United States cannot be easily labeled; nor do they represent a specific type of person or understanding of Islam (despite what negative larger political and societal opinions may claim). On the other hand, the intense otherization and discrimination targeting those who appear to be Muslim has created a sense of group commonality and cohesion, even across the community's differences.

The paradox of diversity and cohesion is a critical framework for understanding the place and trajectory of American Muslims that we argue is becoming more important in the post-2016 election environment. As scholarship of the American Muslim community grows, we think this framework will be particularly relevant for understanding why there appears to be significant divides within the community in some contexts, while, in other contexts, there is noticeable unity.

Origins of Islam in America

As Calfano and Lajevardi preview in the introductory chapter, and in spite of the common misconception of Muslims as "foreign" or "other," the first Muslims in the United States were navigators on Christopher Columbus's famous voyage, making them as much a part of American history as Europeans (Dana and Franklin 2013). It has also been suggested that Muslims arrived to the Americas before Columbus. Many of the Founding Fathers owned copies of the Qur'an and were extremely familiar with the religion and culture of Islam. Most notably, Thomas Jefferson owned a copy of the Qur'an that was published in London in 1764 (and which was eventually used to swear in U.S. Representative Keith Ellison in 2008). Before 1808, a significant number of Muslims were brought to the United States from Africa as slaves. Although many of these slaves lost their religious ties over time, many succeeded in keeping their link to Islam. The most famous of these slaves was Abdul Rahman Ibrahim Ibn Sori, who was an African prince sold into slavery during the late 1700s and later freed by President John Adams.

Immigration

Like most immigrant communities, Muslims migrated to the United States to find economic opportunity and escape repression. This reality is important when considering the misperception of Muslims as un-American, despite their history of community integration and shared hopes and desires. The largest group of Muslims in the United States is American-born blacks, followed by Arabs. Other large groups include migrants from South Asia, Eastern Europe, Iran, Turkey, the former Soviet Union, and Africa. The key areas of immigration in the United States include Detroit, where Yemenis and Lebanese began to settle, followed by Palestinians, Iraqis, and an additional influx of Lebanese, and Chicago, where Bosnians in particular immigrated first in the early 1900s and again in the 1990s. There was also an expansion of Muslim communities in New York and Los Angeles, which was matched with expanding communities in Texas, Oklahoma, and Florida.

Muslim immigration boomed in the early 1900s, as Eastern Europeans and those escaping from the fragmentation of the Ottoman Empire (primarily in Lebanon and Syria) sought out freedom and prosperity. But anti-immigration sentiment in the 1920s caused immigration to come to a temporary halt, as Muslims and those who did not conform to the Western European "standards" were penalized (Dana and Franklin 2013). A second period of Muslim immigration occurred in the years following World War II. This was precipitated, in part, by various social and political conflicts in the Middle East. There was then an influx of Muslims from all nations fleeing political, social, and economic crises. This immigration increase was enabled by the passage of a 1965 law ending national immigration quotas (Dana and Franklin 2013). Palestinians escaping the Israel-Arab crisis also began making their way to the United States in larger numbers, followed by Iranian nationals of all religious backgrounds, including Muslims, escaping the civil unrest and persecution they faced soon after the 1979 revolution. For many of these refugees, the United States offered the freedom to practice their religion and become involved in politics—an opportunity that may not have existed in their previous home countries if they belonged to a nonmajority sect or were ethnic minorities.

The 2011 Pew study on Muslims in America shows that the top nations of origin for immigrants were Pakistan and Bangladesh, and both countries are expected to remain at the top of the immigration list through 2030 (Dana and Franklin 2013). Latino/a Muslims have also altered the relationship between Islam and immigration in the United States. Although the primary converts in the United States have traditionally been African Americans, a group of Latino/a Muslims in New York City created an organization that lead to Latino conversion beginning in the 1970s (Bowen 2013). Latino/a Muslims have a long history with their faith, with the Pima language's Arabic influence and various archeological discoveries throughout what is now North and South America tying their heritage to West African Muslims who crossed the ocean around 889. The conversion of Latino/a Muslims in the past several decades has also been seen as a rejection and redefinition of dominant social discourses in the United States, with many Latino/as joining African American Muslim groups and mosques, further rejecting racial, economic, and social borders (Bowen 2010).

Higher immigration and fertility rates are expected to cause an increase in the total number of Muslims in the United States to 6.2 million in 2030, up from an approximated 2.6 million at the time of this publication (Dana and Franklin 2013). This increase in the American Muslim population will allow for a more significant presence of Islam in the United States, which will act as a more accurate indicator of the diversity among the widespread

Muslim population throughout the world. It is important to note that the exact number of Muslims in the United States (native and foreign born) is unknown, as the United States Census does not take religion into account despite its social and political importance in U.S. society. Therefore, both the current population and the projected population could be lower or higher than approximated. As a culture of immigrants, it is important to note the importance of the *ummah*, a term used to refer to the global Muslim community, as part of the Muslim American identity. Rather than being in a physical, tangible location, the *ummah* transcends color, race, borders, and culture to provide solidarity to all Muslims. The idea of having a shared identity with other Muslims further complicates the concept of nationality, while also freeing Muslims from being tied to a specific "home" country. As Muslim immigrants continue to move to the United States in search of economic opportunity and personal freedom, they further expand the *ummah* while adding to the extremely diverse existing American Muslim population.

Diversity within the American Muslim Community

The Muslim American community is significantly more diverse than other religious groups within the United States. According to a 2009 Gallup poll, the Muslim population is 28 percent white, 35 percent African American, 18 percent Asian, 1 percent Hispanic, and 18 percent "other" (Younis 2009). This can be compared to Judaism (93 percent white), Protestantism (88 percent white), and Catholicism (76 percent white). This ethnic and racial homogeneity within these religious groups serves both as a comfort for Anglo-Americans and a deterrent for American minority groups, many of which have found themselves searching for a religion that prioritizes diversity and can exist alongside dominant social norms. This is certainly true for many Latino/a Muslims, who seek out an alternative to Roman Catholicism. Observing this trend, Wade Clark Roof suggests that "there are those in the Roman Catholic tradition who are somewhat discontent with the modernizing trends of the Catholic Church. To those people, a religious tradition such as Islam, that attempts to maintain a fairly strict set of patterns and practices, becomes attractive," despite the negative opinions voiced by other members of the Latino/a community (Nieves 2001). In her report on the Latino Muslim community, Viscidi argues that the embrace of Islam in the Latino community can be contributed to the related feeling of being disenfranchised in mainstream American society, which is felt by a population that "had fervor to continue the struggle but no place to go" before finding solitude in Islam (Viscidi 2003).

In the Muslim American Public Opinion Survey (MAPOS), the largest survey of Muslims in the United States ($N = 1,410$), respondents derived from forty different nations of origin and spoke twenty different languages (Dana 2011). According to a Pew report, 63 percent of Muslims in America are first generation, 15 percent are second generation, and 22 percent are third generation or more (Pew Research Center 2011b). Therefore, the Muslim American community is called to appeal to and communicate with a multitude of languages and cultures. Fifty-six percent of Muslim Americans believe that most Muslims want to adopt American customs and lifestyles, although only 33 percent of the general public believes this to be true (Pew Research Center 2011b). In light of this reality, it is important to note that the Muslim community can act as a "melting pot" by allowing different cultures to interact with one another, speak the same language, and learn from American Muslims. It is also important to acknowledge that more than four out of ten Muslim Americans will be native-born by 2030, significantly changing the American Muslim community as a whole (Dana and Franklin 2013).

Regarding gender, a Pew survey determined that 55 percent of U.S. Muslims are male, which is higher than the general public male-to-female ratio of 48 to 52 percent. This is likely due to the fact that immigrants from Muslim countries are disproportionately male. There is also a higher level of conversion among African American males versus females. However, the Latino community is beginning to see a higher level of female converts to Islam. Muslim Americans are also younger than the general population, with 59 percent of the Muslim American population between eighteen and thirty-nine years old, versus 40 percent of the general public. Although marriage rates among Muslim Americans are only 1 percent higher than the general population, family sizes are much larger, at an average of 2.8 children per family, compared to 2.1 in the average American household (Pew Research Center 2011b).

Individual levels of religiosity also vary greatly within the Muslim community. MAPOS determined that 50 percent of respondents saw religion as "important," 38 percent as "somewhat important," and 12 percent as "not too important" (Dana, Oskooii, and Barreto 2011). Thus, like other U.S. religious communities, individuals prioritize and perceive their faith quite differently. While religiosity is a multifaceted concept that cannot be measured by mosque attendance alone, attendance is a crucial factor to consider when exploring the Muslim community in the United States. MAPOS found that 26 percent of Muslims consider themselves to be "very" active within their local mosque, 40 percent "somewhat," 20 percent "not much," and 13 percent "not at all"—despite the common American perception of all Muslims being religious individuals (Dana, Oskooii, and Barreto 2011). The MAPOS survey consisted of 39 percent Arab, 22 percent Asian, 15 percent black, and 7 percent white, reflecting the diversity within the *ummah* that is also present in the aforementioned Gallup findings.

However, although it is clear that Muslims differ by their race and religiosity, the majority sees their fate as linked to what happens to other Muslims in the United States, showing a high level of group consciousness. In addition, there is a distinct difference between young and old Muslims in terms of religious and political involvement. While older Muslims are likely to be extremely or somewhat active in the mosque setting and in their community politically, young Muslims seem to take the anti-Muslim discourse more discouragingly (as we discuss below). Young Muslims are also more likely to be unemployed because of the anti-Muslim discrimination and less likely to have the high levels of optimism that older Muslims retain.

Age, Education, and the Middle Class Muslim

The American Muslim population is predominantly middle class. Roughly 40 percent of Muslims reported earning $50,000 or more annually in 2007, a number that is similar to the annual earnings of the general population. However, in a 2008 Gallup survey, Muslim men and women reported having similar incomes in both the $1,999 a month and less bracket and the $5,000 and more a month bracket, making them significantly more egalitarian regarding income equality between the sexes than other religions. In addition, Muslim women were slightly more likely to earn $5,000 a month or more than the general population. American Muslims are as likely as other Americans to report household incomes of $100,000 or more, and are more likely than the general public to express that they are in excellent or good financial shape. Muslim Americans are also more optimistic in terms of success, with 74 percent believing that most people can get ahead through hard work versus 62 percent of the general public who believe so. This optimism exists in the face of extreme discrimination that is found by Muslim American workers in all levels of our economic system (Younis 2009).

In a 2011 Pew survey, 29 percent of Muslims stated that "negative views about Muslims" was the most important problem facing Muslim Americans. Meanwhile, 20 percent said that "Discrimination/Prejudice/Not treated fairly" was the biggest issue (Pew Research Center 2011a). Research shows that Muslim job candidates face discrimination, particularly in conservative areas. For instance, one study shows that in Republican-dominated states, Christian job candidates receive more interview calls than Muslim candidates with the same application. In the ten states with the highest proportion of individuals who voted for Mitt Romney in 2012, 17 percent of Christians received a call, versus 2 percent of Muslims. The difference dropped to 0 percent in the ten states with the lowest number of Romney voters (Sahgal 2013). This study suggests that discrimination is a significant part of the job market, particularly in conservative states, and judgment of an individual is often based on their religion or ethnicity without any additional knowledge of the person.

Muslims' conservative traditions can also spark discrimination in the American workplace. In July 2008, a Muslim woman in Jazle Park, Michigan, was rejected from a job as an Emergency Medical Services worker for the Detroit Fire Department because she wore a hijab, despite passing all of the necessary tests (Nimer 2001). Two months earlier, a group of six Muslim workers in New Brighton, Minnesota, were fired from Mission Foods because they refused to wear the company uniforms, which violated Islamic modesty requirements. Mission Foods cited safety concerns as the reason for this firing, although the individuals were stationed at tables that did not pose a safety risk. These are just two examples of workplace discrimination faced by the Muslim American population. While Muslims are certainly not the only religious group to base their clothing choices on the desire to present a modest appearance because of their religious ideals, they are the only religious group in the United States to be discriminated against for doing so. It is instances such as these that make it understandable as to why Muslims are 9 percent more likely to be unemployed/looking for work or working only part-time when they would prefer full-time employment than the general public (Pew Research Center 2011b).

Although many Muslim Americans are first generation, 82 percent of those surveyed in MAPOS were American citizens, further debunking the concept of Muslims as "foreign." In addition, over half of the individuals surveyed in MAPOS owned their homes, subsequently adding to their view of the United States as their permanent home (Dana and Franklin 2013). This is in line with their largely middle-class existence. What is not average is that, according to MAPOS, 61 percent of American Muslims have at least a college degree. They follow Jewish Americans as the second most educated religious community in the United States, including a high rate of educated women (Younis 2009).

But, unlike the general public, only 64 percent of adult Muslims are registered to vote, which is the lowest percentage among religious groups (Dana and Franklin 2013). According to MAPOS, 28 percent of these individuals prescribe "none" as their political affiliation despite their high levels of education. This could largely be due to the political isolation and persecution caused by the Republican Party and the hostile post-9/11 social environment and media, as is discussed in the following section.

Political and Academic Discrimination in the United States

Anti-Muslim sentiment exists throughout American society and is largely derived from uneducated and prejudiced teachings and statements by American politicians, news sources, and academics. The U.S. media tend to portray Muslims as exclusively Arabs who are often terrifying, dangerous, violent, and strange, generalizing Muslims as a group that is opposed to freedom and democracy (see, e.g., "Islamophobia" 2017). Events in the Middle East have become the focal points for defining American Muslims, regardless of individual backgrounds, and despite the fact that most Muslims are not from the Arabic-speaking world.

In addition, certain portrayals of instability in the Middle East have been used to propel the scholarly argument that Islam is culturally incompatible with the liberal and democratic values of Western (and American) society. The argument claims not only that Muslims are different and antimodern but also that their beliefs directly conflict with American society. The most significant anti-Muslim/anti-Islam scholars in America are Samuel Huntington and Bernard Lewis (1993), both of whom believed that Muslims are incapable of living in non-Muslim societies because of their religious identities.

While it is true that Western culture and Muslim culture may be different, it is inaccurate to claim that they are incompatible. Rather, as a diverse group of individuals, Muslim Americans take on several cultural identities, making their existence more complex than one definition can encapsulate. This internalization of Lewis and Huntington's ideologies has caused individuals and society as a whole to take their opinions as facts, which has allowed their subjective hatred to isolate and alienate Muslims. In addition, Huntington and Lewis are contradicted by the reality that 52 percent of Muslims claim to follow the Qur'an/hadith "very much" and 9 percent only a little or not at all, disproving the idea that Muslims are more religiously devout than other groups in the United States (Dana 2011).

Although MAPOS has determined that Muslim Americans are highly supportive of the American political system, there is still a significant amount of anti-Muslim discrimination that derives from politicians. Politicians, including Mark Williams, Peter King, Ron Ramsey, Lou Ann Zalenik, and Newt Gingrich, have verbally attacked the Muslim community, with the intention to alienate them from the rest of American society. In 2004, King (R-NY), the chairman of the House Homeland Security Committee, claimed that the majority of American Muslim leaders are the "enemy" and that "Islamic fundamentalists" control the mosques, where terrorists are being "homegrown." King further emphasized his prejudice toward Muslims in a 2011 congressional hearing where he reiterated his claim that U.S. mosques are controlled by "radical" imams. In this hearing, King scrutinized the Muslim American community and falsely elaborated its ties to terrorism without significant backlash or contradiction from fellow politicians or citizens in attendance. In fact, a Gallup poll found that the majority of Americans felt the King hearings were appropriate in March 2011, and, further, a CNN poll found that 40 percent of Americans have an unfavorable impression of Islam (Dana 2011).

Additionally, during the same time period, Gingrich voiced his partiality when discussing the Park51 project (a possible center for Muslims near the site of the 9/11 Ground Zero in New York City), by stating the project would be "an assertion of Islamist triumphalism" and part of "an Islamist cultural-political offensive design to undermine and destroy our civilizations" (Dana, Oskooii, and Barreto 2011). Congressional candidate Zalenik (R-TN), who claimed that attempting to build a mosque in her town was "a political movement designed to fracture the moral and political foundation of Middle Tennessee," mirrored this sentiment (Dana, Oskooii, and Barreto 2011). Large percentages of the public supported these candidates and their statements, showing how deeply rooted anti-Muslim prejudices are in American politics. This has helped cause two views to gain popularity: that Muslims are "un-American" and that Islam is "antimodern," despite empirical research that proves otherwise (Dana and Franklin 2013).

Not surprisingly, 28 percent of Muslim Americans claim that people have acted suspicious of them, 22 percent say they have been called offensive names, 21 percent admit they have been singled out by airport security, 13 percent say they have been singled out by law enforcement, and 6 percent say they have been threatened or attacked (Pew Research Center 2011b). And many Muslim converts have felt this harsh reality not only from society as a whole but also from within their own families. In his *Washington Post* article, C. L. Jenkins claims that one grandmother of a convert he interviewed "was so disappointed by the conversion that she asked her granddaughter to leave her home and refused to support her financially. She saw the defection from Catholicism as a rejection of family and tradition" (Jenkins 2001, C1). Another convert was told by his father that "because you are a Muslim, you cannot be considered a patriot," showing how deeply rooted the idea of Islam as non-Western is in American society ("Changing Faiths" 2013).

The possibility of being the victim of a hate crime is a concern for many, especially since September 11 (Nimer 2001). The June 2008 shooting of a Muslim business owner (which was recorded by a surveillance camera) in Cleveland, Ohio, brought particular attention to the issue. According to a 2009 report by the Council on American-Islamic Relations (CAIR), the man was shot after a group of men overheard him and his son speaking Uzbek and uttering an Islamic prayer in Arabic while pumping gas after work (Council on American-Islamic Relations 2009). Some Muslim American groups report significantly high levels of dissatisfaction because of the adversity and discrimination they regularly face. According to a Pew survey, only 13 percent of African American Muslims are satisfied with U.S. conditions, compared to 29 percent of non–African American Muslims who were native born and 45 percent of Muslim immigrants (Dana and Franklin 2013). These statistics are an outcome of the society-wide internalizing of an anti-Muslim ideology that is foundationless yet deeply rooted in politics, media, and academia in America.

Muslim Americans' Response to Political Discrimination

Several groups have been formed to address the anti-Muslim postures that thrive in U.S. politics and society. CAIR is the most prominent organization and uses its position as a national organization to demand Muslim civil rights and resist anti-Muslim discrimination. One of the key roles of this group is to explain Islam to non-Muslims. This is also true for the Inner-City Muslim Action Network (IMAN),[1] which has reached out to people from all races, religions, and cultures since the 1990s. IMAN is led by Rami Nashashibi, who has worked to reduce gang violence, provide healthy eating, build houses for Muslims, and provide other services for his Chicago neighborhood, gaining him a place on the list of *Islamica Magazine*'s 2007 10 Young Muslim Visionaries Shaping Islam in America.

Powerful female activists have also emerged in the resistance against prejudice, and Ingrid Mattson is perhaps the most notable. A professor at Hartford Seminary, Mattson became the first woman to head the Islamic Society of North America (ISNA) in 2006. Mattson states that the fury that derived from events on September 11 caused gender issues to take a back seat in her community, with civil society becoming a priority instead. According to Mattson, this has allowed Muslim women to find "a very rich area for activity." She claims that "the only area where there's a limitation is religious leadership—the Imam," and predicts that "we will have some communities in the future that have female imams," which would lead to a sense of equality that critics of the Muslim community could not deny (Dana and Franklin 2013, 118).

---

1. This IMAN is not to be confused with the Los Angeles–based community center the Iranian-American Muslim Association of North America, which also uses the acronym IMAN.

Resistance to Mosques and Park51, and the Impacts of 9/11

Despite the evidence that mosques have a positive influence on Muslim Americans and their communities, several political bodies have displayed resistance to the presence of mosques and Muslim community centers. American society's perception of U.S. Muslims has deteriorated since 9/11, and Islam has been linked to "un-Americanness" in the eyes of many. The National Republican Trust Political Action Committee (NRTPAC) created an online video advertisement titled *The Audacity of Jihad*, in which images of the 9/11 attack overlap with militants shooting rifles in the desert—a depiction of Muslims that is both quite common in Western media and inaccurate. One of the key claims made by the narrator is that "mosque supporters" rejoiced in 9/11 murders. The NRTPAC's depiction of all Muslims as violent, anti-American terrorists is aligned with the views of many anti-mosque groups that believe that mosques are fundamentally different than other religious institutions.

In addition to 9/11, much of the anti-Islam sentiment in America derives from the proposal of the aforementioned Park51 project, a Muslim community center located in Manhattan near Ground Zero. Although the proposal for Park51 was initially endorsed by the Manhattan community board by a 29–1 vote, a national opposition movement forced a retraction of the endorsement. Some antimosque activists made extreme claims, as seen when activist Pamela Geller appeared in media claiming "the 'Monster Ground Zero Mosque' is aimed at Islamic domination and expansionism" (Dana, Oskooii, and Barreto 2011). Tea Party leader Mark Williams described Park51 as a mosque where "the worship of the terrorists' monkey-god" would take place (Dana, Oskooii, and Barreto 2011). Importantly, when surveyed on the proposal to build Park51, 72 percent of Muslim respondents said it should be allowed, 20 percent said it should not be allowed, and 15 percent said it should be permitted but is a bad idea (Pew Research Center 2011a). This high number of nonsupportive Muslims shows the awareness within their community of anti-Muslim discourse in America and the intolerance that Muslims would face if the building of Park51 were to take place.

The national resistance to Park51 fueled resistance to new mosques in other areas of the country as well. One of the most significant cases of intolerance occurred in Murfreesboro, Tennessee, where the growing Muslim population was not permitted to expand its Islamic center because "Islam is not a religion and that the center was a conspiracy to impose Sharia law on the United States" (Pew Research Center 2011b). A similar situation occurred in Temecula, California, when a group called Concerned Community Citizens claimed that a new mosque in the area would clash with the rural atmosphere and turn the community into a "haven for Islamic extremists" (Pew Research Center 2011b). In Longview, Texas, when a group of forty to fifty Muslims proposed the construction of a 2,500-square-foot mosque, some neighbors protested the mosque by putting signs that said "Jesus" in their yards, while others complained about the mosque creating traffic problems. When asked about the resistance, spokesperson Saleem Shabazz stated, "I was hoping that we could accomplish this without any conflict but at the same time I kind of expected it" ("Neighbors Oppose" 2012). However, to reduce anti-Muslim thought in the area, it is noteworthy that members of a nearby Presbyterian church held educational sessions about Islam and invited leaders of the mosque to speak to the church's members, showing the importance of support in the local community. A member of the church stated, "We didn't want the Muslim community to think that was an example of all Christian congregations. . . . We wanted to reach out to our neighbors in the Muslim community and not react out of fear" (Evans 2012). Longview's mosque was an example of successful relationship and community building within their environment, a story that is uncommon given the prejudice that overshadows support in most American communities.

The anti-Islam attitude in America has spread beyond Muslims, as non-Muslims with Muslim affiliations or Muslim-sounding names or appearances encountering public scrutiny. This is most evident in the case of former President Obama, who had his Christian faith, integrity, and commitment to America doubted because of his middle name, Hussein, and Kenyan-Muslim heritage; during the presidential campaign, he was charged with being a Muslim in an attempt to derail his candidacy. This criticism came from the media, the public, and the elected officials of the U.S. government itself and has continued even after the election. In July 2008, state senator Kevin Bryant (R-SC) posted a photo on his blog depicting a T-shirt that showed Obama and Osama Bin Laden with the text, "The difference between Obama and Osama is just a little B.S." (Pew Research Center 2011a). In the same month, advisor Jim Pinkerton was hired by Republican presidential candidate Mike Huckabee and became known for advocating "a cop in front of every mosque just for safekeeping" (Pew Research Center 2011b).

The Role of the Mosque in Muslim American Politics

Despite the discrimination faced by Muslims in America, there is a strong tie between faith and political involvement in the Muslim community. Mosques provide a setting for Muslims to have a common identity in the *ummah* while also embracing their ethnic diversity. Most mosques in America are composed of all groups (U.S.-born, Arab, Asian, and all others), and some even include Sunni and Shia Muslims praying side-by-side. Mosque involvement is directly related to a strong sense of group commonality, with more active members reporting that they have "a great deal" in common with American Muslims with different backgrounds and nationalities. Furthermore, MAPOS found that mosque attendees are more likely to identify as American Muslims, rather than identifying as their nationality of origin. Thus, despite the critique of Islam as being opposed to positive American qualities, mosques actively allow Muslims from all nations to integrate socially and politically into American society.

Mosques are simultaneously celebrated as supportive to immigrant incorporation and criticized for being "fronts of terrorist organizations" (Pew Research Center 2011a). Yet, like churches and synagogues, they are religious institutions that support and promote political and civic engagement within American culture. Compared to 70 percent of nonreligious Muslims, 81 percent of religious Muslims follow American politics closely. Mosque attendance is correlated with greater involvement in one's community groups and organizations that help the poor, and Muslims who are involved in their mosque report 2.6 acts of civic participation annually on average, rather than 1.7 acts on average reported by those who are not actively involved in their religious community (Pew Research Center 2011b).

The strongest level of support between Islam and politics occurs within the Muslims who are the most religious. According to MAPOS, 77 percent of nonreligious Muslims believe that Islamic teachings are compatible with American politics, while 95 percent of religious Muslims believe this to be so (Pew Research Center 2011b). In addition, religiously devout Muslims are more likely to support political participation and civic engagement, allowing them to integrate with American politics and culture. This is a direct contradiction to the claims of Representative King and others who believe that mosques fuel "Islamic fundamentalists" rather than involved American citizens.

King is further contradicted by the Muslim American National Opinion Survey (MANOS), which reveals that religious fundamentalism is nearly identical among Muslims and Christians. MANOS shows that the general American public is 11.5 percent more likely than foreign-born Muslims and 7.8 percent more likely than U.S.-born Muslims to believe that "right and wrong in U.S. law should be based on God's law," showing that the U.S. population as a whole is more fundamentalist in relation to politics than the Muslim population (Gillum 2013). In addition, Pew's U.S. Religious Landscape Survey shows that Protestant Christians are as likely as Muslims to believe that their holy book should be taken literally, which calls for a reconsideration of the implications of fundamentalism in American society.

Age also plays a significant role in the Muslim community. A Pew survey determined that Muslims under thirty years old are more "religiously observant" and "accepting of Islamic extremism" because of frustrations with politics than older Muslims. In addition, 42 percent see a conflict between faith and modern life in the United States, compared to 28 percent of older Muslims (Dana and Franklin 2013). The number of Muslims who say that there is a great deal or fair amount of support for extremism in the Muslim American community is significantly lower than how the general public sees Muslim American support for extremism (21 percent versus 40 percent), and only 6 percent of this 21 percent consider the Muslim community to show "a great deal" of support (Pew Research Center 2011a). It is important to note that "extremism" is not specifically defined in this study. In addition, as Islam transcends national borders and ethnicities, it is impossible to say that all Muslims share the same political behaviors and thoughts.

Muslim youth are less engaged in political life than older Muslims, and are the least likely of all religions to be registered to vote, with only 51 percent of Muslim youth registered versus 78 percent of Protestant youth (Younis 2009). This is likely due to the sense of alienation that is caused by anti-Muslim politicians throughout all levels of government. American Muslim youth are also more politically diverse than the general public portrays them to be, with 39 percent describing their political views as "moderate," 28 percent as "liberal" or "very liberal," and only 20 percent as "conservative" or "very conservative" (Younis 2009). In contrast, 70 percent of all Muslim Americans claim to be Democrat, 11 percent Republican, and 19 percent do not have a preference, showing the political development that occurs within the Muslim American community. This could largely be affected by the idea that half of American Muslims say that the GOP is unfriendly toward them, while only 7 percent believe the same for the Democratic Party (Pew Research Center 2011b).

Conclusions

Although Muslims are often processed as "foreign" to American culture and politics, Islam has existed in America since at least the voyage of Christopher Columbus, making it a significant and overlooked part of history within the Americas. While many Muslims are foreign-born, they have immigrated to the United States in order to escape repression and find economic opportunity. These desires are shared with virtually all other immigrant groups, allowing Muslims to relate to other groups, particularly within the Latino community. The Muslim America population is expected to increase significantly in the next twenty years, making it an important community to understand and communicate with culturally, socially and politically.

Although imam and author Feisal Abdul Rauf argues that America is an "ideal place to practice Islam" (Dana 2011), it is clear that this practice occurs in the face of adversity throughout the nation. Despite the fact that Muslims are primarily middle-class, hardworking American citizens, the general American population holds biases against them that are deeply rooted in the American political, academic, and religious realms. This has been particularly true since the 9/11 attacks, which revolutionized how Muslim Americans are treated by neighbors, relatives, politicians, and all others. These challenges appear to be increasing over time.

It is evident in the aforementioned survey data throughout this chapter that the *ummah* is composed of diverse individuals and cannot be pigeonholed into one specific religious or cultural stereotype. Muslim Americans differ greatly by race, gender, age, political opinions and involvement, language, and original nationality. It is because of this diversity, among other reasons, that politicians, academics, policy makers, and journalists should participate in further research about Muslims as a way to counter prejudice and misinformation.

REFERENCES

Bowen, P. D. 2010. "Early U.S. Latina/o–African-American Muslim Connections: Paths to Conversion." *Muslim World* 100 (4): 390–413.

———. 2013. "U.S. Latina/o Muslims since 1920: From 'Moors' to 'Latino Muslims.'" *Journal of Religious History* 37 (2): 165–184.

"Changing Faiths: Hispanic Americans Leaving Catholicism for Islam." 2013. *BBC*, August 21. Available at http://www.bbc.co.uk/news/world-us-canada-23774334.

Council on American-Islamic Relations. 2009. "The Status of Muslim Civil Rights in the United States, 2009: Seeking Full Inclusion." Available at https://d3n8a8pro7vhmx .cloudfront.net/cairhq/pages/1990/attachments/original/1503993036/CAIR-2009 -Civil-Rights-Report.pdf?1503993036.

Dana, K. 2011. "Muslims in America: A Profile." Dubai Initiative Working Paper, October. Available at https://www.belfercenter.org/sites/default/files/legacy/files/Dana %20WP%20--%20Muslims%20in%20America.PDF.

Dana, K., and S. Franklin. 2013. "Islam in America." In *Islam for Journalists: A Primer on Covering Muslim Communities in America*, edited by Lawrence Pintak and Stephen Franklin, 96–127. Columbia, MO: Donald W. Reynolds Journalism Institute.

Dana, K., K. Oskooii, and M. A. Barreto. 2011. "Mosques as American Institutions: Muslim Incorporation in American Politics." APSA 2011 Annual Meeting Paper. Available at https://papers.ssrn.com/sol3/papers.cfm?abstract_id=1901746.

Evans, G. 2012. "Islamic Mosque Nearly Complete in Northern Longview." *Longview News-Journal*, June 5. Available at https://www.news-journal.com/news/local/ islamic-mosque-nearly-complete-in-northern-longview/article_a7714155-aaf9 -56f3-a40f-d6ea815af5da.html.

Gillum, R. 2013. "There Is No Difference in Religious Fundamentalism between American Muslims and Christians." *Washington Post*, December 16. Available at http://www.washingtonpost.com/blogs/monkey-cage/wp/2013/12/16/no-difference-in-religious-fundamentalism-between-american-muslims-and-christians.

"Islamophobia in the USA." 2017. *Al Jazeera*, May 3. Available at https://www.aljazeera.com/programmes/aljazeeraworld/2017/05/islamophobia-usa-170501131435789.html.

Jenkins, C. L. 2001. "Islam Luring More Latinos: Prayers Offer a More Intimate Link to God, Some Say." *Washington Post*, January 7, p. C1.

Lewis, B. 1993. "Islam and Liberal Democracy." *The Atlantic*, February. Available at https://www.theatlantic.com/magazine/archive/1993/02/islam-and-liberal-democracy/308509.

"Neighbors Oppose Construction of Mosque on Longview Street." 2012. *Islamophobia Today*, January 25. Available at http://www.islamophobiatoday.com/2012/01/25/neighbors-oppose-construction-of-mosque-on-longview-street.

Nieves, E. 2001. "A New Minority Makes Itself Known: Hispanic Muslims. *New York Times*, December 17. https://www.nytimes.com/2001/12/17/us/a-new-minority-makes-itself-known-hispanic-muslims.html.

Nimer, M. 2001. "The Status of Muslim Civil Rights in the United States, 2001." Available at http://www.swissinfo.ch/media/cms/files/swissinfo/2002/08/arabic.pdf.

Pew Research Center. 2011a. "Muslim Americans: No Signs of Growth in Alienation or Support for Extremism." Available at http://www.people-press.org/2011/08/30/muslim-americans-no-signs-of-growth-in-alienation-or-support-for-extremism.

———. 2011b. "A Portrait of Muslim Americans." Available at http://www.people-press.org/2011/08/30/a-portrait-of-muslim-americans.

Sahgal, N. 2013. "Study: Muslim Job Candidates May Face Discrimination in Republican States." Pew Research Center, November 26. Available at http://www.pewresearch.org/fact-tank/2013/11/26/study-muslim-job-candidates-may-face-discrimination-in-republican-states.

Viscidi, L. 2003. "Latino Muslims a Growing Presence in America." *Washington Report on Middle East Affairs* 22 (5). Available at https://www.wrmea.org/003-june/latino-muslims-a-growing-presence-in-america.html.

Younis, M. 2009. "Muslim Americans Exemplify Diversity, Potential." Gallup, March 2. Available at http://www.gallup.com/poll/116260/muslim-americans-exemplify-diversity-potential.aspx.

American Muslim Women in the Age of Trump (and Beyond)

ANWAR MHAJNE AND

BRIAN R. CALFANO

Most of the work in this book focuses on the experiences of Muslims in the United States generally. This chapter concerns the relative experiences Muslim women have had in America since 9/11, with particular attention paid to the legacies of Western mentalities about the Muslim and Arab worlds (especially the Middle East), security policies enacted in the United States after 9/11, and the specific expectations placed on Muslim women (in part) because of their gender. We also address ways that scholars can use newer research methodologies to gain leverage on questions about Muslim women in the United States.

Though both Muslim women and Muslim men experienced social and political pressures related to the fallout from 9/11, we suggest that the experiences and perceptions of American Muslims may diverge along gender identity lines in the Trump political era and beyond. Some of this difference is due to the nature of how Islam is practiced. While certain interpretations of Islamic texts might be highly egalitarian, the practice of Islam around the world has left women in a generally less advantageous position than men (see Ahmed 1992). Like in all religions, but perhaps especially the Abrahamic faiths that claim that God has set forth knowable expectations for social behavior, divine revelation can be interpreted for multiple, sometimes diametrically opposed, purposes. These purposes include interpretations of the Qur'an about the treatment of women (El-Sohl and Mabro 1994; Barlas 2019). Though scholars have warned about the tendency to overemphasize the argument that Islam disproportionately disadvantages women (see Peters 1999), there is enough evidence to suggest that the experiences of women

Muslims differ generally from those of men across nations and cultures. And these differences are palpable for Muslim women in America, particularly given the scrutiny and stereotyping confronting Muslims more generally in the Trump political era (see Calfano, Lajevardi, and Michelson 2017).

Since most Islamic teaching and practice developed outside the United States, it is instructive to briefly review the dynamics of gender rights within the wider Muslim world. While Islam is truly a global religion in terms of adherent distribution, it is also true that much of the influential thinking about practicing Islam, including gender relations between Muslims, comes from the Arab world (see Calfano 2014). Note that we use the term Arab broadly in this case to mean the greater Middle East/North African region (including Afghanistan and Iran, though the ethnic groups in those states do not identify as Arab). This is to distinguish between Muslims living in other parts of Africa and Asia.

The articulation of alternative and more liberal-feminist constructs within Islam notwithstanding, the continuing controversy surrounding women's rights and Islam is spurred by traditionalist Islamism's influence across state borders—a reality even more pronounced in the social media age (Seymen 2011). Clearly, there is a history of patriarchal interpretation in Islam that has caused immense difficulty for women, but what does this mean for American Muslim women in this new era of Trump?

Hate Crimes and the Hijab

As discussed in Chapter 1, American Muslims have been the subject of political and social scrutiny, particularly in the wake of the 2016 presidential primary where anti-Muslim rhetoric among Republican candidates was especially pronounced. One of the main outcomes from the 2016 election was President Donald Trump's attempt to ban travelers from select Muslim-majority countries. Another post-2016 outcome was a spike in the number of hate crimes against women wearing a hijab (Center for the Study of Hate Crime and Extremism 2016). Perhaps not surprisingly, and according to a recent survey by the Institute for Social Policy and Understanding, 38 percent of Muslims expressed fear for their safety from white supremacist groups (Mogahed and Chouhoud 2017). Moreover, a fifth of American Muslims said in recent survey they have made plans to leave the country "if it becomes necessary" (Center for the Study of Hate Crime and Extremism 2016, 4).

This same survey indicates differences between Muslim women's and men's experiences with Islamophobia after the 2016 election. For example, 47 percent of Muslim women said they fear for their personal safety compared to 31 percent of men. Muslim women in the survey also reported higher rates of emotional trauma versus their male counterparts (19 versus 9 percent respectively). Moreover, and perhaps as a way to cope with challenging circumstances, Muslim women reported an increase in donations to Muslim organizations more so than men (29 percent versus 19 percent) (Center for the Study of Hate Crime and Extremism 2016).

Of course, the targeting of Muslims in America is not new. Since September 11, there has been considerable discussion about the growth of Islamophobia (see Allen 2010; Kumar 2012; Poynting and Mason 2007; Sayyid and Vakil 2010; Zempi and Chakraborti 2015; Selod 2015). And, though it might seem a distant event by some standards, the government response to 9/11 left a negative, lasting impact on American Muslims, particularly Arab men. As Nada Elia notes, "In the immediate aftermath of 9/11, thousands of Arab American men were rounded up, arrested, deported, or otherwise disappeared" (2006, 157). Within days of the attacks, the federal government detained men of Middle Eastern and South Asian descent in a nationwide dragnet. By November 5, 2001, the Department of Justice announced that 1,147 people had been detained. The government refused to provide the most basic information (even to detainees' families) about who had been arrested. Those in custody included American citizens and legal residents (in addition to visa holders).

Legislation enabling religious and racial profiling was enacted after 9/11 (Beydoun 2016). Most notably, Congress passed the USA Patriot Act on October 24, 2001, which "sent a message to the American people that ethnic and religious profiling was acceptable, even necessary, so long as it was directed at [Arab and Muslim] groups" (Cainkar 2009, 111). In December 2002, the government launched the National Security Entry-Exit Registration System (NSEERS). Although dissolved in 2011, the system functioned for a decade as "a sweeping immigration tracking program that almost exclusively targeted Muslim immigrants, nonimmigrants, and permanent residents" (Beydoun 2016). NSEERS required, among other things, temporary foreign visitors from twenty-five countries (most of which are Muslim majority) to register in person with the U.S. Citizenship and Immigration Service (USCIS) if they have stayed in the United States for more than thirty days.

At the same time, the 9/11 attacks, and the policies implemented in their aftermath, amplified the visibility of Arabs and Muslims as American minority groups (Alsutany 2008; Cainkar 2009). Barbara Perry (2014) notes that the reactions to the 9/11 attack and vilification of Muslims were immediate. The FBI investigated more than 40 possible hate crimes by September 18, 2001; the number had increased to 145 by October 11 of that year (Perry 2014). Though much of the public and government backlash was directed at

Muslim men, the effects of hate crimes and increased government scrutiny had a disproportionate impact on *women*. With Muslim men targeted by the government, the job of keeping families and communities functional fell to Muslim women, many of whom did not have the personal or financial resources to assume these responsibilities in the short term. Indeed, women had to deal with the emotional, legal, political, and financial costs of Muslim male imprisonment.

Somewhat ironically, Muslim women became more visible in political discourse after 9/11, as the Bush administration sought to cast its policy decisions under the guise of gender liberation (Abu-Lughod 2002; Elia 2006; Maira 2009; Nader 2012; Razack 2005; Puar 2007). For example, then first lady Laura Bush referenced Muslim women as a justification for the war in Afghanistan in a November 2001 radio address: "Because of our recent military gains in much of Afghanistan, women are no longer imprisoned in their homes. They can listen to music and teach their daughters without fear of punishment. The fight against terrorism is also a fight for the rights and dignity of women" (Bush 2001).

As positive as Bush's sentiments might look from a Western perspective, her quote actually falls under the four-stage gendered logic of empire. First, the logic holds that "women have inalienable rights within universal civilization." Second, it assumes that "civilized men recognize and respect these rights." Third, this logic contends that "uncivilized men systematically abrogate these rights." Finally, "such men (the Taliban) thus belong to an alien (Islamic) system." This imperial logic "genders and separates subject peoples so that the men are the Other and the women are civilizable. To defend our universal civilization we must rescue the women. To rescue these women we must attack these men" (Cooke 2002, 227).

This empire view portrays Muslim women, especially veiled women, as victims in need of saving. As various scholars have shown, Western imperialist states have used this perspective to justify colonial projects in the Global South, including Muslim majority countries (Spivak 2010; Ahmed 1992; Abu-Lughod 2002; Cloud 2004; Lorber 2002; Mishra 2007; Zine 2002; Razack 2008; Al-Saji 2010; Selod 2015). The supposed need for Western intervention in Muslim-majority countries is also steeped in the three personas that Muslim women have occupied in the Western imagination (see Bullock and Jafri 2000). The first is the belly-dancer character: "the mysterious and sexualized woman of the 'Orient'" (Perry 2014, 81). The second is the terrorist Muslim woman (Perry 2014). The third is the oppressed Muslim woman, "often represented as the hijab (headscarf) wearer" (Perry 2014, 81; see also Dana et al. 2018).

The hijab has received particular attention in the West, partly because of its relative ubiquity among women in Muslim communities. According to

Sonia Ghumman and Ann Marie Ryan, the term *hijab* originates "from the Arabic word *hajaba*, which means to cover" (2013, 674). However, in the West, "the *hijab* has come to more exclusively refer to the Muslim headscarf itself" (674). Leila Ahmed (1992, 2005) finds that American Muslim women wore the hijab for individualistic reasons that combine existing symbolic meanings in different and new ways (see also Unkelbach et al. 2010; Ghumman and Ryan 2013). She suggests that the hijab has attained new meanings in the United States relative to the Middle East. By taking on the hijab, young American Muslim women emphasize their Muslim identity as a form of resistance to the inferiority narrative attached to Muslims.

But the veil became increasingly vilified in the West after 9/11 as a symbol of gender oppression and Islamist terrorism (Ahmed 1992; Haddad, Smith, and Moore 2006; Razack 2008). These stereotypes are commonly presented as justification for expressions and acts of hostility toward veiled Muslim women. They underpin "the dehumanization of veiled Muslim women by removing any sense of agency on the part of the veil wearer" (Zempi and Chakraborti 2015, 45). The stereotypes, therefore, render Muslim women "as 'easy targets' for verbal abuse and physical attacks when they are seen in public" (45). Women who wear the hijab are more likely to be targeted because of their clear association with Islam (Cesari 2004; Poynting and Mason 2007; Sheridan 2006; Ghumman and Ryan 2013; Saeed 2016; Dana et al. 2018). R. Laurence Moore (1986) suggests that individuals who use visible religious markers indicating minority religious practices usually face discrimination at a greater level than others. And scholars have found an increase in Islamophobic attacks on veiled Muslim women in the United Kingdom, United States, and in other Western countries over the last decade and a half (see Allen and Nielsen 2002; Cainkar 2009; Githens-Mazer and Lambert 2010).

Importantly, the reasons for "Islamophobic violence against women are both the same and different from those underlying violence against men" (Perry 2014, 80). Sahar Aziz notes that, like her male Muslim counterparts, the Muslim woman "bears the brunt of entrenched stereotypes that portray Muslims as the primary threat to American national security. But, unlike her male counterpart, the headscarved Muslim woman is caught at the intersection of discrimination against religion, women, and the racialized 'Muslim other'" (2012, 222). Even though Muslim men experience racial profiling at airports and other places, some veiled Muslim women became a target of intrusive body searches. Some women were required to take off their veil, in violation of their religious beliefs (Zahedi 2011). Veiled Muslim women in the United States "were often put in a position of having to defend their status as an American when they were out in public" (Selod 2015, 83).

They were also "more likely to be interrogated about their lack of American values by strangers in public spaces compared to American Muslim men and American Muslim women who did not wear the hijab" (85). These women "are put in the uncomfortable situation of defending their religious beliefs and practices in relation to their values as American citizens" (86). Therefore, the bodies of veiled American Muslim women become "a site of contestation between American and Islamic values" (87).

Sunaina Maira argues that obsession in the United States with "oppressed" Muslim women "coexists with a desire to rescue them from their tradition in order to bring them into the nation" (2009, 641). This is accompanied by "a deep anxiety about Muslim and Arab men as potential terrorists and religious fanatics who are antithetical to Western liberal democracy and ultimately inassimilable" (641). Yet despite the narrative portraying Muslim women as victims in various studies (e.g., Asani 2003; Cole and Ahmadi 2003; Haddad 2007; Razack 2008; Shaheen 2001; Srivastava 1987), Muslim women are not free from stereotypes that depict Muslims "as evil, barbaric, backwards, terrorists, religious fundamentalists, and uncivilized" (Ghumman and Ryan 2013, 675). The Muslim woman is also portrayed as a real security threat and placed "within a continuum of extremes, fluctuating between the victim who needs to be saved and a physical and existential threat that needs to be defeated" (Saeed 2016, 68). This may be especially the case for veiled women who are "caught between the stereotypical oppressed Muslim and the potential hidden terrorist" (69).

In response to this scrutiny, some Muslim women have started wearing the hijab as a "symbol of solidarity and resistance to efforts to eradicate the religion of Islam" (Haddad 2007, 253). Others choose to challenge the negative perception of Islam through civic engagement and participation in Muslim organizations. They use various public platforms to defend their religion and assert their "American-ness." This marks a shift "from keeping a low socio-political profile, as had been the case before September 11, 2001, to demonstrating their integration in American society and claiming their place in civic and political spaces" (Zahedi 2011, 184). Armed with their knowledge of Islam and their dedication to it, Muslim women in America have played an important role in challenging misperceptions about Islam and the Americanness of the Muslim citizen by serving as public educators.

This brings us to the 2016 election of Donald Trump, which pushed anti-Muslim (and antiwomen) rhetoric to new heights in American political discourse. One of Trump's early policy proposals was a ban on Muslim immigration (Woodruff 2016). Trump first announced the idea of a ban in December 2015. Following a shooting in San Bernardino, California, his campaign released a statement claiming, "Donald J. Trump is calling for a total and complete shutdown of Muslims entering the United States until our country's representatives can figure out what is going on." The Muslim ban later morphed into the vague notion of "extreme vetting." Trump's anti-Muslim rhetoric exacerbated fears connecting Islam and terrorism. A 2015 CBS poll found that 25 percent of Americans supported Trump's Muslim ban (Salvanto et al. 2015). A March 2016 poll showed greater support for the ban, with 51 percent in favor (P. Moore 2016). A nationwide 2016 poll by Reuters/Ipsos in all fifty states found that Trump supporters were more than twice as likely as Clinton supporters to have negative views of Islam (58 percent to 24 percent) (Flitter and Kahn 2016). And a June 2016 survey by the Texas Politics Project found that 76 percent of Republicans support the ban, compared to 26 percent of Democrats (Texas Politics Project 2016).

The difference between Clinton and Trump supporters' backing of the ban could be attributed to their understanding of the relationship between Islam and violence. Republicans are more likely than Democrats to say they are "very worried" about the increase in Islamic extremism around the world (83 percent to 53 percent) and in the United States (65 percent to 38 percent) (Pew Research Center 2015). Additionally, there is a wide partisan divide over the perceived role of Islam in increasing violence, according to a 2015 Pew study. Republicans (68 percent) were more likely than Democrats (30 percent) to say that Islam encourages violence. Republicans were also more likely than Democrats to say that Muslims should be surveilled more than other types of religious people (49 percent to 20 percent). By vilifying the entire global Muslim community, Trump's rhetoric provides many Americans with the specter of a unified and tangible enemy.

As a result of Trump's rhetoric and policy ideas (and the hijab as visible identity marker), Muslim women are placed in a position to perform as objects of political debate, regardless of whether they wish to. Perhaps the best example of this was Munira Ahmed, a thirty-two-year-old Bangladeshi American who became one of the resistance faces to the Trump administration's anti-Muslim discourse when protestors carried signs with her image during the Women's March in January 2017. The image, by Shepard Fairey (the artist known for his portrait of Barack Obama's "Hope" campaign theme), shows Munira wearing the American flag as a hijab. This image counters the narrative of Muslims as anti-American. It also strikes at the heart of the expectations Muslims confront to perform "good citizenship." According to Maira, there are two "modes of expressing cultural citizenship for Muslim Americans after 9/11" (2009, 633)—"good" and "bad" Muslim citizenship—categories that are "heavily gendered and Orientalized" (641) (see also Calfano 2018).

"Good citizenship" is performed by "testifying loyalty to the nation and asserting belief in its democratic ideals, often through public testimonials that emphasize that Muslims are peaceful, loyal U.S. citizens" (Maira 2009, 634). In contrast, "bad" Muslims are enemies of the West and constitute a threat for national security and U.S. democracy (636). This dynamic compels Muslims to demonstrate their patriotism and loyalty to the United States. For instance, after 9/11, there was an increase in the number of American flags on the windows of Muslim stores, in cabs, and on the lawns of Muslim Americans who live in New York City—all in an attempt to convey "good" citizenship (Benjamin 2010). This compelled demonstration of patriotism also sheds light on the centrality of women as a site of contestation and negotiations between Islam and American values.

Importantly, Muslim women may use their identity to advance the collective well-being of their families and coreligionists in America. As later chapters in this volume show, a heightened sense of Muslim identity may be a key behavioral motivator, but more must be understood about how the unique experience of being an American Muslim woman interacts with the identity mechanisms explored by our colleagues. Of the various paths available, none seem more promising than more fully exploring the potential differences between women and men in the Muslim community. Though we have highlighted apparent gender-based differences within the American Muslim community in this chapter, the extant literature has not explored gendered identity differences among Muslims using quantitatively based research designs featuring the kind of randomized interventions used in the study of psychological identity.

We use the following section to consider additional ways to gain leverage in the study of Muslim women in the social and political contexts they inhabit. Focus is specific to use of random assignment in experimental research design whose application has developed substantially in the religion and politics subfield. Our contention is that further development in understanding the effects of gendered identity requires the encouragement of new research paths.

New Paths in Understanding Muslim Women and American Politics

We identify three major theoretical areas ripe for further exploration by scholars using an experimental framework. By "experimental," we specifically mean research designs that use random assignment for the collection of quantitative data (for a discussion of these designs the religion and politics literature, see Djupe and Calfano 2013). These three areas have psychological identity components that may have variable influence on Muslim opinions and behavior. These psychological aspects are best assessed through methodology that intentionally seeks to direct cognition of specific types (e.g., reflection on thoughts about one's faith, community, family, political views, etc.) while not directing this cognition in others. Following the psychology literature in religion and political science (see Calfano, Michelson, and Oldmixon 2017), we argue that the use of experimental design is the most advantageous strategy to get at the effect that underlying mental processes may have for Muslim women and to identify any differences that exist between women and men. These designs would provide a significant addition to the insights afforded by qualitative approaches (e.g., seeking to supplement rather than replace qualitative studies).

In play as part of the continuing backdrop in understanding Muslim women in this heightened period of political scrutiny are the distinctions between "good" and "bad" citizens and the three personas we identified above: the exotic(ized) belly-dancer, the terrorist Muslim woman, and the oppressed Muslim woman. Each of these are templates that the public and policy makers might use as lenses through which to understand American Muslim women (and their approach to politics) in the coming months and years. Scholars should be sensitive to the distinct effects these personas have on American Muslim women as they contest their citizenship and rights in the American political system.

Each of these three topics also intersects with the larger question of Muslims exercising their citizenship rights, and, quite rightly, the topics intersect with each other. The first regards devoutness, which is an important puzzle because, as Chapter 2 shows, the extent to which American Muslims practice their faith and/or draw inspiration from it is much more variable than conventional wisdom (and Muslim stereotypes) assumes. Studies on devoutness among female Muslims in the Middle East present interesting leads for American scholars, especially given that women have been found to exhibit higher levels of devoutness than Muslims males in that region (see Calfano 2014 for a review). Those findings suggest that any political behavior Muslim women undertake may be partially the result of relatively higher devoutness levels than Muslim men exhibit in the United States. If this is true, it also suggests that the reaction from Muslim women to Trump and others using anti-Muslim rhetoric springs from a motivation not to diminish their faith, but to ensure that it is respected within and by the American political system. The irony here, of course, is that we began this chapter by discussing the extent to which some have contorted Islam to be a repressive force against women. But this has not stopped Muslim women from claiming their faith as a core point of identity, by also demonstrating a semblance of devoutness by wearing the most common physical manifestation of their faith. It is this complexity that we find so important to better understand by extending the methodological approaches used to study American Muslim women.

The second topic concerns identity, and it can easily be seen as deriving from devoutness, at least for some. But it is also important to underscore, as others do in this volume, that Muslim identity is a variable construct. On the surface (given our recounting earlier in the chapter about the experiences of Muslim women before and during the Trump political era), it might be tempting to consider Muslim women as readily accepting their Muslim identity at the top of any self-concept hierarchy. Yet the reality of countless identity studies across disciplines cautions us against this assumption. Instead, it is better for scholars to assume a variable identity where women Muslims have the latitude to conceptualize and act as Muslims, but are also free to identify according to any number of other labels. More interesting still is for scholars to compare the relative levels of identity variability between Muslim women and men, and to draw conclusions about how these differences (to the extent they exist), affect political opinion and behavior between sexes. Though a later chapter in this volume offers some initial insights on this question, much remains to be assessed on this topic.

The third topic is family. Given the general distribution of social role expectations throughout much of the Muslim world, Muslim women act as the primary caregivers for children and other relatives. While this expectation is not limited to the Muslim world, there are few, if any, countervailing voices suggesting more gender balance in shouldering family responsibilities (which means Muslim women are more likely than their non-Muslim counterparts to be expected to provide family care). Muslim family life is also important as a way to understand one of the core institutions by which Muslim youth are introduced to the American political, economic, and social structures. Thus, what Muslim women say and do in their families may have substantial impact on the next generation of Muslims in America. And how women respond to the rhetoric and related challenges of the Trump political era may indicate much about the examples young Muslims are exposed to in determining their own sense of identity.

As with the devoutness and identity items in understanding how Muslim women view their family life and responsibilities, scholars should be sensitive not to assume that women view their family role in a monolithic manner. Instead, it is perhaps more realistic to assume that American Muslim women hold a combination of views about their roles—some that may even be contradictory and wrapped up in commitment to religious devoutness and other identity constructs. The necessity of a research focus on the family topic, however, is that, along with the hijab, it is an experience that predominantly affects women differently from Muslim men. Indeed, part and parcel of a family focus is to understand how male Muslims see their family roles as well. The same goes for devoutness and identity. In other words, while we expect differences to manifest on these major topics between Muslim women and men, it is critical to establish what both women and men perceive, think, and do in regard to each in order to create an insightful picture of Muslim life in this era of contested citizenship.

Research designs used to understand more about these three topics can (and do) take various forms, but the use of an experimental design whereby subjects (for example, Muslim women, men, or both) are introduced to some intervention at random can be used to help determine how devoutness, identity, and family influence, and are influenced by, what Muslim women do and how they think relative to men. One of the most direct ways to examine effects from these topics would be to use a set of survey questions that ask Muslim respondents about their relative levels of religious devoutness, with these religion questions randomly placed either toward the beginning or end of the survey. In the middle of the survey would be questions of related political interest to researchers. These might include perceptions of scrutiny from government actors or non-Muslims in society, relative levels of political activity, self-conscious emotions related to images of the "good" citizen archetype discussed above, reactions to the kind of patriarchal or "empire"-driven narratives referenced previously, and virtually any other related outcome of interest to researchers. Similar question order set-ups can be used to derive insights about identity and family-related topics.

The premise behind these "question-order" experiments is that randomly determining a select number of respondents to reflect on question topics at the start of a survey—prior to asking someone about their perceptions about key outcome topics—might affect how the topics positioned at the start of the survey answer questions about the outcome topics (i.e., priming thoughts). And if there is a gender-based difference to these responses, such an effect is also detectable through the random assignment in an experiment. Returning to the devoutness example, if researchers suspect that priming one's relative level of religious devoutness affects their perceptions of scrutiny about their religious practice as a Muslim, positioning questions about frequency of prayer and participation in mosque-based activities (for example) at random ahead of questions about perceived government and social scrutiny might show a significant statistical effect for the devoutness items for those randomly exposed to the devoutness questions earlier in the survey. Furthermore, splitting the respondents along gender lines may show different effect patterns that demonstrate clear gender-based differences. For example, if the assumption about women Muslims being more religiously devout holds true, there would be different hypothesized expectations for how priming religious devoutness in Muslim women affects perceived scrutiny vis-à-vis men.

This research design approach could be used in substituting questions about one's identity or family for devoutness—the premise is the same (even if the hypothesized impacts might not be). More elaborate designs featuring "real world" or "in the field" artifacts like social media may also prove useful in expanding the study of Muslim women. The takeaway point from this chapter's discussion, however, remains constant: there is enough evidence in media and current events to suggest that interpretations of Islam, the post-9/11 context in the United States, legacies of imperialism, and individual-level factors (including religious devoutness and identity) differentiate the experiences of Muslim women from men, and researchers should work to understand these differences in both the Trump political era and beyond.

REFERENCES

Abu-Lughod, Lila. 2002. "Do Muslim Women Really Need Saving? Anthropological Reflections on Cultural Relativism and Its Others." *American Anthropologist* 104 (3): 783–790.

Ahmed, Leila. 1992. *Women and Gender in Islam: Historical Roots of a Modern Debate.* New Haven, CT: Yale University Press.

———. 2005. "The Discourse of the Veil." In *Postcolonialisms: An Anthology of Cultural Theory and Criticism*, edited by G. Desai and S. Nair, 315–338. New York: Bloomsbury.

Allen, Christopher. 2010. *Islamophobia.* New York: Routledge.

Allen, Christopher, and Jørgen S. Nielsen. 2002. "Summary Report on Islamophobia in the EU after 11 September 2001." Available at fra.europa.eu/sites/default/files/fra_uploads/199-Synthesis-report_en.pdf.

Al-Saji, Alia. 2010. "The Racialization of Muslim Veils: A Philosophical Analysis." *Philosophy and Social Criticism* 36 (8): 875–902.

Alsultany, Evelyn. 2008. "The Prime Time Plight of the Arab Muslim American after 9/11." In *Race and Arab Americans before and after 9/11*, edited by Amaney Jamal and Nadine Naber, 204–228. Syracuse, NY: Syracuse University Press.

Asani, Ali S. 2003. "'So That You May Know One Another': A Muslim American Reflects on Pluralism and Islam." *Annals of the American Academy of Political and Social Science* 588:40–51.

Aziz, Sahar F. 2012. "From the Oppressed to the Terrorist: Muslim American Women Caught in the Crosshairs of Intersectionality." *Hastings Race and Poverty Law Journal* 9:191–263.

Barlas, Asma. 2019. *Believing Women in Islam: Unreading Patriarchal Interpretations of the Qur'an.* Rev. ed. Austin: University of Texas Press.

Benjamin, Mark. 2010. "What Islamophobia Really Threatens." *Salon*, September 30. Available at https://www.salon.com/2010/09/29/american_muslim_terrorism_report.

Beydoun, Khaled A. 2016. "Islamophobia: Toward a Legal Definition and Framework." *Columbia Law Review* 116. Available at https://columbialawreview.org/content/islamophobia-toward-a-legal-definition-and-framework.

Bullock, Katherine H., and Gul J. Jafri. 2000. "Media (Mis)Representations: Muslim Women in the Canadian Nation." *Canadian Woman Studies* 20:35–40.

Bush, Laura W. 2001. Radio address, Crawford, TX, November 17. Available at https://www.bushcenter.org/publications/articles/2013/02/radio-address-by-mrs-laura-w-bush-crawford-tx-november-17-2001.html.

Calfano, Brian Robert, ed. 2014. *Assessing MENA Political Reform: Post–Arab Spring: Mediators and Microfoundations.* Lanham, MD: Lexington Books.

———. 2018. *Muslims, Identity, and American Politics.* New York: Routledge.

Calfano, Brian Robert, Nazita Lajevardi, and Melissa R. Michelson. 2017. "Trumped Up Challenges: Limitations, Opportunities, and the Future of Political Research on Muslim Americans." *Politics, Groups, and Identities* 5:1–17.

Calfano, Brian Robert, Melissa Michelson, and Elizabeth Oldmixon. 2017. *A Matter of Discretion: The Politics of Roman Catholic Priests in the US and Ireland.* Lanham, MD: Rowman and Littlefield.

Cainkar, Louis A. 2009. *Homeland Insecurity: The Arab American and Muslim American Experience after 9/11.* New York: Russell Sage Foundation.

Center for the Study of Hate Crime and Extremism. 2016. "Special Status Report: Hate Crime in the United States." Available at https://assets.documentcloud.org/documents/3110202/SPECIAL-STATUS-REPORT-v5-9-16-16.pdf.

Cesari, Jocelyne. 2004. *When Islam and Democracy Meet: Muslims in Europe and in the United States.* New York: Palgrave Macmillan.

Cloud, Dana L. 2004. "'To Veil the Threat of Terror': Afghan Women and the Clash of Civilizations in the Imagery of the US War on Terrorism." *Quarterly Journal of Speech* 90:285–306.

Cole, Darnell, and Shafiqa Ahmadi. 2003. "Perspectives and Experiences of Muslim Women Who Veil on College Campuses." *Journal of College Student Development* 44:47–66.

Cooke, Miriam. 2002. "Islamic Feminism before and after September 11th." *Duke Journal of Gender Law and Policy* 9:227–235.

Dana, Karam, Nazita Lajevardi, Kassra A. R. Oskooii, and Hannah Walker. 2018. "Veiled Politics: Experiences with Discrimination among Muslim Americans." *Politics and Religion*, June 13. Available at https://doi.org/10.1017/S1755048318000287.

Djupe, Paul A., and Brian R. Calfano. 2013. *God Talk: Experimenting with the Religious Causes of Public Opinion.* Philadelphia: Temple University Press.

Elia, Nada. 2006. "Islamophobia and the 'Privileging' of Arab American Women." *NWSA Journal* 18:155–161.

El-Sohl, Fawzi Camillia, and Judy Mabro, eds. 1994. *Muslim Women's Choices: Religious Belief and Social Reality.* Oxford: Berg.

Flitter, Emily, and Chris Kahn. 2016. "Republicans, Democrats Sharply Divided over Muslims in America: Reuters/Ipsos Poll." *Reuters*, July 15. Available at https://www.reuters.com/article/us-usa-election-poll-muslims/republicans-democrats-sharply-divided-over-muslims-in-america-reuters-ipsos-poll-idUSKCN0ZV20C.

Ghumman, Sonia, and Ann Marie Ryan. 2013. "Not Welcome Here: Discrimination towards Women Who Wear the Muslim Headscarf." *Human Relations* 66:671–698.

Githens-Mazer, Jonathan, and Robert Lambert. 2010. *Islamophobia and Anti-Muslim Hate Crime: A London Case Study*. Exeter, UK: University of Exeter European Muslim Research Centre.

Haddad, Yvonne Yazbeck. 2007. "The Post-9/11 Hijab as Icon." *Sociology of Religion* 68:253–267.

Haddad, Yvonne Yazbeck, Jane I. Smith, and Kathleen M. Moore. 2006. *Muslim Women in America: The Challenge of Islamic Identity Today*. Oxford: Oxford University Press.

Kumar, Deepa. 2012. *Islamophobia and the Politics of Empire*. Chicago: Haymarket Books.

Lorber, Judith. 2002. "Presidential Address: Heroes, Warriors, and Burqas; A Feminist Sociologist's Reflections on September 11." *Sociological Forum* 17:377–396.

Maira, Sunaina. 2009. "'Good' and 'Bad' Muslim Citizens: Feminists, Terrorists, and US Orientalisms." *Feminist Studies* 35:631–656.

Mishra, Smeeta. 2007. "Saving Muslim Women and Fighting Muslim Men: Analysis of Representations in the *New York Times*." *Global Media Journal* 6:1–20.

Mogahed, Dalia, and Youssef Chouhoud. 2017. "American Muslim Poll, 2017: Muslims at the Crossroads." Institute for Social Policy and Understanding. Available at https://www.ispu.org/wp-content/uploads/2017/03/American-Muslim-Poll-2017 -Report.pdf.

Moore, Peter. 2016. "Divide on Muslim Neighborhood Patrols but Majority Now Back Muslim Travel Ban." *YouGov*, March 28. Available at https://today.yougov.com/ topics/politics/articles-reports/2016/03/28/divide-muslim-neighborhood-patrols.

Moore, R. Laurence. 1986. *Religious Outsiders and the Making of Americans*. Oxford: Oxford University Press.

Nader, Laura. 2012. *Culture and Dignity: Dialogues between the Middle East and the West*. New York: John Wiley.

Perry, Barbara. 2014. "Gendered Islamophobia: Hate Crime against Muslim Women." *Social Identities* 20:74–89.

Peters, Ruud. 1999. "Islamic Law and Human Rights: A Contribution to an Ongoing Debate." *Islam and Christian-Muslim Relations* 10:5–14.

Pew Research Center. 2015. "Views of Government's Handling of Terrorism Fall to Post-9/11 Low." December 15. Available at http://www.people-press.org/2015/12/15/views -of-governments-handling-of-terrorism-fall-to-post-911-low.

Poynting, Scott, and Victoria Mason. 2007. "The Resistible Rise of Islamophobia: Anti-Muslim Racism in the UK and Australia before 11 September 2001." *Journal of Sociology* 43:61–86.

Puar, Jasbir K. 2007. *Terrorist Assemblages: Homonationalism in Queer Times*. Durham, NC: Duke University Press.

Razack, Sherene. 2005. "Geopolitics, Culture Clash, and Gender after September 11." *Social Justice* 32:11–31.

———. 2008. *Casting Out: The Eviction of Muslims from Western Law and Politics*. Toronto: University of Toronto Press.

Saeed, Tania. 2016. *Islamophobia and Securitization: Religion, Ethnicity and the Female Voice*. New York: Palgrave Macmillan.

Salvanto, Anthony, Jennifer De Pinto, Sarah Dutton, and Fred Backus. 2015. "Poll: Solid Opposition to Ban on Muslims Entering U.S." *CBS News*, December 11. Available at https://www.cbsnews.com/news/poll-solid-opposition-to-ban-on-muslims -entering-us.

Sayyid, Salman, and AbdoolKarim Vakil, eds. 2010. *Thinking through Islamophobia: Global Perspectives*. El Paso, TX: Cinco Puntos Press.

Selod, Saher. 2015. "Citizenship Denied: The Racialization of Muslim American Men and Women Post-9/11." *Critical Sociology* 41:77–95.

Seymen, Atasoy. 2011. "The Turkish Example: A Model for Change in the Middle East?" *Middle East Policy* 18:86–100.

Shaheen, Jack. 2001. *Reel Bad Arabs: How Hollywood Vilifies a People*. Northampton, MA: Interlink.

Sheridan, Lorraine P. 2006. "Islamophobia Pre– and Post–September 11th, 2001." *Journal of Interpersonal Violence* 21:317–336.

Spivak, Gayatri Chakravorty. 2010. "Can the Subaltern Speak?" In *Can the Subaltern Speak? Reflections on the History of an Idea*, edited by Rosalind C. Morris, 21–78. New York: Columbia University Press.

Srivastava, Ramji. 1987. "A Comparative Study of Awareness and Expression of Male and Female Sex Trait Stereotypes among Majority and Minority Communities." *Perspectives in Psychological Researches* 10:57–68.

Texas Politics Project. 2016. "Banning Muslims from Entering U.S. (June 2016)." Available at https://texaspolitics.utexas.edu/set/banning-muslims-entering-us-june-2016#party-id.

Unkelbach, Christian, Hella Schneider, Kai Gode, and Miriam Senft. 2010. "A Turban Effect, Too: Selection Biases against Women Wearing Muslim Headscarves." *Social Psychological and Personality Science* 1:378–383.

Woodruff, Betsy. 2016. "Trump Attorney General Pick Jeff Sessions Argued for a Religious Test to Ban Muslims." *Daily Beast*, November 19. Available at https://www.thedailybeast.com/trump-attorney-general-pick-jeff-sessions-argued-for-a-religious-test-to-ban-muslims.

Zahedi, Ashraf. 2011. "Muslim American Women in the Post–11 September Era: Challenges and Opportunities." *International Feminist Journal of Politics* 13:183–203.

Zempi, Irene, and Neil A. Chakraborti. 2015. "'They Make Us Feel Like We're a Virus': The Multiple Impacts of Islamophobic Hostility towards Veiled Muslim Women." *International Journal for Crime, Justice and Social Democracy* 4:44–56.

Zine, Jasmin. 2002. "Muslim Women and the Politics of Representation." *American Journal of Islamic Social Sciences* 19:1–22.

The Unbearable Whiteness
of Being Middle Eastern

Causes and Effects of the Racialization
of Middle Eastern Americans

Nazita Lajevardi, Melissa R. Michelson,

and Marianne Marar Yacobian

As the previous three chapters underscore, identity politics are a persistent and salient factor in American politics. Indeed, African Americans, Latinos, and other national-origin and racial groups have formed panethnic coalitions to increase their political power and fight for equality and justice. Conversely, other identity groups have fought to instead be recognized as white. The assimilation stories of the Polish, Irish, Catholics, and Italians fit into this mold, as do, to a lesser extent, the stories of Jews and Latter-Day Saints. From the early 1900s up to 9/11, Middle Eastern and Muslim Americans followed a similar trajectory in their battle for whiteness. And for the most part, they were successful. But after 9/11, and especially with the election of Donald Trump as president of the United States, a new period of identity politics has arrived, in which the whiteness of some groups is increasingly called into question, particularly among members of the white nationalist (a.k.a. alt-right) groups empowered by Trump's victory.

We focus on Middle Eastern and Muslim Americans' battle for recognition as white and how the preferred ethno-racial identities of members of this community help us understand their political attitudes and behaviors. First, we review the history of the battle to be recognized as white by various U.S. subgroups, and particularly by Middle Eastern and Muslim Americans. Second, we propose how these identities have been highlighted and activated since 2015, largely because of the Trump campaign and the early actions and policies of his administration. Next, we describe our hypotheses about identity and describe findings from our unique data collection effort in California in 2013 and in an online sample of Muslim Americans in 2017. Last, we discuss how our findings help predict what we expect to see from Muslim American and Middle Eastern Americans moving forward.

Absorption of Middle Eastern Identity under Muslim American Panethnicity

After 9/11, legislators, the news media, and the American public struggled to identify the national enemy. Indeed, the news media's discussion of Arab Americans, Middle Eastern Americans, Muslim Americans, and national-origin Americans all increased as society struggled in its identification of the correct and relevant group responsible for the terrorist attack (Lajevardi 2017). Initially, there was an emphasis on the study of Arab Americans, reflecting the George W. Bush administration's "war on terror" in Iraq. Even then, the war was understood by some to be targeting the Middle East, given Arab Americans' diverse faiths and national origin backgrounds and the inclusion of Afghanistan in the war. But it was not until the increased proliferation of what was referred to as Islamic terrorism (also sometimes referred to as ISIS, ISIL, or Daeesh), and the Syrian refugee crisis, that public focus settled on Muslim Americans.

Over time, and certainly with the 2016 presidential election, it became clear to scholars that Muslim Americans were the panethnic group being repeatedly identified and demonized by legislators and in the media (Lajevardi 2017). The identification of Muslim Americans as the central group worthy of study, however, does not capture the repeated and negative association that Arab Americans, Middle Eastern Americans, and national origin Americans experienced in the years that followed the 9/11 attacks. This shift in focus has muddied public understanding of the distinction between these groups and complicated the ability of members of these various communities to buy into the strong panethnic identity imposed on them. The political decision to focus on Muslim Americans as the internal enemy in the war on terror has led to the decreased visibility of Middle Eastern Americans. As we document later in this chapter, members of the public often conflate members of these groups, ascribing Muslim identities to non-Muslims of Middle Eastern descent. Sometimes, these non-Muslim Middle Eastern Americans suffer Islamophobic discrimination and even violence. In addition, because Muslim American identity has been stigmatized, individuals have, in turn, been discouraged from developing panethnic (or pan-religious) identities, perhaps choosing to instead identify with their national origin group or other salient identity. This dilutes the Muslim community's potential political power and thus its ability to work to fight back against stigmatization and Islamophobia. In the following section, we explore Middle Eastern American identity—a label that we contend has been subsumed by Muslim Americans in recent years—but also identifies the nuanced activation of Muslim American identity among those Middle Eastern Americans who struggle with their identification as "others" in society.

How Middle Easterners Became White

For centuries, the definition of race has changed to fit the sociopolitical paradigm and agenda of a certain time (Omi and Winant 2004). Some groups were accepted as normal, and others were not, often for vague and fundamentally flawed reasons not necessarily related to skin color, hair texture, or other seemingly distinctive ascriptive characteristics of various communities. Yet, while socially constructed and artificial, race permeates every factor of the American sociopolitical order, allowing governments and individuals to define and categorize members of the polity (Glenn 2002). As Haney López asserts, "Race determines our politics. It alters electoral boundaries, shapes the disbursement of local, state, and federal funds, fuels the creation and collapse of political alliances, and twists the conduct of law enforcement" (1994, 3). Yet, while race is an omnipresent and powerful factor in American politics, it is also "constantly being transformed by political struggle" (Omi and Winant 1994, 55).

Today, the U.S. Census Bureau collects information on Middle Easterners under the "white" classification. Even if a Middle Eastern individual indicates their race as "Other" and identifies as Middle Eastern, the census "corrects" that data to classify the individual as racially white. This conforms with the bureau's current official definition of white, as "a person having origins in any of the original peoples of Europe, the Middle East, or North Africa" (U.S. Census Bureau 2018). Census policy notwithstanding, most Americans and Middle Easterners understand Middle Easterners to belong to a separate, panethnic group that is phenotypically distinct from the majority white population. In fact, major efforts were underway to include a Middle Eastern North African (MENA) category to the 2020 Census (Arab American Institute 2018). The Census Bureau does not collect information on religious affiliation.

These already-enacted policies (and potential policies) interact with the focus by the media on Muslim Americans to generate barriers to the political power of Middle Eastern Americans, with negative consequences for members of both groups. Middle Eastern Americans are encouraged to identify as Middle Eastern as part of a clearly delineated panethnic group, separate from (and not aligned with) Muslim Americans. At the same time, as noted above, Middle Eastern Americans are often mistakenly identified as Muslim and then victimized by Islamophobic rhetoric and violence. Their ability to mobilize against those threats, and to ally with Muslim Americans in order to destigmatize that community, is undermined by that same stigmatization and by government policies that remind Middle Easterners they are a separate community. At the same time, and for Muslim Americans, the lack of government policies that identify them as a politically relevant group (including the ongoing policy of not collecting information about the size of the community through the census) discourages their political cohesion and minimizes their political power at the same time that they are demonized by the Trump administration and by media coverage.

Thus, to understand the current political trends among Middle Easterners, we must first understand what it means to be *both* Middle Eastern and white. The dynamic poses a twofold problem—one that identifies Middle Easterners as a geopolitical threat assumed to exist from Islam and yet simultaneously as members of the dominant racial group. By ascertaining the intrinsic flaws in defining Middle Easterners as white, to be simultaneously included and excluded, we shed light on the group's political activism and political invisibility.

The Battle for Whiteness

Historically, whiteness came with many legal, economic, and sociopolitical privileges. The 1790 Naturalization Act restricted naturalization to "free white persons," thereby restricting voting rights and other political power to European immigrants. Many states allowed only white citizens to own or lease land. These restrictions stayed in place, with only minor adjustments to allow for African Americans and former slaves to become citizens, until the McCarran-Walter Act of 1952. Thus, over time, many individuals, including those hailing from the Middle East, fought to be recognized as white by the legal system (Tehranian 2009).

The definition of whiteness changed over time to benefit or further marginalize groups of people. For example, the borders of whiteness were originally drawn within Europe, but geopolitical influences eventually led to drawing borders that encompassed Europe (Omi and Winant 2004). The social construction of whiteness became a vehicle for the perpetuation or alleviation of oppression. Until 1952, political and economic pressures generated by U.S. law incentivized individuals from many backgrounds to fight for legal recognition as "white."

While for many groups this recognition was elusive (e.g., for Japanese Americans), for Arabs and Persians the attainment of whiteness was successful: the government considers them white, and they are directed to check the "white" box for race on the U.S. Census and other governmental forms.[1] This enabled Arab Americans and Middle Easterners to own land and be granted rights and privileges only afforded to whites. The groups were also less likely than other minorities to fight the same battles for civil rights, voting rights, and racial equality as other racial minorities and immigrant groups did.

However, this "white" racial formation would prove complex in its effects. Currently, Middle Easterners are not eligible for affirmative action programs that have hiring preferences and government contracts or funding to individuals; nor does being Middle Eastern allow for special consideration for acceptance to colleges and universities. And, official whiteness notwithstanding, Middle Easterners in the United States have increasingly been the target of both public and private discrimination. John Tehranian notes:

> The assumption that Americans of Middle Eastern descent have not suffered systemic racial prejudice in American society is disingenuous. Indeed, quotidian realities quickly reveal the problematic governmental categorization of Middle Easterners as white. As any Arab, Turkish, or Iranian American will tell you, Middle Easterners are infrequently treated as white people in their daily lives. (2009, 38)

The historical and institutionalized discrimination of Middle Easterners dating back to events like the Palestinian-Israeli conflict, the Persian Gulf War, the wars in Iraq and Afghanistan, and systemic racial profiling post-9/11 has led to an almost socially acceptable discrimination in the name of patriotism and national security.

Today, discrimination has recently reached new heights. Since the 2016 presidential campaign, much of this discrimination toward Middle Easterners—and by extension Muslim Americans—has translated into increased episodes of hate crimes, the rampant proliferation of negative attitudes, and the implementation of policies targeting Middle Eastern and Muslim Americans. On January 27, 2017, just a week into his administration, President Trump signed an executive order (EO 13769) to ban individuals from seven predominantly Muslim countries from entering the United States (Iran, Iraq, Libya, Somalia, Sudan, Syria, and Yemen; five of these seven countries are part of the Middle East). The immigration order, popularly known as the

---

1. For a case involving naturalization of a Japanese immigrant, see *Ozawa v. United States*, 260 U.S. 189 (1922). For a case involving naturalization of a Syrian immigrant, see *Dow v. United States*, 226 F. 145 (4th Cir. 1915).

Muslim Ban, was the immediate target of numerous protests and legal challenges. Two states (Washington and Minnesota) filed lawsuits against EO
13769; a national temporary restraining order was issued on February 3 and
later upheld by the United States Court of Appeals for the Ninth Circuit on
February 9. This led the Trump administration to announce it would replace
the executive order with a new one.

A second executive order on immigration (EO 13780) was issued on
March 6, 2017, dropping Iraq from the list of banned countries and making
other changes. Yet this second effort was similarly challenged in the courts,
and was blocked by Hawaii's U.S. District Judge Derrick Watson on March
15 on the grounds that the state of Hawaii was likely to prove that EO 13780
was, in fact, a Muslim ban (Levine and Rosenberg 2017). In an op-ed written
for *CNN*, National Iranian American Council president Trita Parsi and former U.S. Marine Adam Weinstein commented, "This ban is a blueprint for
ridding the United States of Muslims and turning the remaining Muslim
population into second-class citizens" (Parsi and Weinstein 2017). In late
June 2017, the U.S. Supreme Court agreed to hear the issue, but before the
planned hearing date, the Trump administration withdrew the order and
replaced it with a third version of the travel ban, this time removing Sudan
and adding Chad, North Korea, and Venezuela to the list of banned countries. The third iteration of the travel ban suffered a similar fate as its prede-
cessors: on October 17 it was blocked by the same federal judge in Hawaii,
who noted that the ban "suffers from precisely the same maladies as its predecessor," despite the window-dressing addition of two non-Muslim countries (Rubin 2017). Another injunction was issued at the same time by Maryland district judge Theodore D. Chuang, who noted that Trump's tweets
helped convince him that the ban was an "inextricable re-animation of the
twice-enjoined Muslim ban" and thus likely unconstitutional (Zapotosky
2017). On December 22, the Ninth Circuit Court of Appeals held that Trump
lacks authority under federal immigration laws to issue such sweeping restrictions, writing that the president "cannot without the assent of Congress
supplant its statutory scheme with one stroke of a presidential pen" (S. M.
2018). The case, *Trump v. Hawaii*, heard oral arguments in April 2018, with
a decision in favor of the president in June 2018. "In a 5-to-4 vote, the court's
conservatives said that the president's power to secure the country's borders,
delegated by Congress over decades of immigration lawmaking, was not undermined by Mr. Trump's history of incendiary statements about the dan-
gers he said Muslims pose to the United States" (Liptak and Shear 2018).

Although Trump's efforts to impose a Muslim ban both faced immediate
and significant legal and popular resistance (see Collingwood, Lajevardi,
and Oskooii 2018), they also fueled Islamophobia and negative attitudes

about Muslims and Middle Easterners. The few supporters of the travel ban insisted that this was not a *Muslim ban* per se but, rather, a ban on countries, many of which are Middle Eastern, and their citizens that threatened our national security. Supporters pointed out that there was no religious litmus test. Thus, it was mostly a ban on threatening Middle Eastern countries. But this characterization was futile. FBI statistics for 2015 showed a 67 percent increase in hate crimes against Muslim Americans (Federal Bureau of Investigation 2016). The Southern Poverty Law Center reported a spike in anti-Muslim hate crimes after Trump was elected, particularly against women in hijab. In the last two months of 2016, 34 attacks on mosques were reported, and in the ten days immediately after the election, 49 hate crimes against Muslims were reported (Southern Poverty Law Center 2016). In addition, some hate crimes were reported against individuals incorrectly identified by their attackers as Muslim or Middle Eastern Americans. This includes the case of a Florida man who set fire to a convenience store he believed was owned by Muslims (but was actually owned by U.S. citizens of Indian descent) (Morlin 2017) and the case of a Kansas man who shot and killed two people he thought were Iranian but who in fact were of Indian origin (Associated Press 2017). According to the Southern Poverty Law Center, and as seen in Figure 4.1, the number of anti-Muslim groups in the United States spiked 198 percent, from just 34 in 2015 to 101 in 2016.

In addition to his executive orders, Trump has fueled anti-Muslim hate through his incendiary rhetoric and through his initial staffing choices. He has proposed creating a national database of Muslims and has supported surveilling mosques. He also frequently shared a false story about shooting Muslims with bullets dipped in pig blood and has declared, "Islam hates us" (Mathias 2017). His first choice as national security advisor, retired general Mike Flynn, had previously described Islam as a "malignant cancer" and tweeted that fear of Muslims was rational (Potok 2017).

The characterization of Muslim Americans and Middle Easterners as the "enemy alien" is observable in some of the evidence discussed above, such as in the number of hate crimes reported in the months immediately following Trump's electoral victory. Mosques were vandalized and set on fire, Muslim and Middle Eastern individuals and leaders were threatened with or were victims of violent assault, and racist fliers and propaganda against Muslims appeared on university campuses. This builds on the anti-Muslim sentiment that has been institutionalized in a number of states. Between 2013 and 2015, ten states approved "anti-Islam" laws and two states revised their textbooks in response to anti-Islam campaigns (CAIR 2016).

The rampant proliferation of negative and discriminatory attitudes, behaviors, and policies raises questions about the ability of Middle Eastern and

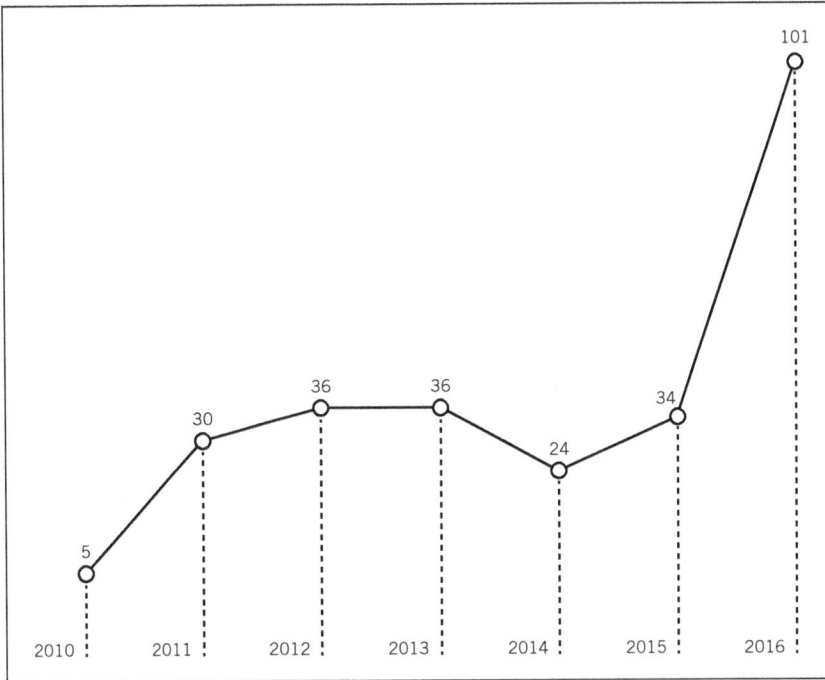

Figure 4.1 Increase in anti-Muslim groups over time
Source: Southern Poverty Law Center, n.d.

Muslim Americans to continue to take advantage of the privileges of whiteness that they were legally afforded long ago. While it may be that they have been legally granted the protections and privileges of whiteness, those protections and privileges do not extend to everyday societal and political experiences. American society has increasingly condemned antiblack, anti-Latino, and anti-Asian discrimination, but often racism against Middle Easterners and Muslim Americans is tolerated and even encouraged (Mc-Carus 1994). Tehranian notes, "Middle Easterners have come to represent enemy aliens, and even an enemy race, in the popular imagination" (2009, 70).

The rampant proliferation of discrimination against Middle Eastern Americans may be connected to the activation and focus on Muslim American identity since 2015. Muslims have experienced the greatest increases in news media coverage relative to blacks and Latinos. In 2000, the year prior to 9/11, Muslims, blacks, and Latinos appeared in 1.87 percent, 4.95 percent, and 3.5 percent of all available news media broadcasts, respectively. However, the relative salience and importance of each of these groups shifted drastically fifteen years later. In 2015, the news media covered Muslims nearly 1.5 times more than blacks and twice as much as Latinos, America's two largest racial minority groups; Muslims are mentioned in 14.2 percent of all available transcripts, compared to blacks and Latinos who are mentioned in 9.86 percent and 7.1 percent of 2015 transcripts, respectively (Lajevardi 2017). Given the increase in media focus on Muslims, attention on Muslims *in* America has arguably risen dramatically in American society.

Causes and Effects of Identity Activation

What is less well understood, and what we explore here, is the impact of these activated identities as Muslim Americans and Middle Eastern Americans (racialized identities) on political behavior. We hypothesize that Middle Eastern Americans who are racialized have distinctive sets of political attitudes and behaviors as compared to nonracialized Middle Eastern Americans, including increased cynicism and stronger feelings of political efficacy. In addition, we posit that this racialization empowers individuals to become more involved in the political arena and be more attentive to politics. We explore these questions with a unique data set collected in 2013, as well as data on Muslim Americans collected in early 2017.

In July 2013, we fielded a team of researchers in Southern California (Orange County and Los Angeles County) to collect in-person paper surveys from Middle Easterners. Over the course of two days (Saturday and Sunday, July 13 and 14), we visited two Islamic community centers and a shopping center frequented by Middle Easterners. The data collection effort overlapped with an important month in the Islamic calendar, Ramadan, which ensured a good pool of potential respondents at the community centers, both of which were used during this time to mark the holiday and the end of daily fasting.

Surveys were available in English, Arabic, and Farsi. The team of researchers—faculty, undergraduates, and graduate students—included individuals fluent in these languages. Three of the researchers collecting surveys were male and three were female. At each location, individuals were approached by a researcher and asked if they would be willing to complete the paper survey. No direct compensation was offered for participation, but those who completed a survey were given a paper ticket and invited to place it into one of several available sealed boxes with slits on top. The box was labeled as designated for a variety of charities, placed on a table situated far enough away from the researchers to indicate to participants that their choice would not be observed. One dollar was pledged for each ticket deposited. Thus, participants were compensated for their participation through the ability to direct a small donation to their preferred charity. In addition, by tracking tickets, we were able to record which charity was chosen by each respondent, providing additional information about their behavioral identity. Additional information about this aspect of the data is provided below.

Overall, the two-day effort yielded 133 surveys, including 100 in English, 4 in Arabic, and 29 in Farsi. About half ($N = 63$) of respondents chose to direct their donation to Action Against Hunger, a humanitarian organization that fights hunger in the Middle East; 15 chose the Red Cross, 53 chose to donate to the Islamic community center at which the survey was collected, and 2 respondents chose the Jewish Federation of Greater Los Angeles. The small sample size notwithstanding, these data provide a unique opportunity to explore Middle Eastern American political attitudes and behaviors. A growing body of research studies Muslim Americans (Ayers and Hofstetter 2008; Barreto and Bozonelos 2009; Barreto and Dana 2010; Jamal 2005) and Arab Americans (Cho, Gimpel and Wu 2006; Gimpel, Cho and Wu 2007); Middle Eastern Americans make up a broader group, yet one that is increasingly considered panethnic (Love 2006).

Our first hypothesis is that Middle Eastern Americans with racialized identities will have distinct sets of political attitudes. Matt Barreto and Karam Dana (2010) note that Muslims who live close to one another are more likely to vote and identify as Democrats, which they attribute to a higher levels of linked fate and perceived discrimination. Similarly, we hypothesize that Middle Eastern Americans with racialized identities will be more likely to be political active and more likely to prefer the Democratic Party. Finally, we hypothesize that Middle Eastern Americans with racialized identities will be more likely to choose to donate their one-dollar ticket to Action against Hunger—the charity operating to fight hunger in the Middle East—rather than to a religious or "American" charity.

Our main independent variable is whether the respondent considers "Middle Eastern" to be a distinctive racial category. We posit that some individuals who consider Middle Easterners to be a distinctive racial category may not initially self-identify as such because of the whitewashing so prevalent in surveys that ask for racial self-identification. Overall, sixty-five respondents self-identified their race as Middle Eastern, while sixty-eight did not. Of the latter, a majority ($N = 42$, 62 percent) said later in the survey that they consider Middle Eastern to be a distinct racial category. We rely on *distinct* as the indicator of racialized identity. Our dependent variables of interest are reported partisanship, political interest, reported nonelectoral political participation, and the charity respondents chose to give their one-dollar ticket. Political participation includes an additive index of three reported behaviors: (1) whether the respondent has made a political donation in the last year, (2) whether they have attended a political meeting, and

TABLE 4.1: CROSSTABS AND MEANS: RACIALIZATION IN THE MIDDLE EASTERN AMERICANS SURVEY

	Middle Eastern *is not* a distinct race ($N = 52$)	Middle Eastern *is* a distinct race ($N = 81$)
% Democrats	36.54%	44.44%
Mean political participation (0–3)	.615 (SE = .138)	.531 (SE = .096)
Mean political interest (0–2)	1.083 (SE = .102)	1.099 (SE = .072)
Donation to AAH	36.54%	54.32%

Source: Lajevardi, Michelson, and Yacobian 2013.
Note: SE = standard error.

(3) whether they have worked for a political campaign. See Table 4.1 for a list of descriptive statistics about the respondents.

We first explore our hypotheses with simple crosstabs and differences in means. As shown in Table 4.1, these results are suggestive, but none reach traditional levels of statistical significance. Overall, individuals who report that Middle Eastern is a distinct race are more likely to be Democrats, more likely to be interested in politics, and more likely to have donated their one-dollar ticket to Action against Hunger, but they are slightly less likely to report engaging in nonelectoral participation.

The politicization of this Middle Eastern community is particularly visible when compared to data on participation by other ethno-racial groups, including (non-Latino) whites, blacks, Latinos, and Asian Americans from the 2012 Cooperative Congress Election Study (CCES).[2] In our study, 26 percent of Middle Eastern Americans reported donating to a political campaign, 17.7 percent reported attending a local political meeting, and 15.6 percent reported working on a political campaign; these rates of participation are all substantially larger than those reported by Anglo, black, Latino and Asian respondents to the CCES, as shown in Table 4.2. It is possible that racialized Middle Eastern Americans are more wary of reporting such behavior because of their racialized identity, despite being more likely to be politically active. In other words, that they are racialized may make them suspicious of any attempts to find out how they are engaging in the political arena.

We next explored our hypotheses with multivariate models, allowing for inclusion of other data collected in the surveys such as age, national origin, education, whether they rent or own their home (a proxy for income/class), and frequency of religious attendance. None of these models resulted in robust coefficient estimates. Future studies with larger data sets will help clar-

2. Study data are available at https://cces.gov.harvard.edu.

TABLE 4.2: NONELECTORAL PARTICIPATION PERCENTAGES FROM MIDDLE EASTERN AMERICANS SURVEY AND 2012 CCES

	Middle Eastern Americans	Racialized Middle Eastern Americans	Nonracialized Middle Eastern Americans	CCES Anglos (non-Latino whites)	CCES blacks	CCES Latinos	CCES Asians
Donation	21.8	20.99	23.08	32.6	28.4	19.1	17.2
Local meeting	19.55	17.28	23.08	15.6	10.9	9.9	7.7
Political campaign	15.04	14.81	15.28	9.7	10.6	5.7	4.7

Source: Lajevardi, Michelson, and Yacobian 2013; Cooperative Congressional Election Study.

ify the predictors and covariates relevant to Middle Eastern political participation. Elsewhere, we have used these data to show that political participation by Middle Eastern Americans is predicted by variables found to be significant for Anglos (non-Hispanic whites) and that they are less racialized than other, traditional minority groups (Lajevardi, Michelson, and Yacobian 2013). In that analysis, Persians were more likely than non-Persians to report attending local meetings or working on a political campaign. However, these differences do not persist when controlling for socioeconomic variables (income, education, and age). These data also indicate that political interest is a strong predictor of participation (consistent with Rosenstone and Hansen's [1993] psychological resources model; see also Leighley and Vedlitz 1999). Overall, testing a variety of theories and models, education and political interest are consistently statistically significant and substantively large predictors of reported political participation.

Looking back, we hypothesized that our findings reflected the dilution of Middle Eastern identity and the ongoing and increasing focus on Muslim Americans by politicians and the media (as noted earlier in this chapter). In other words, the fact that respondents with racialized Middle Eastern identities were not more likely to report political interest or participation may be reflective of the tendency of individuals in that community not to think of their Middle Eastern identity as a political identity. We hypothesized that different findings might result from an examination of strong Muslim American identities. We turn now to our exploration of that hypothesis.

Muslim American Survey

In early 2017 we conducted an online survey of Muslim Americans aimed at measuring the degree to which the Trump administration had activated their Muslim identities. Data on 215 Muslim American respondents were collected by Survey Sampling International between February 28 and March 6. Respondents were asked to rate four questions on their Muslim American identity and were asked to rate the extent to which they agreed with the statements. These statements were adopted from "national identity" measures long relied on in political psychology, which aim to capture attachment to the group and its symbols (Gustavsson 2017; Citrin, Wong, and Duff 2001; Huddy 2001, 2015; Huddy and Khatib 2007; Collingwood, Lajevardi, and Oskooii 2018). Muslim identity is thus related to a sense or feeling of being Muslim. Respondents were asked to rate the following four statements: (1) "My Muslim American identity is an important part of my 'self'"; (2) "Being a Muslim American is an important part of how I see myself"; (3) "I am proud to be a Muslim American"; and (4) "Sometimes, I dislike being a Muslim American." Respondent attitudes toward these statements were measured using a five-item Likert scale. Answer categories and their scores were as follows: (1) strongly disagree, (2) somewhat disagree, (3) neither agree nor disagree, (4) somewhat agree, and (5) strongly agree. Item 4 was reverse coded so that increasing values indicated a stronger Muslim American identity. The average for all for items was 4.03, indicating that respondents in the sample held strong levels of Muslim American identity.

We also asked respondents whether they approved of the job Donald Trump was doing as president of the United States, and whether they had participated in any of the major protests that took place over the weekend after Trump's first executive order on immigration (the "first" Muslim ban). Only 27.9 percent of the sample said that they approved of the president, while 72.1 percent disapproved. Responses were highly correlated with strength of Muslim American identity: the mean Muslim American identity was 3.74 among those who approved and 4.14 among those who disapproved, and this difference is statistically significant ($p < 0.05$). The correlation with protest participation, in contrast, exhibits a negative correlation. Only 36.3 percent of respondents had protested, and those who participated reported weaker levels of Muslim American identity than those who did not, 3.83 versus 4.12, and the difference is statistically significant ($p < 0.05$). In other words, Muslims with strong religious identities are more likely to disapprove of President Trump, but they are significantly less likely to participate in protests against his anti-Muslim policies.

Discussion and Conclusion: The Shifting Power of Identity

Panethnic identity is often imposed from above rather than resulting from ground-up organizing and mobilizing (Espiritu 1993). While this lumping together can bring advantages such as increased political power, it also suppresses and dilutes the identities of component groups (Beltrán 2010). In the case of Muslim American identity, we have seen considerable evidence that this lumping has also often included individuals who do not actually identify as Muslim, further erasing their true voices in the polity. The continued conflation of various subgroups (Middle Eastern, Arab, Muslim, etc.) dilutes the visibility of these subgroups and makes more difficult efforts to identify and understand their political attitudes and behavior.

At the same time, the post-9/11 lumping and association of these groups, heightened by the 2016 presidential election campaign and anti-Muslim policies passed at the state and national levels in 2015 and 2016, has generated a clear focus on Muslim Americans as a distinct and stigmatized community. The proliferation of hate groups, Islamophobia, and increased hate crimes is accompanied by a stronger sense of Muslim American identity that some have seen as increasing politicization and political participation. Data from our 2013 and 2017 surveys indicate that Middle Eastern Americans and Muslim Americans are responding to this hostile political climate with increased interest in politics but less political behavior. Scholars examining other minority communities have found that threat motivates increased participation (Barreto et al. 2009; Flippen et al. 1996; Grant and Brown 1995; Marcus, Neuman, and MacKuen 2000; Miller and Krosnick 2004; Pantoja and Segura 2003). Other research shows, however, that fear has a demobilizing effect (Sampaio 2015). There is certainly grounds for increased fear among members of the Muslim American and Middle Eastern American communities, given the recent increases in the number of hate groups and of Islamophobic violence. How a community responds to threat may depend on whether that threat generates fear (anxiety) or anger (Albertson and Gadarian 2015). Further research is needed to determine if our findings persist across time and with larger samples, as the anti-Muslim sentiment that spiked after 9/11 and after Trump's election recedes, and comparing how different responses to threat (i.e., anxiety or anger) affect political participation.

Most Middle Eastern Americans are Muslim, but millions are not. Most Middle Eastern Americans are of Arab descent, but many are not. Yet Middle Eastern American and Muslim American attitudes matter, perhaps now more than ever as they are a growing segment of the population with visible communities in many parts of the country. Additional research is needed on the shared and unique politicizations of these groups and their political attitudes and behavior, as well as how the groups overlap in their identities and political action, or how individuals respond when overlapping identities may recommend divergent responses.

REFERENCES

Albertson, Bethany, and Shana Kushner Gadarian. 2015. *Anxious Politics: Democratic Citizenship in a Threatening World*. New York: Cambridge University Press.

Arab American Institute. 2018. "2020 Census: Reaching an Accurate Count." April 26. Available at http://www.aaiusa.org/2020census.

Associated Press. 2017. "Suspect Apparently Thought He Shot 'Iranian People' in Kansas Bar Attack That Killed Indian Man." *Los Angeles Times*, February 27. Available at http://www.latimes.com/nation/nationnow/la-na-911call-bar-shooting-20170227 -story.html.

Ayers, John W., and C. Richard Hofstetter. 2008. "American Muslim Political Participation following 9/11: Religious Belief, Political Resources, Social Structures, and Political Awareness." *Politics and Religion* 1 (1): 3–26.

Barreto, Matt A., and Dino N. Bozonelos. 2009. "Democrat, Republican, or None of the Above? The Role of Religiosity in Muslim American Party Identification." *Politics and Religion* 2 (2): 200–229.

Barreto, Matt A., and Karam Dana. 2010. "The American Muslim Voter: What Explains Voting When Nobody Cares?" Paper presented at the annual meeting of the American Political Science Association, September 2–5, Washington, DC. Available at https://papers.ssrn.com/sol3/papers.cfm?abstract_id=1644103.

Barreto, Matt A., Sylvia Manzano, Ricardo Ramirez, and Kathy Rim. 2009. "Mobilization, Participation, and Solidaridad: Latino Participation in 2006 Immigration Protest Rallies." *Urban Affairs Review* 44 (5): 736–64.

Beltran, Cristina. 2010. *The Trouble with Unity*. New York: Oxford University Press.

CAIR (Council on American-Islamic Relations). 2016. "Islamophobia and Its Impact in the United States." Available at http://islamophobia.org/images/ConfrontingFear/ Final-Report.pdf.

Cho, Wendy K. Tam, James G. Gimpel, and Tony Wu. 2006. "Clarifying the Role of SES in Political Participation: Policy Threat and Arab American Mobilization." *Journal of Politics* 68 (4): 977–991.

Citrin, Jack, Cara Wong, and Brian Duff. 2001. "The Meaning of American National Identity: Patterns of Ethnic Conflict and Consensus." In *Social Identity, Intergroup Conflict, and Conflict Reduction*, edited by Richard D. Ashmore, Lee Jussim, and David Wilder, 71–100. New York: Oxford University Press.

Collingwood, Loren, Nazita Lajevardi, and Kassra A. Oskooii. 2018. "A Change of Heart? Why Individual-Level Public Opinion Shifted against Trump's 'Muslim Ban.'" *Political Behavior* 40 (4): 1035–1072.Espiritu, Yen. 1993. *Asian American Panethnicity: Bridging Institutions and Identities* . Philadelphia: Temple University Press.

Federal Bureau of Investigation. 2016. "Hate Crime Summary." Available at https://ucr .fbi.gov/hate-crime/2015/resource-pages/hate-crime-2015-_summary_final.

Flippen, Annette, Harvey Hornstein, William Siegal, and Eben Weitzman. 1996. "A Comparison of Similarity and Interdependence as Triggers for In-Group Formation." *Personality and Social Psychology Bulletin* 22:882–893.

Gimpel, James G., Wendy K. Tam Cho, and Tony Wu. 2007. "Spatial Dimensions of Arab American Voter Mobilization after September 11." *Political Geography* 26 (3): 330–351.

Glenn, Evelyn Nakono. 2002. *Unequal Freedom: How Race and Gender Shaped American Citizenship and Labor*. Cambridge, MA: Harvard University Press.

Grant, Peter, and Rupert Brown. 1995. "From Ethnocentrism to Collective Protest: Responses to Relative Deprivation and Threats to Social Identity." *Social Psychology Quarterly* 58:195–212.

Gustavsson, Gina. 2017. "National Attachment—Cohesive, Divisive or Both? The Divergent Links to Solidarity from National Identity, National Pride, and National Chauvinism." Paper presented at "Liberal Nationalism and Its Critics: Normative and Empirical Questions" conference, Oxford, June 20–21.

Haney López, Ian. 1994. "Social Construction of Race: Some Observations on Illusion, Fabrication, and Choice." *Harvard Civil Rights–Civil Liberties Law Review* 29:1–63.

Huddy, Leonie. 2001. "From Social to Political Identity: A Critical Examination of Social Identity Theory." *Political Psychology* 22 (1): 127–156.

———. 2015. "Group Identity and Political Cohesion." *Emerging Trends in the Social and Behavioral Sciences: An Interdisciplinary, Searchable, and Linkable Resource*, May 15. Available at https://onlinelibrary.wiley.com/doi/10.1002/9781118900772 .etrds0155.

Huddy, Leonie, and Nadia Khatib. 2007. "American Patriotism, National Identity, and Political Involvement." *American Journal of Political Science* 51 (1): 63–77.

Jamal, Amaney. 2005. "The Political Participation and Engagement of Muslim Americans Mosque Involvement and Group Consciousness." *American Politics Research* 33 (4): 521–544.

Lajevardi, Nazita. 2017. "A Comprehensive Study of Muslim American Discrimination by Legislators, the Media, and the Masses." Ph.D. diss., University of California, San Diego.

Lajevardi, Nazita, Melissa R. Michelson, and Marianne Marar Yacobian. 2013. "The Unbearable Whiteness of Being Middle Eastern: Causes and Effects of the Racialization of Middle Eastern Americans." Poster presented at the annual meeting of the American Political Science Association, August 20–September 1, Chicago.

Leighley, Jan E., and Arnold Vedlitz. 1999. "Race, Ethnicity, and Political Participation: Competing Models and Contrasting Explanations." *Journal of Politics* 61 (4): 1092–1114.

Levine, Dan, and Mica Rosenberg. 2017. "Hawaii Judge Halts Trump's New Travel Ban before It Can Go into Effect." *Reuters*, March 15. Available at http://www.reuters .com/article/us-usa-immigration-court-idUSKBN16M17N.

Liptak, Adam, and Michael D. Shear. 2018. "Trump's Travel Ban Is Upheld by Supreme Court." *New York Times*, June 26. Available at https://www.nytimes.com/2018/06/ 26/us/politics/supreme-court-trump-travel-ban.html.

Love, Erik Robert. 2006. "Divided or United? Panethnicity among Middle Eastern Americans in Detroit." Ph.D. diss., University of California, Santa Barbara.

Marcus, George, Russell Neuman, and Michael MacKuen. 2000. *Affective Intelligence and Political Judgment.* Chicago: University of Chicago Press.

Mathias, Christopher. 2017. "The Number of Anti-Muslim Hate Groups in the U.S. Tripled in 2016." *Huffington Post*, February 15. Available at http://www .huffingtonpost.com/entry/anti-muslim-hate-groups-triple-southern-poverty-law -center_us_58a46e2ee4b03df370dc2d9a.

McCarus, Ernest Nasseph, ed. 1994. *The Development of Arab-American Identity.* Ann Arbor: University of Michigan Press.

Miller, Joanne, and Jon Krosnick. 2004. "Threat as a Motivator of Political Activism: A Field Experiment." *Political Psychology* 25:507–523.

Morlin, Bill. 2017. "Arsonist Claims He Wanted to Run Muslims out of America." Southern Poverty Law Center, March 15. Available at https://www.splcenter.org/hatewatch/2017/03/15/arsonist-claims-he-wanted-run-muslims-out-america.

Omi, Michael, and Howard Winant. 2004. "Racial Formations." *Race, Class, and Gender in the United States* 6:13–22.

Pantoja, Adrian, and Gary Segura. 2003. "Fear and Loathing in California: Contextual Threat and Political Sophistication among Latino Voters." *Political Behavior* 25:265–286.

Parsi, Trita, and Adam Weinstein. 2017. "Why Trump's Travel Ban Is Still a Muslim Ban." *CNN*, March 7. Available at http://www.cnn.com/2017/03/07/opinions/travel-ban-is-still-a-muslim-ban-opinion-parsi.

Potok, Mark. 2017. "The Year in Hate and Extremism." Southern Poverty Law Center, February 15. Available at https://www.splcenter.org/fighting-hate/intelligence-report/2017/year-hate-and-extremism.

Rosenstone, Steven, and John M. Hansen. 1993. *Mobilization, Participation and Democracy in America*. New York: Macmillan.

Rubin, Jennifer. 2017. "Another Travel Ban Loss." *Washington Post*, October 18. Available at https://www.washingtonpost.com/blogs/right-turn/wp/2017/10/18/another-travel-ban-loss.

Sampaio, Anna. 2015. *Terrorizing Latina/o Immigrants: Race, Gender, and Immigration Politics in the Age of Security*. Philadelphia: Temple University Press.

S. M. 2018. "Donald Trump's Travel Ban Heads Back to the Supreme Court." *The Economist*, January 23. Available at https://www.economist.com/blogs/democracyinamerica/2018/01/travelling-ban.

Southern Poverty Law Center. n.d. "Anti-Muslim." Available at https://www.splcenter.org/fighting-hate/extremist-files/ideology/anti-muslim (accessed March 16, 2017).

———. 2016. "Ten Days After: Harassment and Intimidation in the Aftermath of the Election." Available at https://www.splcenter.org/20161129/ten-days-after-harassment-and-intimidation-aftermath-election.

Tehranian, John. 2009. *Whitewashed: America's Invisible Middle Eastern Minority*. New York: New York University Press.

U.S. Census Bureau. 2018. "Race: About." Available at https://www.census.gov/topics/population/race/about.html.

Zapotosky, Matt. 2017. "Second Judge Rules against Latest Entry Ban, Saying Trump's Own Words Show It Was Aimed at Muslims." *Washington Post*, October 18. Available at https://www.washingtonpost.com/world/national-security/second-judge-rules-against-latest-travel-ban-saying-trumps-own-words-show-it-was-aimed-at-muslims/2017/10/18/5ecdaa44-b3ed-11e7-9e58-e6288544af98_story.html.

What Is More "American" to Do When the FBI Knocks on Your Door?

Muslim Americans' Debates on Engagement with Law Enforcement

AHMET SELIM TEKELIOGLU

I n early 2017, a number of Muslim institutions decided they would return federally funded grants from the of Department of Homeland Security's Countering Violent Extremism (CVE) program (Wang 2017; Montemayor 2017; for a primer on CVE programs, see McKenzie 2016). The CVE program was initiated by the Obama administration; CVE, as well as its predecessor in the United Kingdom, Prevent, are both controversial programs. These initiatives essentially argue that it is possible to identify certain indicators that help predict if a person is on the path to radicalization. They seek to "counter" such radicalization by engaging individuals and communities in question.

In this chapter, I examine how the "question of radicalization" has become a key part of the way government agencies perceive Muslim Americans in the post-9/11 era. These programs, run by city, state, and federal law enforcement agencies, structure Muslim Americans' relationships within civic and political life. Focusing on the period 2013–2017, I consider how Muslim Americans debate, and often disagree, about the nature and proper mode of engagement with law enforcement agencies. I draw my data from fieldwork conducted in three research sites: the greater Los Angeles area, Boston, and the San Francisco Bay area.[1] I argue that, for many American Muslims,

---

1. I thank the Contending Modernities Program at Notre Dame University for its generous support of my fieldwork in California and Boston during the 2013–2014 academic year. For a summary of my research for the Contending Modernities Program's Public Ethics and Citizenship in Plural Societies research group, see Tekelioglu 2016.

barriers to social citizenship, if not legal citizenship, come as a direct consequence of their adversarial relationship with local or federal law enforcement
agencies. America's foreign policy toward the Muslim-majority world adds
yet another layer of difficulty in the already stereotyped images of American
Muslims and, in turn, negatively influences American Muslims' perception
of American pluralism (Morey and Yaqin 2011).

The Delicate Balance between Freedoms and Security

In a world where asymmetric, hybrid security threats are more pervasive
than ever, the question of security poses significant dilemmas for governments and citizens alike. One of these dilemmas centers on balancing between security of citizens and their basic rights. Contrary to popular belief,
Western democracies are not immune to the multiple problems and contra-
dictions that arise from these dilemmas. From freedom of information to
complex ethical questions involving issues such as child pornography and
freedom of religion, problems associated with the freedom-security nexus
have been important challenges for American democracy.

Muslim Americans occupy the lion's share in the center of the question
of security-freedom nexus. Law enforcement agencies interact with faith
communities from all religious backgrounds in a number of venues that
require enhanced channels of communication and cooperation. In the case
of Muslim Americans, these interactions are exponentially more problematic, sensitive, and potentially divisive. They happen at airports where Transportation Security Agency officers interact with Muslims traveling for annual pilgrimage to Mecca and have to wear special attire. In the nation's
prisons, Muslim inmates' demands for religious accommodation require
cooperation of prison administrators to provide religious services, literature,
and specific diets (Price 2014; MPAC 2012). Threats (Wyloge 2015; Kaplan
2015) and vandalism against houses of worship and hate crimes call for the
immediate attention of law enforcement agencies. Muslim organizations
have developed safety-kit guidelines for use in mosques (for an example, see
MPAC 2011). Clearly, Muslim Americans' citizenship practices include various modes of engagement with law enforcement agencies, but these same
agencies may also be engaged in violation of Muslim freedoms and rights.

From Watts Riots to 9/11

Law enforcement agencies in Boston, the Bay Area, and Los Angeles have
become integral actors in interfaith events, civic meetings, and the wider
landscape of ethno-religious and moral diversity. This, of course, was not

new in the wake of violent events involving racialized groups. In Los Angeles, for example, in the post–Watts Riots period the police department (LAPD) and the sheriff's department (LASD) created community liaison groups. Over time, the LAPD and LASD created liaisons for Asian and Pacific Islander, Hispanic, African American, LGBT, and Sikh communities (among others) as part of their outreach efforts (for an example, see LAPD, n.d.).

At the micro level, community policing also puts security agencies in closer contact with an increasingly diverse population, although most local police forces continue to be understaffed and underfunded to adequately implement proper community policing protocols (McCampbell 2010).

In the last decade and a half, law enforcement officials have become key actors in the wider civic landscape of the three research sites I discuss in this chapter. In Los Angeles, interfaith leaders organize press conferences with the LAPD and LASD to declare their opposition to religious extremism. Officers take part in interfaith panels, organize periodic meetings with the U.S. Muslim community (LAPD 2013, 2015), attend Ramadan dinners, and are given awards at events. In Boston, the police department and Muslim communities cooperate on a number of initiatives, and the police superintendent joined a swearing-in ceremony for a newly promoted Muslim captain at the city's largest mosque, the Islamic Society of Boston Cultural Center (ISBCC) (ISBCC 2014). Community leaders in Boston are briefed by the police following major events that involve Muslims (ISBCC 2015). Meanwhile, in the Bay Area, Muslim Americans invite police officers to their communities and conduct community awareness programs (Muslim Community Association 2017).

These partnerships point to an increased sense of awareness on the part of both Muslim community members and law enforcement agencies, reinforcing that Islam and American Muslims have come to occupy a special place in the nation's religiously diverse landscape. But while other religious and ethnic communities have also experienced problematic engagement with the police and the FBI, the Muslim community's relationship with law enforcement agencies has become more intense and controversial compared to other religious minorities. Additionally, alternative paths followed by Muslim organizations and civic leaders in their relationship with law enforcement agencies have created deep schisms among American Muslims, both nationally and locally.

For example, in Los Angeles in 2014, the largest Iranian American religious and cultural center, Iranian-American Muslim Association of North America (IMAN), pulled out of the Islamic Shura Council of Southern California, an umbrella organization that brings together almost eighty mosques and other Muslim organizations. In an interview, IMAN leaders told me that the development was rooted in the fact that they viewed the leadership of the Shura Council as too hostile against the LAPD and LASD. Today, a major component of American Muslims' conversations about civic engagement is centered on the very question of what constitutes the proper mode of engagement with local and federal agencies. Below, I contextualize post-9/11 securitization and then offer two vignettes that help explain the complex web of discursive disagreement within American Muslim community about its relationship with law enforcement agencies.

Securitization of Muslim Life after 9/11

There is little disagreement among a wide spectrum of American Muslim stakeholders that the new terrain of suspicion, Islamophobia, and discussion surrounding national security in 9/11's aftermath created crucial problems for American Muslims. Despite pronouncements to the contrary, law enforcement agencies indiscriminately targeted Muslim organizations, charities, and leaders (Bakalian and Bozorgmehr 2009, 156–176). Most American mosque communities initiated "know your donor programs" with the help of FBI, thereby informing the government of any donations over $5,000 to help fight allegations of extremists financing mosques ("Islamic Society" 2002). The ramifications of ongoing surveillance culture and reliance on informants from the early 2000s continue to be an important source of the rift between Muslim communities and law enforcement agencies (Ali et al. 2011; CAIR 2013).

To make the matters worse, a number of transnational events over the last decade, such as the Madrid and London bombings of 2004 and 2005 and the 2013 Boston Marathon bombing, helped extend the fear of homegrown Islamic terrorism to the center of American debates (Brooks 2011; Mueller and Stewart 2012; Schanzer, Kurzman, and Moosa 2010). The "Muhammad cartoon" controversy in Denmark, the anti-Muslim video released in 2011, and the 2015 attack on *Charlie Hebdo* sparked debates about Islam's position on freedom of speech and apostasy. The rise of the Islamic State in Iraq and Syria and affiliated groups in the Middle East and Africa served as the impetus behind creation of CVE programs (for a background on philosophical questions related to Islam and the phenomenon of ISIS, see Zaytuna College 2014; Dagli 2015; Wood 2015). This shifting context not only exacerbated the already negative perceptions of Islam in the public sphere but also placed the global Muslim community in a defensive posture. Additionally, about a dozen American Muslims from different backgrounds—converts, second-generation Muslims, and recent immigrants—were arrested on charges of plotting to carry out attacks in America or providing material support to extremist Muslim organizations abroad (Bharath 2015). These developments raised a number of questions, including whether Muslim minorities living in the West were susceptible to the appeal of a dogmatized and violent interpretation of Islam.

Communal Response: Condemnation, Cooperation, Contestation

In response to these questions, American Muslim organizations emphasize that reporting suspicious activities and threats is not only a civic duty but also a religious obligation (CAIR, n.d.). In numerous declarations that seek to underline that Muslims should not allow their religion to be defined by isolated yet vocal extremist interpretations, organizations refute dogmatic and violent interpretations by referencing Qur'anic interpretations that point to Muslim's obligations to adhere to national law (MPAC 2013; Al-Yaqoubi 2015). American Muslim leaders continue to join other faith leaders to condemn attacks against houses of worship in the United States and abroad (Casiano 2015). They co-organize press conferences with the LAPD and LASD that condemn transnational events that involve Muslim extremists, such as those who attacked a mall in Kenya ("LAPD Chief" 2013), and join forces with civic leaders to speak against the tension between Muslims and Coptic Christians in the Middle East following the release of a hateful "innocence of Muslims" movie.[2]

In these events, American Muslim leaders reemphasize their opposition to terrorism, extremist interpretations, and acts of violence against members of other faith traditions, while also underlining their commitment to a multicultural and multireligious America and to the nation's security. And yet Muslims continue to face the question "Where are the Muslim leaders condemning these attacks?" in their daily lives, in interfaith gatherings, and in the media.

The Silver Lining

In the post-9/11 period, the Muslim community has witnessed a rise in interfaith dialogue efforts, civic and political participation, and the desire to build broad societal coalitions. My interlocutors emphasize that for all the

---

2. A clip of the press conference is available at http://www.mpac.org/assets/files/2012/mideast-violence-over-muhammad-film/copt_muslim_press_conf-audio-raw_trimmed.mp4.

problems generated by the increased scrutiny from intelligence agencies toward mosques, umbrella associations, and charities across the nation, the post-9/11 era also triggered the professionalization of their organizations, fostered proactive rather than reactive initiatives, and increased internal discipline and wider support from the Muslim population.

Nonetheless, Islam's protagonists frequently question American Muslims' "loyalty," and others argue that Muslim Americans are susceptible to radicalization—that "moderate Muslims" were an exception to the rule. One of the primary indicators of "loyalty to the country" is measured by a popular question on many polls: "Does your religion or country come first?" In 2007, American Muslims did put more emphasis on their religion (47 percent), but so did a significant number of Christians (42 percent) (Jamal 2005). Mahmood Mamdani's (2002) conceptual construct "good Muslim/ bad Muslim" helps explain the abundance of public views about Islam in the post-9/11 era. It also sheds light on how some government and policy circles view Muslims. But at the same time, the complex nature of American Muslim leaders' engagement with law enforcement agencies, the widespread acceptance of a hybrid model that overcomes the duality of cooperation-contestation model (for a reflection that is attentive to debates on authority, see Grewal 2014), requires a more nuanced analysis, exactly because Mamdani's otherwise helpful framework does not adequately foreground the agency of American Muslims.

There is now a discursive battle among American Muslim organizations about what constitutes the proper form of engagement with law enforcement agencies. This debate is shaped by a wide repertoire of discursive and practical layers that are often defined by simultaneous processes of cooperation and contestation. These new sites of cooperation and contestation between religious minorities and security agencies point to a maturation of American Muslims' agency and their crucial role as visible reminders of a pluralistic America. At the same time, and in line with the broader debates about the term *American Muslim identity* and what it entails, these debates point out that the contours of political negotiations and corresponding paradigms for American Muslim identity and outlook take shape in an often chaotic and horizontally diverse framework.

I use the next section to examine the development of LASD's Muslim American Homeland Congress and the Young Muslim American Leaders Advisory Council (Young MALAC) programs. Both were conceived by the Muslim Community Affairs Unit (MCAU) at LASD—along with the LAPD's Muslim Mapping Project (Downing 2007), which was discarded in 2007 after strong backlash from Muslim community and civil rights organizations. I present debates around these programs with a specific focus on alternative citizenship discourses that illustrate the process of cooperation and contestation between American Muslims and their government at the local, state, and federal levels.

The CIA and American Muslim Youth

On November 9, 2013, I attended an event at California State University, Long Beach that included speeches by Jihad Turk, the president of Islamic graduate school Bayan Claremont, and Ali Saleh, a second-generation Lebanese American city council member from Bell, California. Turk was born in the United States to a mixed faith couple and had decided to study Islam in Medina. Saleh, who was active in the Shi'i Al Hussain Youth Center in Bell, had faced backslash during his first run for the city council in 2009 from local groups because he was Muslim. In 2010 he emerged as the face of popular civic mobilization against a corruption scandal in Bell (Abdulrahim 2010) and received overwhelming support from the Latino community to become the first Muslim on the city council.

Other speakers included an executive from the tech giant Oracle, who told the audience that corporate America did not care about a person's faith. The female panelist was a Muslim volunteer chaplain at Southern California prisons who attends the prominent Islamic Institute of Orange County. She urged the audience to not be caught in the struggles of "back home": "If I am here and I am thinking on what's happening in the Middle East, I am losing a lot. In chapter 36, Verse 12 of the Qur'an Allah tells us we will be held accountable for what we did. . . . You will make a change here, not there. . . . Prophet emphasized this when he moved to Medina." All speakers underlined the importance of interfaith alliances and urged the largely young audience to be civically engaged and invest in understanding other walks of life.

The messages that were delivered at this event were not necessarily different than speeches you would hear in any other mainstream youth meeting. The distinctive aspect of this event, however, was that it was sponsored by the Department of Homeland Security, FBI, CIA, LASD, and LAPD. Importantly, some Southern California Muslims were fiercely against the federal sponsors. CAIR-LA's executive director Hussam Ayloush wrote this on social media:

> Why are the CIA & FBI part of a Muslim youth conf? I haven't seen them sponsor Jewish or Catholic youth events. At a time when the CIA is found guilty of committing torture, kidnapping, and murder on foreign soil and when the FBI is guilty of hiring criminals to act

as agent provocateurs to entrap Muslim youth and new converts, I find it distasteful and objectionable that they will be given access to our youth. Am I the only one who sees a problem with that? (2013)

In an interview, Aylosuh told me that he pushes against CIA- and FBI-sponsored Muslim youth events but strongly advocates for engagement with local law enforcement agencies. He argues that such events will signal to the youth that "they are different than other youth with different faith backgrounds and it is ok for federal agencies to sponsor Muslim events" (November 22, 2013, Orange County, CA). According to Aylosuh, CIA and FBI sponsorship of Muslim events carried the risk of hampering future self-perceptions of young American Muslims. The CIA representative at the event, who was busy organizing informational documents at the CIA table in the back of the ballroom, however, saw no problem with their participation. When I asked her about opposition to their sponsorship, she said they were invited to the event just as they are invited to any college job fair.

Overseeing the Long Beach event was Sergeant Muawiya (Mike) Abdeen, a nineteen-year veteran of the LASD and the head of its MCAU. A Palestinian-born naturalized citizen, Abdeen joined the LASD in 1996. Following 9/11, when all law enforcement agencies were scouting for Arabic-speaking agents, he joined the local counterterrorism task force. In time, Abdeen would become the LASD's main face in the Muslim community. Abdeen acknowledges that it took him and his team a while to win over the Muslim community. He vocally criticizes some of the leading Muslim leaders in Southern California for being uncooperative, for being too hostile toward law enforcement agencies, and blames some communities for "staying behind their closed doors and then complaining when their neighbors do not know them." He cited, as an example of a model relationship, the case of the Islamic Center of San Gabriel Valley (ICSGV) that had to fight off neighborhood opposition to its expansion project. Abdeen argues that the ICSGV had realized the importance of becoming more open to its neighbors, including the LASD. When the then secretary of homeland security Jeh Johnson visited Los Angeles to have conversations with the Muslim community about the CVE Initiative in November 2014, the ICSGV hosted the meeting (Masunaga 2014; see also Advancing Justice 2014 and Islamic Shura Council of Southern California 2014 for community reactions to this particular meeting).

Self-identifying as a secular Muslim, Abdeen told me that "secular Muslims are more integrated to America, those who are more religious are busy with events overseas and tend to become too political and isolationist" (October 31, 2018, Whittier, CA). Inside the LASD, Abdeen had it difficult too. He says that before the MCAU was formed, training materials about Islam for new recruits was "full of stereotypical material" (for an example, see CAIR 2012). Abdeen helped develop a new curriculum that allowed for better cultural training. He credits former sheriff Lee Baca for creating the MCAU. Baca had seen the need to develop better relations with Muslim community, and had realized early on that the culture of surveillance and spying was alienating the Muslim community. In the aftermath of 9/11, federal and local law enforcement agencies relied on informants who could direct them to extremists in Muslim communities. As the use of these informants, especially by the FBI (see ACLU, n.d.; Al Jazeera 2014), became more widespread and community outreach efforts were sometimes utilized toward intelligence gathering, the mistrust between Muslim communities and law enforcement agencies increased. In 2006, a year after the July 7 London bombings, Baca created the Muslim American Homeland Congress (MAHC) with the participation of leading Southern California Muslim organizations to develop a forum between the LASD and the Muslim community (Los Angeles County Sheriff's Department 2010).

Despite the Muslim community's tense relationship with the LASD, sparked in part because of the latter's unwillingness to provide religious accommodation for Muslim inmates in LASD-run correctional facilities, Baca built a rapport with the Muslim community and became a strong voice in support of American Muslim communities during the radicalization hearings organized by Representative Peter King of New York in March 2011 (see the discussion of this event in Chapter 2). The hearings became a politicized platform for a number of anti-Muslim voices who argued that there was a primordial link between Islam and violence. Baca argued using examples from his department's outreach activities that wholesale accusations against American Muslims would exacerbate their feeling of being singled out and only further alienate an otherwise civically engaged, peaceful community (Baca 2011; Lopez 2010).

The year after Sheriff Baca announced the formation of the MAHC, the LAPD announced a program that, according to its chief architect Deputy Chief Mike Downing, would enable the LAPD to identify Muslim communities that were particularly at risk of being radicalized. Downing argued in 2007 that engagement with Muslim communities helped elevate "moderate Muslim voices" and that "in preserving good will and buy in by Muslim communities, law enforcement is, in fact, advancing its intelligence agenda by fostering an environment that maximizes tips and leads surfacing from those same communities. The long-term solution to this radicalization problem will come from Muslim communities themselves" (LAPD 2007).

Under the new program, the LAPD would collaborate with local academics to "map the Muslim community" to identify its geographic distribution and those areas that "may be susceptible to violent ideologically-based extremism and then use a full-spectrum approach guided by an intelligence-led strategy." When Downing's plan was picked up by the local media, Muslim and civil rights groups raised their voices against it. CAIR argued the LAPD was conflating Los Angeles's Muslim community with isolated Muslim enclaves in some European countries and was furthering the notion that Muslim Americans were treated through the prism of national security. Downing's close ally, Muslim Public Affairs Council (MPAC) founder Dr. Maher Hathout, argued he had more in common with his Christian neighbors in the Los Angeles suburb of Arcadia than with some of his Muslim neighbors (Masunaga 2014).

The backlash from Muslim community and civil rights organizations against the initiative was so harsh that then LAPD chief William Bratton quickly shelved the program (Winton and Watanabe 2007). In a press release, Bratton emphasized that the project would only work if the Muslim community participated in it and that LAPD had heard their reservations clearly (LAPD 2007). When New York City mayor Bill de Blasio tapped Bratton for the position of police commissioner in 2013, some Muslim activists voiced their concerns because of Bratton's initial defense of the Muslim mapping project. After all, de Blasio was looking for someone who could undo the blistering damage of the monitoring and surveillance of Muslim businesses and student organizations by the New York Police Department (NYPD) (Associated Press, n.d.; MACLC, CLEAR, and AALDEF 2013). For Muslims, the NYPD program was a clear indication of law enforcement's approach to Muslim Americans.

Government monitoring of religious and racial groups have left a considerable mark in American history, but it had been limited mostly to "cultish" religious groups (Richardson and Robbins 2010, 354–355). In a testament to the mainstreaming of Islam in America, when it was revealed that a number of prominent figures in the national Muslim community were subject to surveillance by the federal government, interfaith and civil rights leaders called on the Obama administration to end the practice (Savage and Apuzzo 2014).

To be sure, the post-9/11 anti-Muslim bias against American Muslims and their opposition to law enforcement discrimination have allowed Muslim communities to establish new partnerships with interfaith coalitions, communities of color, ethnic minorities, and (at times) sexual minorities (Vali 2012). Specifically, in Los Angeles and New York, Muslim activists formed bonds with community organizations that sought to dispel stop-and-frisk policies, racial discrimination, and targeting of minorities. In Boston, interfaith leaders came to the aid of Black Lives Matter activists who were charged with jail time following a protest they organized (Gibbons et al. 2015). In Oakland, Muslim scholars and activists partnered with marginalized communities to protest a new surveillance center, arguing that indiscriminate surveillance is against the spirit of Islam and that of American constitution (Craun 2014).

These debates about and confrontations with law enforcement agencies also generate a new discourse that emerges frequently in American Muslim leaders' broader repertoire. These public voices argue that immigrant Muslims come from contexts where law enforcement is widely perceived as an authoritarian force that largely enjoys impunity even when they are acting against established laws. By asserting their rights and seeking venues of cooperation with law enforcement agencies, American Muslims—both U.S.-born and immigrants—would come to appreciate their constitutional rights.

The CVE Debate and "the Patriotic Thing" to Do When FBI Knocks on Your Door

"The patriotic thing to do when FBI knocks on your door," argues CAIR–Bay Area's Zahra Billoo, "is to tell them you will get back to them with your lawyer present. You do not invite them in for *chai*." This is why civil rights and policy advocacy groups continue to express their anxiety with the post-9/11 pattern of engagement whereby Muslim outreach was placed under the authority of special operations bureaus or counterterrorism task forces in local and federal law enforcement agencies (Kaste 2015). This is typified by Downing, who is based not at the Community Relations Bureau but runs the LAPD's Counter-Terrorism and Special Operations Bureau (Freedman 2015). Although law enforcement agencies are aware of the barriers this placement builds, the CVE initiative seems poised to entrench this practice. With varying degrees, most American Muslims see a problem in this approach. Some choose to work with the White House and pursue formal engagement with law enforcement, while others emphasize faulty presumptions that guide the initiative and draw attention to securitization of Muslim identity as a result of CVE programs.

While leaders of organizations such as MPAC and CAIR are careful to keep their disagreements on policy preferences and tactics civil, their differences are important to highlight. Though they both draw on similar interpretive frameworks regarding the Qur'an and Islamic history, CAIR is focused more on Muslim civil liberties (see Bilici 2012, 136), while MPAC places more emphasis on political advocacy. Despite these parallels, the divergent preferences and vocabularies employed by CAIR and MPAC were clearly seen when the White House's CVE program was launched. CAIR and its offices

across the nation, including in Los Angeles, strongly opposed CVE on principle, while MPAC referenced its own Safe Spaces initiative and potential
benefits of cooperation with the Obama administration (Al-Marayati 2015).

The CVE initiative seems to verify one scholar's observation that post-
9/11 era and transnational developments create a particular reality for
American Muslims' performative place in America's pluralistic society, that
they inherit "pluralism under special circumstances" (Moore 2010, 33–35;
see also Breen-Smyth 2014). Muslims increasingly recognize that, while part
of the country and the political elite grant them a public role and legitimacy,
there are others who have found ample public space to delegitimize and se-
curitize Muslim Americans. Ever since the U.S. Attorney's office designated
Los Angeles (Bennett, Rubin, and Kim 2014) as one of the three pilot cities
(Los Angeles Interagency Coordination Group 2015)—along with Boston
(U.S. Attorney's Office, District of Massachusetts 2015) and Minneapolis
(U.S. Attorney's Office, Minneapolis 2015)—these perceptions and dynamics
have become all the more crucial.

On the one hand, the rationale for the selection of these three cities was
the already advanced relationship law enforcement agencies have with the
Muslim community. The CVE Summit in Washington (see Hudson 2015)
created a flurry of positive (MPAC 2015) and critical (Arab American Association of New York 2015) commentary, public posturing, and a heated
debate on the potential implications of a CVE-specific engagement with
Muslim communities. Even though President Obama gave a reassuring
speech at the summit (White House 2015), many observers (Barzegar and
Powers 2015), including some who were part of the meetings (MPAC 2015),
pointed out that the political scene in Washington is malleable—and it already has changed for the negative in its approach to Muslims under the
Trump administration.

What is potentially harmful in the long run is that although the Los
Angeles, Minneapolis, and Boston district attorneys were careful to not present their CVE approach as specifically targeting Muslim populations and
referenced concerns about the program in their reports (see Jacobs 2015), the
division within the Muslim community between supporters of these initiatives and dissenters has become noticeable. The dissenters have correctly
pointed out that the White House approach was modeled after failed initiatives used in Britain (Thomas and Sanderson 2011, 1029–1031) and that allowing the government to approach Muslim Americans from a security lens
would only engender further securitization of Muslim identity in America.

They have also highlighted that these programs also carried the risk to
make state-led promotion of theological interpretations, thereby violating
the First Amendment (Rascoff 2012). Significantly, in Los Angeles, the in-

volvement of key actors of the city's Muslim institutions in the CVE debate created a deep schism in the community. Alternative visions about engagement with law-enforcement agencies within the American Muslim communities also created potential fault lines in the already sensitive relationship between the larger Muslim community and black Muslims. While some African American leaders and programs are highlighted in the Los Angeles presentation to the CVE Summit, other leaders pointed out that the CVE programs had the potential to turn into the problematic law enforcement programs similar to COINTELPRO that targeted the civil rights movement in the 1950s and 1960s (Hill 2015).

Those who deeply disagree about law enforcement engagement share a concern toward the future of Muslim American citizenship practices. Although some see more harm in allowing the federal and local government to single out Muslim communities, others argue that Muslim Americans should not feel apologetic for collaborating with government agencies, and that a combative stance against CVE programs would only create a void that will be filled with anti-Muslim security experts.

These alternative sentiments are not limited to the CVE debate alone. They extend into a number of related debates in the larger American Muslim ecology such as the White House iftar boycotts and Muslim Leadership Initiative trips to Israel (see, for example, Shaikh 2015). Both of these issues have been the subject of several local and national community forums over the last few years with a focus on the question of how to manage different views, strategies, and preferences regarding a host of issues that face Muslim Americans (see, for example, Institute for Social Policy and Understanding 2015). And whether they build their arguments about complex issues such as the benefits of boycott or engagement, multiple stakeholders at different ends of these debates continue to collaborate on a number of platforms and issues. In other words, intrafaith differences reverberate in political, economic, and social issues as a testament to the complexity of questions that face faith communities. These conversations continue unabated under the Trump administration as a number of American Muslim mosques and nonprofit organizations have been identified as recipients of Department of Homeland Security CVE grants (see, for example, Department of Homeland Security 2016) and others rejected the funds (Wang 2017; see also "Minneapolis Public School" 2015 for a controversial CVE initiative in a Minnesota public school). While the Trump administration's belligerent approach to Muslim identity seems to have unified American Muslims, developing a meaningful path forward on law enforcement engagement that is attentive to civil rights and avoids marginalization of American Muslims remains a high priority on community leaders' agendas.

REFERENCES

Abdulrahim, Raja. 2010. "Activist Raises Profile of Bell's Lebanese Community." *Los Angeles Times*, September 8. Available at http://articles.latimes.com/2010/sep/08/local/la-me-bell-lebanese-20100908.

ACLU (American Civil Liberties Union). n.d. "Fazaga v. FBI." Available at https://www.aclusocal.org/en/cases/fazaga-v-fbi.

Advancing Justice. 2014. "Los Angeles Based Groups Serving American Muslim Communities Question Federal Government's 'Countering Violent Extremism' Programs as Ill-Conceived, Ineffective, and Stigmatizing." November 13. Available at https://www.advancingjustice-la.org/sites/default/files/20141113-Coalition-CVE-Statement.pdf.

Ali, Wajahat, Eli Clifton, Matthew Duss, Lee Fang, Scott Keyes, and Faiz Shakir. 2011."Fear, Inc.: The Roots of the Islamophobia Network in America." Center for American Progress, August. Available at https://cdn.americanprogress.org/wp-content/uploads/issues/2011/08/pdf/islamophobia.pdf.

Al Jazeera. 2014. "Informants." *YouTube*, July 20. Available at https://www.youtube.com/watch?v=CMRns4ViuEY.

Al-Marayati, Salam. 2015. "Seek Understanding and Stop Infighting on Countering Violent Extremism." *Altmuslim*, June 12. Available at http://www.patheos.com/blogs/altmuslim/2015/06/seek-understanding-and-stop-infighting-on-countering-violent-extremism.

Al-Yaqoubi, Shaykh Muhammad. 2015. *Refuting ISIS: A Rebuttal of Its Religious and Ideological Foundations*. Middletown, DE: Sacred Knowledge.

Arab American Association of New York. 2015. "Joint Statement Regarding Upcoming Summit on Countering Violent Extremism." February 17. Available at http://www.arabamericanny.org/jointstatementoncve.

Associated Press. n.d. "Highlights of AP's Pulitzer Prize–Winning Probe into NYPD Intelligence Operations." Available at https://www.ap.org/about/awards-and-recognition/highlights-of-aps-pulitzer-prize-winning-probe-into-nypd-intelligence-operations.

Ayloush, Hussam. 2013. Facebook post, October 21. https://www.facebook.com/hussam.ayloush/posts/10151770256829825.

Baca, Lee. 2011. "The Extent of Radicalization in the American Muslim Community and the Community's Response." Available at https://homeland.house.gov/files/Testimony Baca_0.pdf.

Bakalian, Anny, and Mehdi Bozorgmehr. 2009. *Backlash 9/11: Middle Eastern and Muslim Americans Respond*. Berkeley: University of California Press.

Barzegar, Abbas, and Shawn Powers. 2015. "Muslim NGOs Could Help Counter Violent Extremism." *Washington Post*, February 17. Available at http://www.washingtonpost.com/blogs/monkey-cage/wp/2015/02/17/muslim-ngos-could-help-counter-violent-extremism.

Bennett, Brian, Joel Rubin, and Victoria Kim. 2014. "L.A. Chosen for Pilot Program on Dissuading Militant Recruits." *Los Angeles Times*, September 22. Available at http://www.latimes.com/local/la-me-terror-jihad-program-20140923-story.html.

Bharath, Deepa. 2015. "Orange County Muslims on Edge over ISIS, after Two Anaheim Men Arrested on Suspicion of Supporting Terrorists." *Orange County Register*, June 2. Available at http://www.ocregister.com/articles/community-663933-muslim-extremism.html.

Bilici, Mucahit. 2012. *Finding Mecca in America: How Islam Is Becoming an American Religion*. Chicago: University of Chicago Press.

Breen-Smyth, Marie. 2014. "Theorising the 'Suspect Community': Counterterrorism, Security Practices and the Public Imagination." *Critical Studies on Terrorism* 7 (2): 223–240.

Brooks, Risa A. 2011. "Muslim 'Homegrown' in the United States: How Serious Is the Threat?" *International Security* 36 (2): 7–47.

CAIR (Council on American Islamic Relations). n.d. *American Muslim Civic Pocket Guide: Your Rights and Responsibilities as an American Muslim*. Washington, DC: CAIR.

———. 2012. *An Analysis of Sam Kharoba's "A Law Enforcement Guide to Understanding Islamist Terrorism."* Washington, DC: CAIR.

———. 2013. *Legislating Fear: Islamophobia and Its Impact in the United States*. Washington, DC: CAIR.

Casiano, Louis. 2015. "Orange County Religious Leaders Say Places of Worship Must Be Free of Violence." *Orange County Register*, January 25. Available at http://www.ocregister.com/articles/religious-649196-people-stern.html.

Craun, Dustin. 2014. "Lighthouse Mosque Protests Proposed Building of Oakland Spy Center." *Medium*, February 18. Available at https://medium.com/@dustincraun/light house-mosque-protests-proposed-building-of-oakland-spy-center-46451caaf425.

Dagli, Caner K. 2015. "The Phony Islam of ISIS." *The Atlantic*, February 27. Available at http://www.theatlantic.com/international/archive/2015/02/what-muslims-really -want-isis-atlantic/386156.

Department of Homeland Security. 2016 "EMW-2016-CA-APP-0025." Available at https://www.dhs.gov/sites/default/files/publications/EMW-2016-CA-APP-00253 %20Full%20Application.pdf.

Downing, Michael P. 2007. "Statement of Michael P. Downing before the Committee on Homeland Security and Governmental Affairs." October 30. Available at http:// assets.lapdonline.org/assets/pdf/Michael%20DowningTestimonyfortheU.S.Senate -Final.PDF.

Freedman, Samuel G. 2015. "Los Angeles Police Leader Makes Outreach to Muslims His Mission." *New York Times*, March 6. Available at http://www.nytimes.com/2015/03/ 07/us/lapd-deputy-chief-muslims.html.

Gibbons, John, Sarah Gibb Millspaugh, Jason M. Lydon, Heather Concannon, Will Green, Katie Omberg, M. Lara Hoke, et al. 2015. Letter to Marian Ryan. July 13. Available at http://www.scribd.com/doc/271570603/Interfaith-Clergy-Letter-in -Support-of-Somerville-18.

Grewal, Zareena. 2014. *Islam Is a Foreign Country: American Muslims and the Global Crisis of Authority*. New York: New York University Press.

Hill, Margari Aziza. 2015. "Logging It All: CVE and Schisms in the Muslim Community." *Islamic Monthly*, March 4. Available at http://theislamicmonthly.com/logging -it-all-cve-and-schisms-in-the-muslim-community.

Hudson, John. 2015. "Inside the Fight Over Obama's Terror Summit." *Foreign Policy*, February 17. Available at http://foreignpolicy.com/2015/02/17/inside-the-fight-over -obamas-terror-summit.

Institute for Social Policy and Understanding. 2015. "Debating Boycott vs. Engagement: #ISPUDebate2015 at 52nd Annual ISNA Convention." *YouTube*, September 10. Available at https://www.youtube.com/playlist?list=PLtO3SZoCiKcWAdhhoRcfIwx 7id-750a5L.

ISBCC (Islamic Society of Boston Cultural Center). 2014. "Haseeb Hossein Appointed Captain at ISBCC." *YouTube*, October 31. Available at https://www.youtube.com/watch?v=DVIpgRnPsMw.

———. 2015. Facebook post, June 3. Available at https://www.facebook.com/ISBCC.org/posts/885422824830171.

Islamic Shura Council of Southern California. 2014. Letter to Jeh Johnson. December 1. Available at http://origin.library.constantcontact.com/download/get/file/110 2150755525-390/JehJohnsonDHS_CVE_120114.pdf.

"Islamic Society Breaks Ground in Roxbury." 2002. *Mass Moments*, November 7. Available at https://www.massmoments.org/moment-details/islamic-society-breaks -ground-in-roxbury.html.

Jacobs, Sally. 2015. "Fighting the Lure of the Galaxy of Jihad." *Boston Globe*, May 3. Available at https://www.bostonglobe.com/metro/2015/05/02/fighting-lure-galaxy -jihad/21OT0v7wmPZm6tP7oKzrKL/story.html.

Jamal, Amaney. 2005. "The Political Participation and Engagement of Muslim Americans: Mosque Involvement and Group Consciousness." *American Politics Research* 33 (4): 521–544.

Kaplan, Michael. 2015. "Anti-Muslim Protests Scheduled Nationwide: 'Global Rally for Humanity' Calls on Demonstrations in Front of Mosques across US Cities." *International Business Times*, September 30. Available at http://www.ibtimes.com/anti -muslim-protests-scheduled-nationwide-global-rally-humanity-calls-demonstra tions-2120625.

Kaste, Martin. 2015. "Counterterrorism Cops Try to Build Bridges with Muslim Communities." *NPR*, December 21. Available at https://www.npr.org/2015/12/21/ 460536774/2-la-counterterrorism-cops-build-bridges-with-muslim-community.

LAPD (Los Angeles Police Department). n.d. "Community Relationship Division." http://www.lapdonline.org/home/content_basic_view/2034.

———. 2007. "LAPD's Community Engagement Initiative." November 15. Available at http://www.lapdonline.org/newsroom/news_view/37004.

———. 2013. "Police Chief Charlie Beck to Host Muslim Community Forum." March 8. Available at http://www.lapdonline.org/olympic_news/news_view/53116.

———. 2015. "Police Chief Charlie Beck to Host Muslim Community Forum." April 1. Available at http://www.lapdonline.org/newsroom/news_view/58374.

"LAPD Chief, Interfaith Leaders Call for Peace, Unity in Wake of Kenya Attack." 2013. *CBS Los Angeles*, September 27. Available at http://losangeles.cbslocal.com/2013/09/ 27/lapd-chief-inter-faith-leaders-call-for-peace-unity.

Lopez, Robert J. 2010. "Sheriff Baca Argues with Republican Congressman about Islamic Group." *Los Angeles Times*, March 17. Available at http://latimesblogs.latimes .com/lanow/2010/03/baca-argues-with-republican-congressman.html.

Los Angeles County Sheriff's Department. 2010. "Muslim Community Affairs Unit." Available at http://shq.lasdnews.net/content/uoa/MCA/MCAOverviewJan2010 _LoRes.pdf.

Los Angeles Interagency Coordination Group. 2015. "The Los Angeles Framework for Countering Violent Extremism." Available at https://www.dhs.gov/sites/default/ files/publications/Los%20Angeles%20Framework%20for%20CVE-Full%20Report .pdf.

MACLC (Muslim American Civil Liberties Coalition), CLEAR (Creating Law Enforcement Accountability and Responsibility), and AALDEF (Asian American Legal Defense and Education Fund). 2013. "Mapping Muslims: NYPD Spying and Its

Impact on American Muslims." Available at http://www.law.cuny.edu/academics/clinics/immigration/clear/Mapping-Muslims.pdf.

Mamdani, Mahmood. 2002. "Good Muslim, Bad Muslim: A Political Perspective on Culture and Terrorism." *American Anthropologist* 104 (3): 766–775.

Masunaga, Samantha. 2014. "Homeland Security Head Aims to Build Trust in L.A. Muslim Community." *Los Angeles Times*, November 13. Available at http://www.latimes.com/local/california/la-me-1114-mosque-visit-20141114-story.html.

McCampbell, Michael S. 2010. "The Collaboration Toolkit for Community Organizations: Effective Strategies to Partner with Law Enforcement." U.S. Department of Justice, September. Available at https://www.hsdl.org/?view&did=12717.

McKenzie, Robert L. 2016. "Countering Violent Extremism in America: Policy Recommendations for the Next President." Brookings Institution, October 18. Available at https://www.brookings.edu/research/countering-violent-extremism-in-america-policy-recommendations-for-the-next-president.

"Minneapolis Public School CVE Program." 2015. *C-Span*, March 9. Available at http://www.c-span.org/video/?c4530677/minneapolis-public-school-cve-program.

Montemayor, Stephen. 2017. "Homeland Security Announces Two Counterextremism Grants for Minnesota." *Star Tribune*, June 24. Available at http://www.startribune.com/homeland-security-announces-two-extremism-grants-for-minnesota/430455753.

Moore, Kathleen M. 2010. *The Unfamiliar Abode: Islamic Law in the United States and Britain*. New York: Oxford University Press.

Morey, Peter, and Amina Yaqin. 2011. *Framing Muslims: Stereotyping and Misrepresentation after 9/11*. Cambridge, MA: Harvard University Press.

MPAC (Muslim Public Affairs Council). 2011. "Security Tips for Places of Worship." September 6. Available at https://www.mpac.org/programs/government-relations/security-tips-for-places-of-worship.php.

———. 2012. "Ensuring Religious Accommodations for L.A. County Muslim Inmates." May 9. Available at http://www.mpac.org/issues/civil-rights/ensuring-religious-accommodations-for-muslim-inmates.php.

———. 2013. "Declaration against Extremism." Available at http://www.mpac.org/assets/docs/2013/MPAC-Declaration-Against-Extremism.pdf.

———. 2015. "When Engagement Brings Results: The White House CVE Summit." February 19. Available at https://www.mpac.org/blog/policy-analysis/when-engagement-brings-results-the-white-house-cve-summit.php.

Mueller, John, and Mark G. Stewart. 2012. "The Terrorism Delusion: America's Overwrought Response to September 11." *International Security* 37 (1): 81–110.

Muslim Community Association. 2017. "Meet and Greet with Santa Clara Police Officers." Facebook post, March 3. Available at https://www.facebook.com/media/set/?set=a.10155181047433623.1073741854.23077583622&type=1&l=2c4740b4b5.

Price, Jessica. 2014. Letter to John L. Scott. March 28. Available at https://www.aclusocal.org/sites/default/files/wp-content/uploads/2014/03/ACLUSoCal-Letter-LASD-3.28.14.pdf.

Rascoff, Samuel J. 2012. "Establishing Official Islam? The Law and Strategy of Counterradicalization." *Stanford Law Review* 64 (1): 125–189.

Richardson, James T., and Thomas Robbins. 2010. "Monitoring and Surveillance of Religious Groups in the United States." In *The Oxford Handbook of Church and State in the United States*, edited by Derek H. Davis, 353–369. New York: Oxford University Press.

Savage, Charlie, and Matt Apuzzo. 2014. "U.S. Spied on 5 American Muslims, a Report Says." *New York Times*, July 9. Available at http://www.nytimes.com/2014/07/10/us/politics/nsa-snowden-records-glenn-greenwald-first-look.html.

Schanzer, David, Charles Kurzman, and Ebrahim Moosa. 2010. "Anti-Terror Lessons of Muslim-Americans." January 6. Available at https://fds.duke.edu/db/attachment/1255.

Shaikh, Ahmed. 2015. "MPAC, Countering Violent Extremism and American Muslim Astroturf: A Critical Review." *Altmuslim*, January 9. Available at http://www.patheos.com/blogs/altmuslim/2015/06/mpac-countering-violent-extremism-and-american-muslim-astroturf-a-critical-review.

Tekelioglu, Ahmet Selim. 2016. "Los Angeles: A Microcosm for National Conversations on Religion, Public Life and Deep Diversity." *Contending Modernities*, January 6. Available at http://contendingmodernities.nd.edu/global-migration-the-new-cosmopolitanism/los-angeles-a-microcosm-for-national-conversations-on-religion-public-life-and-deep-diversity.

Thomas, Paul, and Peter Sanderson. 2011. "Unwilling Citizens? Muslim Young People and National Identity." *Sociology* 45 (6): 1028–1044.

U.S. Attorney's Office, District of Massachusetts. 2015. "A Framework for Prevention and Intervention Strategies: Incorporating Violent Extremism into Violence Prevention Efforts." Available at http://www.justice.gov/sites/default/files/usao-ma/pages/attachments/2015/02/18/framework.pdf.

U.S. Attorney's Office, Minneapolis. 2015. "Building Community Resilience: Minneapolis–St. Paul Pilot Program." Available at http://www.justice.gov/usao-mn/file/642121/download.

Vali, Yusufi. 2012. "From Public Marginalisation to Public Recognition: The Action Is in the Reaction, Part II." In *A New Covenant of Virtue: Islam and Community Organising*, edited by Ruhana Ali, Lina Jamoul, and Yusufi Vali, 31–34. London: Citizens UK and Industrial Areas Foundation.

Wang, Amy B. 2017. "Muslim Nonprofit Groups Are Rejecting Federal Funds Because of Trump." *Washington Post*, February 11. Available at https://www.washingtonpost.com/news/post-nation/wp/2017/02/11/it-all-came-down-to-principle-muslim-nonprofit-groups-are-rejecting-federal-funds-because-of-trump.

White House. 2015. "Background Conference Call by Senior Administration Officials Previewing the White House Summit on Countering Violent Extremism." February 16. Available at https://www.whitehouse.gov/the-press-office/2015/02/16/background-conference-call-senior-administration-officials-previewing-wh.

Winton, Richard, and Teresa Watanabe. 2007. "LAPD's Muslim Mapping Plan Killed." *Los Angeles Times*, November 15. Available at http://articles.latimes.com/2007/nov/15/local/me-muslim15.

Wood, Graeme. 2015. "What ISIS Really Wants." *The Atlantic*, March. Available at http://www.theatlantic.com/magazine/archive/2015/03/what-isis-really-wants/384980.

Wyloge, Evan. 2015. "Hundreds Gather in Arizona for Armed Anti-Muslim Protest." *Washington Post*, May 30. Available at https://www.washingtonpost.com/news/post-nation/wp/2015/05/30/hundreds-gather-in-arizona-for-armed-anti-muslim-protest.

Zaytuna College. 2014. "The Crisis of ISIS: A Prophetic Prediction; Sermon by Hamza Yusuf." *YouTube*, September 19. Available at https://www.youtube.com/watch?v=hJo4B-yaxfk.

Muslim Expectations of U.S. Law Enforcement Behavior

RACHEL M. GILLUM

From Ahmet Tekelioglu's discussion in Chapter 5, it is clear that there is a growing perception among Muslim Americans—especially those born and raised in the United States—that Muslims are being unfairly targeted by the U.S. government and its countering violent extremism (CVE) and counterterrorism (CT) policies (see CHRGJ 2011; Abdo 2006; Bakalian and Bozorgmehr 2009; Peek 2011; Brooks and Manza 2013; Cainkar 2009; Jamal 2008). Many have expressed concern over programs that involve extensive monitoring, indefinite detentions, and other actions that may violate the constitutional rights of nonviolent, noncriminal Muslim citizens—often without proximate cause for suspicion or material benefit to national security (Apuzzo and Goldman 2013; Muslim Advocates 2011).

At the same time that many Muslims face such scrutiny, they are being asked to do more to help stop the threat. Government officials have asserted that Muslim Americans play an important role in keeping the country safe (*Eight Years* 2009; Obama 2015) and, at times, have accused Muslim communities of not doing enough. However, Muslim Americans have indeed been helpful to law enforcement, with some scholars citing Muslim Americans as one of the largest known sources of initial information leading to disrupted terrorism plots since 9/11 (Bergen et al. 2014; Kurzman 2014; New America 2017).

An extended version of this chapter was previously published in Rachel Gillum, *Muslim Americans in a Post-9/11 World: A Survey of Attitudes and Beliefs and Their Implications for U.S. National Security Policy* (Ann Arbor: University of Michigan Press, 2018).

How has the post-9/11 scrutiny affected Muslims' relationship with U.S. law enforcement? In particular, do individual Muslims believe that their religious identity will result in unfair treatment by authorities, or do they trust that they will be treated indiscriminately? Using a randomized survey experiment, I compare Muslims' beliefs about police behavior when the suspect is Muslim American versus some other background. I explore the reasons for the variance in Muslims' levels of trust in the police and attitudes toward government, including the effect of immigrants' experiences with law enforcement in their country of origin. These data suggest that U.S.-born Muslims have internalized negative beliefs about government behavior toward Muslims and are more likely to anticipate that police behavior toward Muslims will be discriminatory. Foreign-born Muslims, however, do not appear to believe that the police treat Muslims differently than non-Muslims, and instead base their judgments of American law enforcement on their experiences in their country of origin. Specifically, immigrant Muslims whose home country had corrupt institutions, including corrupt police forces, are more likely to expect bad behavior from American police forces. These attitudes appear to reflect their lower standards toward government security agencies generally. Conversely, immigrants from less corrupt countries have more positive expectations of American police forces.

This chapter expands our understanding of how Muslim American attitudes toward government are linked to their religious identities and socialization experiences within the United States and abroad. Moreover, this chapter also suggests that some of the policies designed to keep America safe from terrorist attacks may have eroded one of law enforcement's greatest assets in the fight against domestic violent extremism—a relationship of trust and goodwill between the Muslim American community and U.S. government entities. While Muslims continue to be active and helpful toward law enforcement, there are growing concerns over controversial counterterrorism policing methods, as well as the expanded list of behaviors that are considered signs of "radicalization," effectively criminalizing Muslim identities (see Gillum 2018). The implications for this diminished trust are discussed at the conclusion of this chapter.

Perceiving Unfair Policing

Citizens' perceptions of police fairness are key to understanding overall judgments of law enforcement and have implications for community-assisted policing. The perceptions and stories of Muslim Americans, in particular, highlight the importance of creating an environment in which citizens feel safe going to law enforcement with information or when they are in need.

But on what bases do citizens tend to judge police? Empirical research has consistently demonstrated that satisfaction with the police and legal systems are shaped as much by beliefs about whether one is being governed with fairness and objectivity as by the actual outcome one receives (Levi, Sacks, and Tyler 2009; Sunshine and Tyler 2003; Tyler and Fagan 2008). For example, Tom Tyler and R. Folger (1980) found that when citizens are stopped for traffic violations, their evaluations of the interaction with the officer is influenced more by the perceived fairness with which they are treated than by the result itself (i.e., whether they were issued a traffic citation).

Beyond direct personal interactions with law enforcement, research suggests that people's perceptions of how their in-group members are treated also affect their judgments about the legitimacy of specific law enforcement behavior. People tend to sympathize more with individuals who share similar traits and backgrounds. For instance, whites' support for punitive policies such as the death penalty decreases significantly when they learn that the criminal perpetrator is white rather than nonwhite (Gilliam and Iyengar 2000; Hurwitz and Peffley 2005; Eberhart et al. 2004). Jon Hurwitz and Mark Peffley (2005) found that blacks tend to sympathize and be more sensitive toward the treatment of black suspects because they anticipate mistreatment toward black suspects relative to white suspects, whereas white respondents expect police to treat whites and blacks in an identical fashion.

Though Muslim Americans faced scrutiny in the United States long before the 2016 election of President Donald Trump and the fallout from the September 11, 2001, attacks, Muslim Americans have in recent years become even less trusting of law enforcement agencies and police. Many Muslim Americans believe that innocent people are regularly subjected to unwarranted surveillance and observe that Muslims are frequently harassed by airport security and immigration officials (Gillum 2018; Peek 2011; Bakalian and Bozorgmehr 2009; Cainkar 2009). Moreover, pervasive societal discrimination has undermined some Muslims' confidence they will be treated fairly by law enforcement in an investigation. According to a 2011 poll by the Pew Research Center, more than half of Muslim Americans believe that the government's antiterrorism policies single out Muslims for increased surveillance and monitoring, and 43 percent report being called offensive names, singled out by airport security or law enforcement, or physically threatened for being Muslim (Pew Research Center 2011).

These views are most prevalent among U.S.-born Muslims. Elsewhere, I find that Muslims born and raised in the United States have expressed the greatest concern over the treatment of the Muslim American community (see Gillum 2018). With more experience and knowledge of the American system, U.S.-born Muslims hold higher expectations of the American government, similar to other Americans, assuming government representatives and law enforcement officers will uphold American values of fairness, equality, and good governance. Moreover, later generation Muslims are better able to recognize when the government is treating Muslim citizens less well compared to other Americans. Muslim immigrants on the other hand—many of whom were socialized abroad under illiberal regimes—do not necessarily share all of the same expectations of fair and equal governance and may not be able as readily to identify differential treatment when it occurs. These findings echo studies on other American and European immigrant groups where perceptions of discrimination are greater among later-generation immigrants (Garcia-Bedolla 2005; Michelson 2001, 2003a, 2003b, 2007; Maxwell 2008, 2010; Correia 2010). These scholars find that while immigrants tend to be relatively trusting of the government, with greater levels of assimilation and integration, and with later generations, trust in government erodes. In examining Muslim Americans' perceptions of fairness of U.S. law enforcement, I consider how the religious identity of the target of police engagement (the criminal suspect) shifts expectations for fair behavior, and how these patterns vary by the birth place of the respondent.

Data: Muslim American National Opinion Survey (MANOS)

I utilize data from an original and nationally representative survey, the Muslim American National Opinion Survey (MANOS). This survey was administered online in English[1] by the international Internet-based market re-

---

1. Foreign-born Muslims in the United States are believed to have similar, if not higher, levels of English acquisition compared to other American immigrant groups; upwards of 80 percent or more are estimated to be fluent in English (Pew 2011). This limits the degree to which the sample composition would be skewed by being administered in English only. In comparing the composition of the MANOS respondents with a 2011 Pew Research Center survey that was administered in multiple languages, MANOS respondents look remarkably similar to Pew's across several major demographic factors, including those that were not weighted, such as the proportion of Shias to Sunnis. They also match on attitudinal variables such as religiosity. The MANOS survey, however, has a higher percentage (20 percentage points) of U.S.-born respondents compared to Pew. Limiting the analysis to English speakers eliminates concerns of question comprehension and comparability; however, it also runs the risk of skewing the findings of the survey. But given the key questions and findings of this study, including non-English speakers would likely make the findings *more* pronounced. One of the central findings of this chapter is that U.S.-born Muslims tend to hold relatively more critical feelings toward government than immigrant Muslims. Several existing studies find that immigrants in the United States and Europe who speak a different language from the official language of their host country have more positive attitudes toward government than immigrants who speak an official host country language at

search firm YouGov. YouGov administered the survey to individuals living around the United States from a sample of millions of Americans who had previously been surveyed and had identified themselves as Muslim.[2]

MANOS was fielded from February 2, 2013, through March 19, 2013. The data set captures 501 self-identified Muslims living in 45 U.S. states plus the District of Columbia, including foreign-born respondents from 46 different nations. Basic demographic features of the survey respondents are presented in Table 6.1. The survey included standard political questions as well as randomized survey experiments. Because there is no federal census data on the Muslim American population, for sample weighting YouGov relied on the American Social Survey, conducted by the U.S. Census Bureau, as well as the Pew Research Center's 2011 estimates on the composition of the Muslim American community.[3]

Survey Experiment: Attitudes toward Police

To systematically assess American Muslims' perceptions of fairness by U.S. law enforcement, the MANOS data set included a survey experiment focused on police. Respondents were asked about how fairly they believed the police would behave in a theoretical criminal investigation. To assess whether respondents' beliefs about police behavior would change depending on the suspects involved in the investigation, an experimental survey design manipulated the identity of the suspect in question. Respondents were randomly assigned to one of two conditions. In one, the suspect is a presumably a non-Muslim American named Jake Lewis. In the other condition, the suspect is presumably a Muslim American named Umar Sayyid. For each respondent, the response when the suspect is a non-Muslim or a Muslim is observed, but not both.

Subjects were told that "the police have received an anonymous tip that a 23-year-old American citizen, [Jake Lewis/Umar Sayyid], a man without a criminal record, is planning to commit a major crime." Following the prompt, respondents were asked about their expectations of police fairness: "Generally speaking, do you think U.S. law enforcement will treat a person

---

home (Correia 2010; Wortley and Owusu-Bempah 2009; Roder and Muhlau 2012). Including non-English speakers in the data set would only strengthen this relationship. Even so, the absence of even a small group of non-English-speaking Muslims in the survey limits the degree to which this survey can capture the full range of experiences in the Muslim American population.

2. Respondents may have been previously surveyed for a range of different purposes, including, but not limited to, marketing research, product reviews, academic research, and political opinion polling.

3. A full discussion of YouGov's sampling methods, including weighting, is available upon request.

TABLE 6.1: MUSLIM AMERICAN NATIONAL OPINION SURVEY
(MANOS) RESPONDENT DEMOGRAPHIC FEATURES SUMMARY

Foreign born	34%
Second generation	22%
Third generation	44%
Female	49%
Average age	36
Arab	17%
Asian	19%
Black	23%
White	32%
N	501

Note: All respondents are self-identified Muslims. Second-generation Muslims are those
born in the United States with foreign-born parents; third-generation Muslims are
those born in the United States with U.S.-born parents. Respondents were able to identify themselves within multiple racial categories. Thirty-two percent of Muslims identified as white only. Among white-only respondents, 57 percent identify as third generation, 11 percent as second generation, and 33 percent as foreign-born. Among white-
only second-generation respondents, about 38 percent are of Arab descent, and 25
percent are of Turkish descent. Among white-only respondents who were born abroad,
45 percent indicate that they were born in Arab countries, 25 percent in Turkey, and
the remaining from various parts of Europe. Seventy-one percent, 13 percent, and 16
percent of respondents who identify as black are third generation, second generation,
and foreign-born, respectively.

like this fairly?" Answers were ranked on a seven-point scale from completely agree (7) to completely disagree (1) and were rescaled to range from
1–0 in the following analysis.

Differential Perceptions of Fairness

To estimate the effect of the suspect's identity on expectations of law enforcement fairness, Table 6.2 presents a series of predicted probabilities that are
derived from two ordinary least squares (OLS) regressions. The first column
of the table lists the MANOS subgroups under consideration. For each subgroup listed, the second column displays predicted levels of expected fairness when the suspect is a non-Muslim, along with corresponding confidence intervals. The third column displays predicted levels of expected
fairness when the suspect is a Muslim, along with corresponding confidence
intervals. The final column displays the difference between the two conditions for each subgroup of interest. The results are robust to the inclusion of
basic demographic controls—age, income, education, and gender.[4]

---

4. Details of the full models are available upon request.

TABLE 6.2: PREDICTED VALUES OF EXPECTED FAIRNESS OF LAW ENFORCEMENT, BY SUSPECT IDENTITY

	Jake's predicted value (CI)	Umar's predicted value (CI)	Treatment effect
Total	.54 (.50–.57)	.41 (.36–.46)*	–13%
Race			
Arab	.51 (.46–.57)	.46 (.41–.52)	–5%
Asian	.60 (.51–.68)	.48 (.38–.58)*	–12%
Black	.52 (.45–.60)	.28 (.15–.40)	–24%
White	.52 (.46–.58)	.42 (.34–.50)	–10%
Generation			
Foreign-born	.53 (.48–.59)	.53 (.47–.60)	10%
U.S.-born	.54 (.49–.59)	.34 (.28–.41)*	–20%
Race × generation			
Arab only			
Foreign-born	.42 (.34–.50)	.58 (.48–.68)	16%
U.S.-born	.60 (.52–.67)	.35 (.28–.43)*	–25%
Asian only			
Foreign-born	.61 (.52–.70)	.49 (.38–.60)	–12%
U.S.-born	.56 (.39–.73)	.45 (.24–.66)	–11%
Black only			
Foreign-born	.50 (.39–.61)	.44 (.27–.61)	–6%
U.S.-born	.53 (.45–.61)	.26 (.12–.39)*	–27%
White only			
Foreign-born	.55 (.45–.66)	.58 (.47–.68)	3%
U.S.-born	.51 (.43–.58)	.37 (.27–.47)	–14%

Source: Muslim American National Opinion Survey, 2013.

Note: Numbers are predicted values from two OLS regressions, with 95 percent confidence intervals (CI) in parentheses. Perceived fairness is measured by the question: "Generally speaking, do you think U.S. law enforcement will treat a person like this fairly?" Higher values indicate agreement with the statement. Generation, race, gender, income, education, and age are set at zero or their mean.

*$p < 0.1$.

Generational Differences

Looking at the entire sample of Muslim Americans, we see that priming respondents to consider the treatment of Muslims under police scrutiny reduces perceptions of fairness by 13 percentage points, a statistically significant difference. This indicates that on average, Muslim Americans expect U.S. law enforcement to treat Muslim suspects less well than non-Muslim suspects in identical situations.

The next row in Table 6.2 assesses the difference in respondents' expectations of how the police will treat Jake and Umar, by generation. Looking at the "Jake" column, foreign-born and U.S.-born Muslims have nearly identical prior expectations about the conduct that non-Muslim suspects are likely to see from police. There is a striking difference, however, between how foreign-born and U.S.-born Muslims respond to police interacting with a Muslim suspect. While foreign-born Muslims expect equal treatment under the law regardless of the identity of the suspect, Muslims born in the United States are 20 percentage points (a statistically significant difference) less likely to expect the police to treat Muslim suspects fairly.

These results offer evidence that U.S.-born Muslims are significantly more likely to have an internalized expectation about the mistreatment of Muslims by the government. As mentioned previously, this is consistent with research that shows that second-generation immigrants (U.S.-born with foreign-born parents) perceive greater discrimination by the government than their less-assimilated foreign-born counterparts and are more sensitive to the mistreatment of fellow in-group members (Garcia-Bedolla 2005; Michelson 2001, 2003a, 2003b; Maxwell 2008, 2010; Correia 2010). Even though immigrants' experiences under illiberal, corrupt regimes can result in low expectations of the government (as confirmed below), they still on average have more positive views of American law enforcement than do U.S.-born Muslims, when considering how police will behave toward a Muslim.

Generational Differences across Races

A long line of empirical evidence demonstrates that racial minorities in the United States are more likely to be the victims of police violence and racial profiling (Tyler and Huo 2002; Weitzer 2002). Consequently, minority residents tend to perceive that they and other racial-group members are unfairly targeted for aggressive and discourteous treatment by the police because of their race (Brunson 2007; Sharp and Atherton 2007; Garcia and Cao 2005; Cao, Frank, and Cullen 1996; Hurst, Frank, and Browning 2000). It follows, therefore, that Muslims who are racial minorities would be more likely to have hostile or negative interactions with the government because of profiling or being associated by virtue of their race with criminal activity. They may thus be more familiar with instances of police misconduct toward Muslims (or at the very least, open to the idea that police can behave badly) and as a result more likely to expect the mistreatment of Muslims by law enforcement in ambiguous situations.

Moving down Table 6.2, it becomes clear that the effect of generation on perceived fairness discussed above is generally consistent across racial groups. That is, U.S.-born and foreign-born Muslims alike, of all races, anticipate similar levels of police fairness for a non-Muslim suspect, but U.S.-born Muslims expect worse treatment for a Muslim suspect. The largest decreases in expectations of fairness toward a Muslim suspect compared to a non-Muslim are seen among U.S.-born Arab Muslims and black Muslims—25- and 27-point drops, respectively. These differences are statistically significant and suggest that the experiences of Arab and black Muslims may make them particularly sensitive to scenarios that involve Muslim suspects and law enforcement.

The exception to this pattern is Asian respondents. Foreign-born *and* U.S.-born Asians' expectations of fairness also drop, by 12 percent and 11 percent respectively, when considering the treatment of a Muslim suspect compared to a non-Muslim suspect; however, these effects do not quite reach statistical significance (the confidence intervals for the Jake and Umar condition overlap). In other words, Asian respondents generally expect police to treat Muslim and non-Muslim suspects differently. This is consistent, however, with the observation that Asian Americans generally tend to perceive less discrimination than other U.S. minority groups (Pew Research Center 2013).

The data presented in this section point to the importance of generational differences and experiences in explaining perceptions of America's security apparatus. The findings provide additional support for the argument that Muslim immigrants come to the United States with more optimistic expectations of the treatment of Muslim suspects; however, U.S.-born Muslims who have been socialized within the United States, and are thus more familiar with America's security apparatus and its history, hold greater cynicism toward the government when dealing with Muslim suspects.

Foreign Influences on American Muslim Immigrants

The results to this point demonstrate that U.S.-born Muslims hold more pessimistic views toward law enforcement than their foreign-born counterparts, clarifying that this generational difference is based on an increased awareness of *group-based* injustices. That is, U.S.-born Muslims do not hold more negative views of the police overall, but their perceptions of unfairness are directed at the treatment of Muslim Americans specifically. Given that foreign-born Muslims do not seem to perceive group-based mistreatment against Muslims to this same degree, what can be learned about how the views of foreign-born Muslims develop?

Several studies have noted that foreign-born individuals tend to use their experience with social institutions in their home country as a reference to interpret their experiences and evaluate the institutions in a new country (Waldinger and Lichter 2003; De Vos and Suarez-Orozco 1990; Correia 2010; Wortley and Owusu-Bempah 2009). Specifically, negative evaluations of police in one's home country can carry over to result in more negative perceptions of law enforcement in the new destination country, as has been found with Chinese and Korean immigrants to America and Canada (Wu, Sun, and Smith 2010; Pogrebin and Poole 1990). The feature of institutions that has been shown to be most consistently associated with citizens' trust in government is corruption (Delhey and Newton 2005; Rothstein and Uslaner 2005). Compared to fair and impartial institutions, corrupt institutions are more likely to give way to negative experiences of discrimination and unfair treatment.

The extant literature suggests then that when making judgments about the legitimacy and fairness of police in the United States, immigrant Muslims are likely to reference the government institutions in their country of origin. Specifically, Muslims who come from countries with greater levels of corruption and unfair administration of the law may not hold the U.S. government to standards as high as those held by U.S.-born Muslims and may trust governments less than immigrants who come from countries with strong institutions and rule of law and lower levels of corruption. So while on average we observe that U.S.-born Muslims have more negative views toward police than immigrants overall, when comparing foreign-born individuals to each other, we may expect to see variation in attitudes toward police, based on the quality of government institutions in country from which they came.

The Moderating Effect of New Experiences

Regardless of whether an immigrant's prior socialization experience with her home country's institutions was positive or negative, her home frame-of-reference may fade as she spends more time in the United States, acquires new information and experiences, and becomes more integrated in society. Political science and sociology literature finds, in fact, that as immigrants have more contact with government authorities, they become less trusting of the government. Keven Chun, Pamela Organista, and Gerardo Marin (2003) and Henry Chow (2002) find that immigrants who had more previous contact with the police have less respect for law enforcement. Studies have shown that immigrants' experience with immigration officials also directly affects perceptions of other U.S. legal authorities. This is because some immigrants, particularly those from countries with centralized civil service systems, may not distinguish American police officers from immigration officers (Wu, Sun, and Smith 2010; Chaundry et al. 2010).[5]

Based on this line of thinking, the blurring of roles between immigration officials and local police means that immigrants who have gone through the naturalization process—and who have thus had direct experience with U.S. authorities and more socialization as an "American"—are more likely to make judgments of American legal institutions based on their personal interactions in the United States and be less influenced by previous experiences under institutional corruption. Indeed, the naturalization process itself has been shown to increase integration and knowledge of national laws among immigrants (Hainmueller, Hangartner and Pietrantuono 2015; Just and Anderson 2012). Moreover, greater knowledge of society and the government is associated with higher reported rates of discrimination compared to less acculturated immigrants (Finch, Kolody, and Vega 2000). So while Muslim immigrants' expectations of American law enforcement are likely shaped by the quality of institutions in their home country, those preconceived expectations may be updated as immigrants become exposed to the American system, whether through socialization, police contact, or more general contact with government institutions frequented by immigrants.

Measuring Country-of-Origin Corruption

To assess whether the quality of institutions under which foreign-born respondents were socialized affect their perceptions of American law enforcement, I construct a measure of the corruption levels in respondents' country of origin using data from the World Bank's Political Indicators Index—the "Corruption Control" measure (Kaufman, Kraay, and Mastruzzi 2009). The levels of Corruption Control for respondents' respective home countries are presented in Figure 6.1. "Corruption," for the purposes of this analysis, is the inverse of the Corruption Control Index. Higher values of "Corruption" represent poor control of corruption, or higher levels of corruption.

As presented in Figure 6.2, in the MANOS sample, 17 percent of respondents came from countries with a Corruption Control index score greater than 1, meaning that these countries had relatively low levels of corruption. Those countries include Australia, Belgium, Canada, France, Germany, the Netherlands, the United Kingdom, and Qatar. The bulk of the foreign-born

---

5. In addition to this confusion, in the post-9/11 era, local police departments have become increasingly involved in the enforcement of federal immigration laws, which has had a direct impact on levels of scrutiny that Muslim Americans face (Skogan 2009).

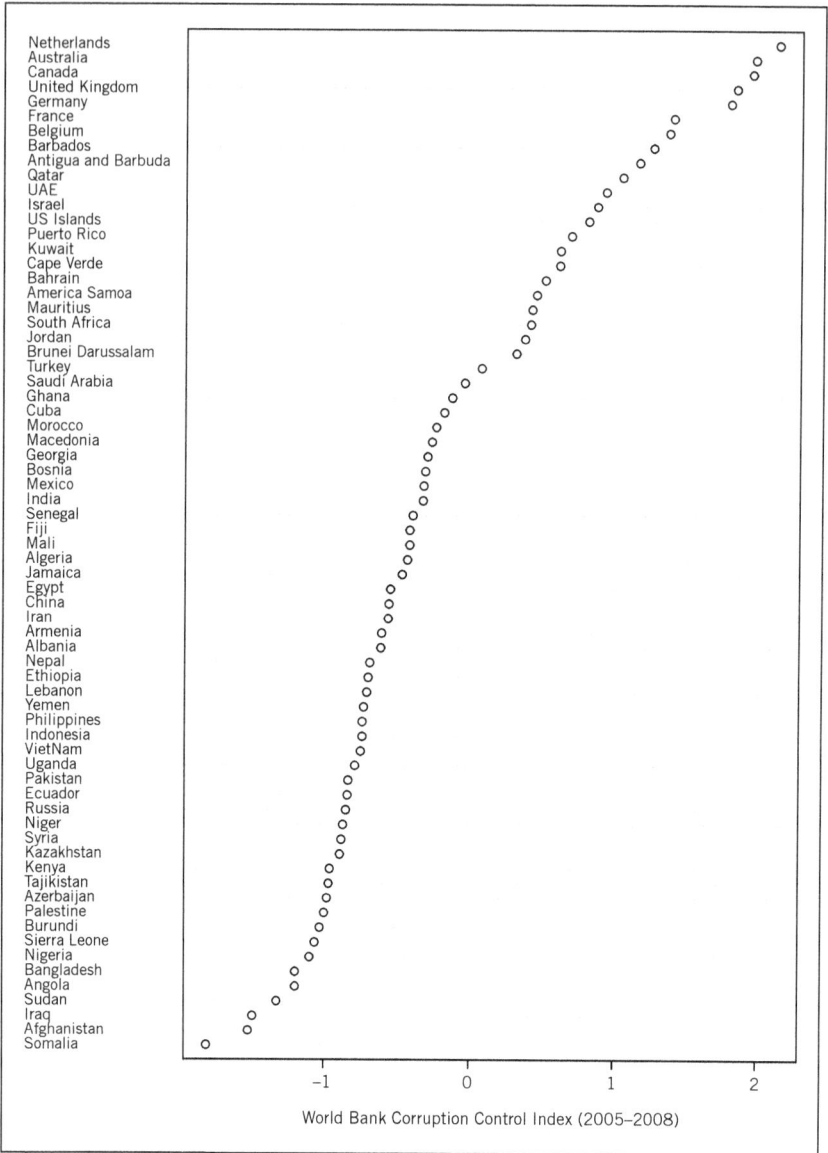

Figure 6.1 Corruption control index by sending country

Source: Kaufman, Kraay, and Mastruzzi 2009.

Note: Index scores are drawn from the World Bank Governance Indicators project. Scores range from 2 to –2; higher values represent better control of corruption (lower levels of corruption). Figures are averaged from 2005, 2006, 2007, and 2008 for more reliable estimates. The "Corruption" variable used in the analysis is the inverse of the Corruption Control Index.

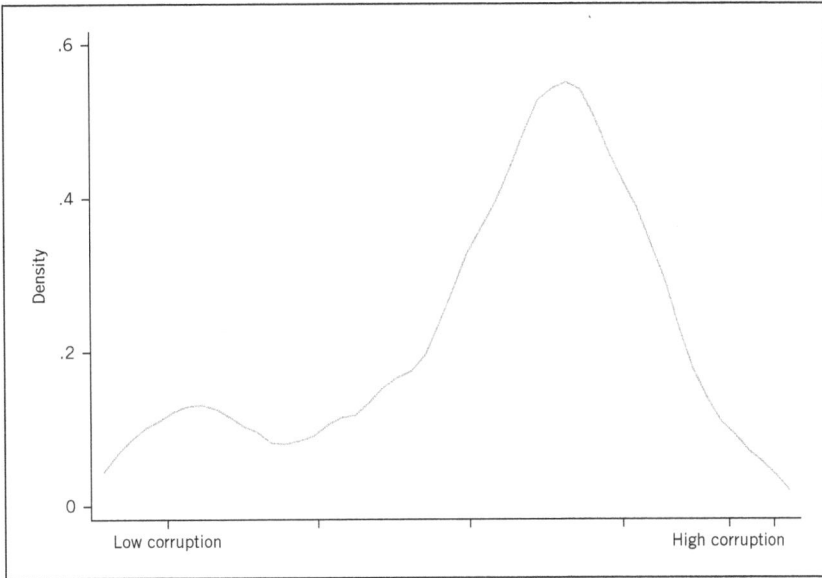

Figure 6.2 Density of respondents by sending-country corruption levels
Source: Data come from the Muslim American National Opinion Survey, 2013, and the World Bank Worldwide Governance Indicators project, 2010, available at https://datacatalog.worldbank.org/dataset/worldwide-governance-indicators.

sample (56 percent) was born in countries with corruption control scores between 1 and 0, with moderate levels of corruption, including countries like Turkey, Jordan, and Israel. Seventeen percent came from countries with scores between 0 and –1, higher levels of corruption, the majority of which are from Pakistan and India. Just 10 percent of foreign-born respondents in this sample came from countries with corruption control index score less than –1, countries with rampant corruption, including Afghanistan, Bangladesh, Nigeria, Sierra Leone, and Somalia.

Foreign-Born Muslims and Sending-Country Effects

Returning to the MANOS data, Table 6.3 presents the results from an OLS regression that estimates the degree to which foreign-born respondents' beliefs about police fairness are related to the levels of corruption in their country of origin. The potential effect of having gone through the naturalization process is also considered. The second model includes an interaction between "Corruption" and "Naturalization," in order to determine whether the effects of home-country corruption depend on whether the respondent is a naturalized citizen. Finally, the third model was developed to assess whether

TABLE 6.3: DETERMINANTS OF EXPECTED FAIRNESS OF LAW ENFORCEMENT AMONG FOREIGN-BORN MUSLIMS

	Model 1	Model 2	Model 3
Corruption (sending-country)	−0.04	−0.09*	−0.11*
	(0.03)	(0.04)	(0.05)
Naturalized	−0.05	−0.07	−0.07
	(0.05)	(0.05)	(0.05)
Naturalized × corrupt		0.09*	0.14*
		(0.05)	(0.06)
Umar (Treatment)	0.06	0.07	0.02
	(0.05)	(0.05)	(0.07)
Umar × naturalized			0.05
			(0.10)
Umar × corrupt			0.11
			(0.11)
Umar × corrupt × naturalized			−0.18
			(0.12)
Controls?	Y	Y	Y
R^2	0.17	0.19	0.21
N	168	168	168

Source: Muslim American National Opinion Survey, 2013.

Note: Numbers use a standard OLS regression with robust standard errors. Perceived fairness is measured by the question: "Generally speaking, do you think U.S. law enforcement will treat a person like this fairly?" Higher values indicate agreement with the statement. Models include foreign-born respondents only and control for age, income, education, and gender.

*$p < 0.1$.

an immigrant's background differentially affects her or his perceptions of fairness depending on the identity of the suspect. To do this, interactions between the identity of the suspect (Umar or Jake) and home-level "Corruption"; the identity of the suspect and "Naturalization"; and a triple interaction between "Corruption," "Naturalization," and the identity of the suspect are included. All models control for age, income, education, and gender. The results of these three estimates are reported as models 1 to 3 in Table 6.3.

Sending-Country Corruption Measures

Model 1 in Table 6.3 confirms that whether the suspect is a Muslim has no direct effect on expectations of police fairness for foreign-born Muslims. Whether law enforcement officers are engaging with a suspect identified as a Muslim or non-Muslim, foreign-born respondents are no more likely to think law enforcement will behave unfairly. The coefficient in model 1 for the level of corruption of one's sending country is negative, as is the coefficient for naturalized citizens; however, neither is statistically distinguishable from zero. This means that we cannot be sure that changes in the level of home-country corruption or naturalization status are necessarily linked to attitudes toward police.

When the interaction of "Corruption" and "Naturalization" is included in model 2, the coefficient of the interaction term is positive and statistically significant. This can be interpreted to mean that the effect of the level of corruption of one's sending country depends on whether the respondent is a naturalized citizen. Specifically, "home-country corruption" only has an effect on perceptions of police fairness if one has not yet become a naturalized citizen. The effect of the interaction in model 2 is visualized in Figure 6.3. Looking first at noncitizen immigrants (solid line), on the left side of the graph, individuals who emigrated from countries with low levels of corruption come to the United States with relatively sanguine prior expectations regarding fair treatment by law enforcement. In other words, the individuals

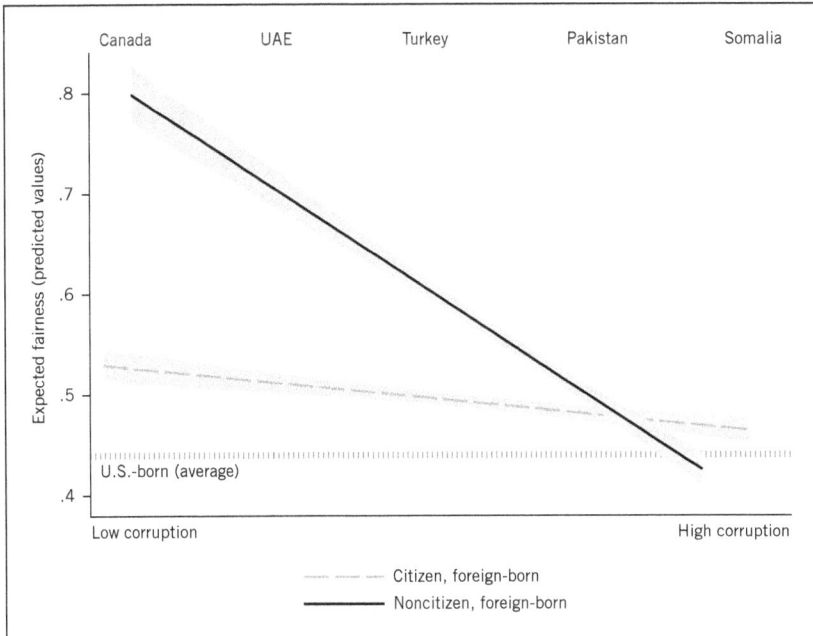

Figure 6.3 Expected perceived fairness among foreign-born naturalized citizens and noncitizens, by home-country corruption level
Source: Data come from the Muslim American National Opinion Survey, 2013.
Note: Numbers are based on results from an OLS regression controlling for age, income, gender, and education.

in the survey who were most optimistic about how fairly police would treat both suspects were foreign-born noncitizens largely from Western democracies with relatively low levels of corruption, such as the Netherlands and Canada.

Moving right across the graph, as levels of country corruption increase, perceptions of fairness decrease for nonnaturalized immigrants. Among Muslim immigrants overall, nonnaturalized immigrants coming from countries with the highest levels of corruption, such as Somalia, Afghanistan, and Iraq, have the most pessimistic views of U.S. law enforcement (and about the same level of pessimism as expressed by U.S.-born Muslims,[6] denoted by the dotted line in Figure 6.3). The observation that among immigrants, noncitizens coming from noncorrupt countries are the most likely to expect fair behavior by police and those coming from highly corrupt countries are the least likely to expect fair behavior, is robust to the inclusion of standard demographics controls, as well as controls for racial identification.[7]

The Naturalization Process

As discussed, the extant literature suggests that immigrants coming to the United States tend to be most optimistic toward the government before they have had a chance to interact with officials, to learn more about the society or have unpleasant experiences. But over time, disillusionment can set in (Correia 2010; Chun, Organista, and Marin 2003; Chow 2002; Michelson 2001, 2003a, 2003b, 2007). This trend also appears in the MANOS data. The positive expectations of those coming from noncorrupt societies disappear by the time Muslims have gone through the naturalization process. As displayed in Figure 6.3, foreign-born naturalized citizens' (dashed line) expectations of fairness do not vary by the corruption level of their country of

---

6. The average score for "Expected Fairness" for U.S.-born Muslims is 0.44 (0.39–0.50) as seen in the dotted line in Figure 6.3. The average for immigrant Muslims is 0.53 (0.46–0.58). This means that U.S.-born Muslims hold overall lower levels of expected fairness than foreign-born Muslims. Among immigrant Muslims from countries with a Corruption Index score greater than 1 (highest levels of corruption: Afghanistan, Bangladesh, Iraq, Sierra Leone, and Somalia), the average level of expected fairness is 0.32 (0.11–0.53). While this score is lower than the average score for U.S.-born Muslims, the difference is not statistically significant, as the confidence intervals overlap. So statistically speaking, U.S.-born Muslims and Muslims coming from the most corrupt countries hold equal levels of expected fairness.

7. The models in Table 6.2 do not include controls for race; however, race is not significantly related to expectations of fairness for foreign-born Muslims, and including race does not change the findings of the model. Full models are available upon request.

origin. This offers some evidence that with more time and experiences in the United States, influences from an immigrants' country of origin may fade.

To judge the importance of the naturalization process, how naturalization affects perceptions of fairness was simulated, while holding other variables at their means. Among those who emigrated from a country with low corruption (corruption-control score higher than 1), moving from noncitizen to citizen, the probability of expecting fair treatment decreases from .80 to .52, a 28-point difference. The difference between noncitizens and citizens becomes smaller as levels of corruption increase. Among those coming from countries with moderate levels of corruption, citizens' probability of expecting fairness is about 10 points less than that of noncitizens. Of those from countries scoring the highest on the corruption measure (corruption-control score less than –1), the probability of expecting fair treatment is lower among noncitizens (.37) than among citizens (.47).

Many of those coming from the most corrupt countries may be refugees, since Iraqi and Somali nationals made up some of the largest percentages of refugees to the United States between 2009 and 2011 (Russell and Batalova 2012). This suggests that refugees' expectations for governance may actually improve somewhat after becoming citizens. In order to assess whether an immigrant's background differentially affects her perceptions of fairness depending on the identity of the suspect, model 3 in Table 6.3 presents interactions between the identity of the suspect, citizenship status, and level of sending-country corruption. The lack of significance indicates that while previous experiences of corruption and familiarity with the U.S. system reduce *overall* expectations of fairness, fairness is not reduced at a greater rate when considering a Muslim suspect versus a non-Muslim suspect. This is in keeping with earlier findings that foreign-born Muslims—regardless of their naturalization status or country-of-origin level of corruption—are not expecting the police to treat the Muslim and non-Muslim suspects differently.

The Effects of Time in the United States on Perceptions of Fairness

How does time in the United States, versus the naturalization process, affect expectations of fairness toward law enforcement? The effect of time is a difficult thing to measure, because it is likely to depend on the age during which one migrated to the United States. For example, the effect of living in America for twenty years is likely to mean something different for those who came to America as infants than for those who came as adults.

To assess the effect of time as a function of age, Figure 6.4 presents the effect of time spent in the United States on predicted values of expected fairness, by age of the respondent. Specifically, the figure shows how this relationship differs based on whether the respondent is under thirty years of age or over. Looking first to immigrants who are over thirty years of age (solid line), on average, time in the United States does not significantly change an individual's attitude toward U.S. law enforcement. Looking then to individuals who are under the age of thirty, attitudes appear to be more malleable with time. Specifically, for individuals who came to the United States at a young age, expectations of fairness drop significantly over time. Among those who have lived almost their entire lives in America, not surprisingly, their expectations of U.S. law enforcement are identical to those of native-born Muslims.

Just as those who came to the United States as children and adolescents are more likely to hold attitudes about law enforcement that are similar to U.S.-born Muslims, it follows that country-of-origin effects should be weak among those who have spent very few years living in the countries where were born. Figure 6.5 presents the marginal effect of home-country corruption on predicted values of expected fairness by the proportion of one's life spent abroad (years lived in the United States divided by age). We see from the figure that home-country corruption does not affect the expectations of

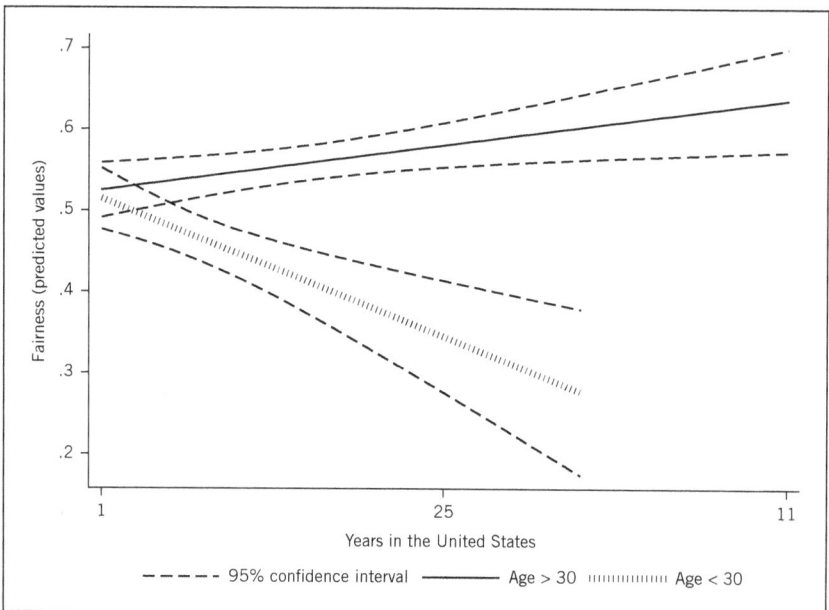

Figure 6.4 Expected perceived fairness among foreign-born Muslims, by time lived in the United States and age
Source: Data come from the Muslim American National Opinion Survey, 2013.
Note: Numbers are based on results from an OLS regression controlling for age, income, gender, and education.

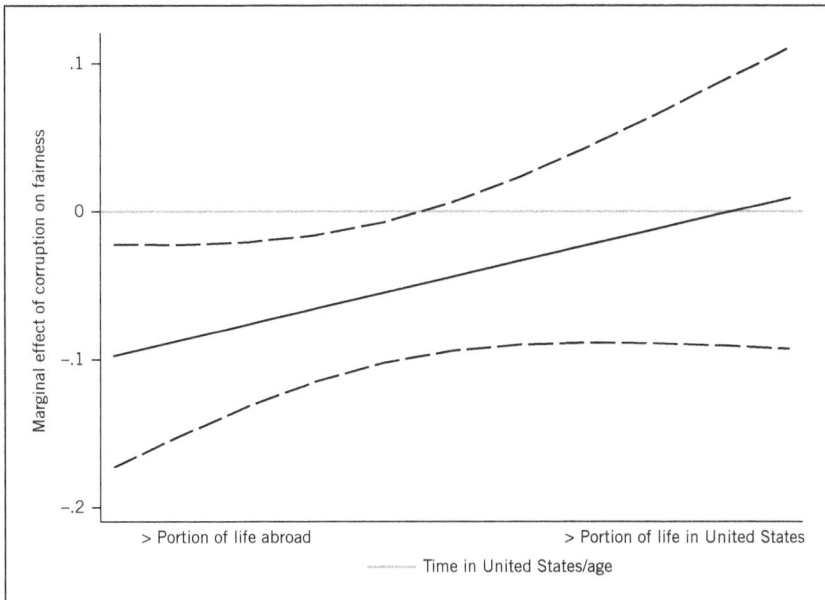

Figure 6.5 Marginal effect of home-country corruption on perceived fairness among foreign-born Muslims, by time lived in the United States
Source: Data come from the Muslim American National Opinion Survey, 2013.
Note: Proportion of life lived in the United States is measured by dividing years of residency by the respondent's age. Numbers are based on results from an OLS regression controlling for age, income, gender, and education.

those who have lived the majority of their lives in the United States (right side of graph). For those who have spent most their lives in their country of origin (left side of graph), home-country corruption significantly reduces expectations of fairness.

Robustness Checks and Limitations

The finding that home-country effects carry over into the United States and then fade as individuals become more familiar with the American institutions is consistent with interviews with immigrant respondents, as well as the related literature. Nonetheless, potential alternative explanations to the theory are assessed here below.

U.S. War Zone Migrants

Could the findings about the impact of home-country corruption on perceptions be veiled by another effect: an immigrant's negative experience with U.S.

foreign policy in his or her country of origin? Among the most corrupt countries are Iraq and Afghanistan, countries where in 2013 (the year the MANOS survey was administered) the United States had stationed troops within each country for at least ten years. In this sample, 8 percent of respondents reported being born in either Iraq or Afghanistan, and about half of them immigrated to the United States after 9/11. All of those who came before 9/11 have become naturalized citizens, and about half who arrived after 9/11 are citizens. Individuals who were born in Iraq or Afghanistan are 28 percentage points less likely to expect fair treatment by law enforcement than other foreign-born respondents. This difference is substantively large and statistically significant, even after controlling for sending-country corruption and citizenship status. This suggests that U.S. foreign policy in immigrants' country of origin may also shape attitudes toward the broader American government, including local police. Removing individuals from Iraq or Afghanistan from the full models in Table 6.3 does not change the substantive results; however, the interaction between citizenship status and corruption now just barely misses statistical significance (perhaps because of a reduced sample size). Naturalization is still significantly related to low levels of expected fairness.

Economic Development and Anti-American Sentiment

While the quality of government institutions is known to shape levels of trust in government (Uslaner 2008), a country's corruption levels are also correlated with its levels of economic development, as well as levels of anti-American sentiment within the country (Gillum 2010). Could corruption also be serving as a veil for either of these effects? Anti-American sentiment is particularly high in the Muslim world and is a popular topic of discussion for political elites in the region (Blaydes and Linzer 2012). It could be that newcomers exposed to high levels of anti-American rhetoric bring with them negative conceptions of the U.S. security apparatus. It could be that newcomers from corrupt, war-ridden countries such as Iraq and Afghanistan, for instance, bring negative conceptions of the U.S. security apparatus, due not only to poor experiences with their country's institutions but also to negative interactions with U.S. military personnel or extensive exposure to anti-American rhetoric.

I examine the potential role of economic development in an immigrant's country of origin on perceptions of fairness. As a robustness check, the models from Table 6.3 were rerun using the International Monetary Fund's 2012 per capita GDP estimates instead of the Corruption measure.[8] While GDP

8. Regression results available upon request.

has a positive effect on expectations of fairness, the effect is not statistically distinguishable from zero. Similarly, the effects of GDP are larger for non-citizens, but this effect is not statistically significant. This means that home-country GDP has no notable impact on perceptions of police fairness for MANOS respondents.

I also rerun the models using the average levels of anti-American senti-ment (based on Pew Research Center's 2007 estimates) in one's sending country in place of the "Corruption" measure. Similar to GDP, while anti-American sentiment has a negative effect on expectations of fairness, the effect is not statistically distinguishable from zero. The effects of anti-Amer-ican sentiment are larger for noncitizens, but this effect is not statistically significant. This means that the level of anti-American sentiment in one's home country is not related to his or her perceptions of police fairness in the United States.

Self-Selection among Naturalized Citizens?

Because naturalization requires action on the part of the respondent, there could be a self-selection effect. In other words, those who choose to natural-ize could be primed to hold more positive views; those with more negative perceptions of the United States would choose *not* to naturalize. While the results show precisely the opposite (naturalized citizens were more likely to hold negative views), it is worth noting whether any other factors that could potentially affect perceptions of fairness are more commonly associated with those who choose to become citizens.

Sixty-one percent of the foreign-born sampled respondents report being naturalized U.S. citizens. Muslims have a very high naturalization rate that is significantly correlated with immigration year. Since it technically takes at least three to five years to become eligible for citizenship, many of the more recent arrivals have not been in the country long enough to apply. Moreover, having gone through the process of naturalization suggests ex-tensive contact with U.S. immigration officials and American legal institu-tions, which is shown to directly affect perceptions of other U.S. legal au-thorities, specifically the police (Wu, Sun, and Smith 2010; Chaundry et al. 2010). To assess whether individuals who choose to naturalize are signifi-cantly different from those who do not, Table 6.4 presents mean levels of a variety of socioeconomic and behavioral indicators. The table reveals that naturalized citizens and noncitizens do not significantly differ on these in-dicators, including age, socioeconomic status, race, political preference, or religiosity.

TABLE 6.4: DEMOGRAPHIC COMPARISONS OF NONCITIZENS, NATURALIZED
CITIZENS, AND U.S.-BORN MUSLIMS

	Foreign-born noncitizen	Foreign-born citizen	U.S.-born
N	69	103	331
Age	38.2 (33.3–43.1)	42.5 (37.9–47.1)	44.1 (40.7–47.5)
Female	.49 (.34–.65)	.35 (.21–.49)	.53 (.44–.62)
Education	4.0 (3.5–4.5)	3.7 (3.4–4.0)	3.5 (3.3–3.7)
Income	5.1 (4.1–6.2)	6.1 (4.6–7.5)	5.7 (5.1–6.2)
Convert	.10 (.02–.18)	.15 (.01–.28)	.42 (.32–.50)
Republican	.11 (.04–.18)	.15 (.05–.26)	14 (.09–.19)
Perceived religious discrimination	.54 (.44–.64)	.52 (.43–.61)	.61 (.56–.66)
Perceived ethnic discrimination	.47 (.38–.57)	.43 (.34–.52)	.52 (.47–.57)
Religiosity (pray)	.78 (.70–.87)	.75 (.66–.83)	.76 (.70–.82)
Anti-U.S. sentiment (home country value)	59.4 (51.6–67.2)	48.6 (39.0–58.2)	

Source: Muslim American National Opinion Survey, 2013.
Note: Means are presented with 95 percent confidence intervals in parentheses. $N = 503$.

Discussion: American Muslim Integration, Foreign-Born Influences, and Trust in Police across Generations

In this chapter, I set out to understand whether Muslims believe that their religious identity will result in differential treatment by authorities, or whether they trust that they will be treated indiscriminately. While past studies have assessed Muslim Americans' interactions with government officials and law enforcement using qualitative interviews (Cainkar 2009; Peek 2010; Bakalian and Bozorgmehr 2009), the experimental design presented in this chapter allows for a more precise measure of the degree to which Muslims have (or have not) internalized beliefs about the differential treatment of Muslims in the United States by law enforcement agencies. Consistent with past studies on perceptions of the government among immigrant groups in the United States and Europe, Muslims who are more familiar with American norms and the government—measured here by generation, naturalization, and time in the United States—generally expect U.S. law enforcement to behave less fairly when conducting criminal investigations. Respondents who are less familiar with the American system, foreign-born Muslims and noncitizens, tend to be more trusting of the police overall.

The findings of this chapter suggest two significant explanations for differential patterns of trust in police across generations. First, what appears to change across generations is an increased awareness of *group-based* injustices. The data demonstrate that U.S.-born Muslims have a greater sensitivity to the differential treatment of Muslim Americans as a group. Muslims born outside the United States tend to expect equal treatment of Muslim and non-Muslim suspects by police, while U.S.-born respondents expect Muslims to be treated significantly worse than non-Muslims. These findings reflect studies that observe that descendants of immigrants are more likely to make direct comparisons between themselves and their nonimmigrant, U.S.-born counterparts in the country. It is the discrepancies that they perceive that drive their perceptions of discrimination by the police and the broader government toward Muslims.

These data also indicate that U.S.-born Muslims do not necessarily have an *overall* negative view of U.S. law enforcement. On average, U.S.-born and foreign-born Muslims hold similar levels of trust in America's security institutions when discussing the treatment of non-Muslims. The groups differ in their beliefs about the police only when considering the treatment of Muslims in the United States. This potentially offers more nuance to studies that have similarly found reduced trust among second-generation immigrants toward the government. It may be that the decrease in trust on the part of immigrants and their children over time does not represent their belief that entire institutions are inevitably untrustworthy but are more of an indication that they have internalized their status in the society.

Second, the analysis suggests that foreign-born Muslims' attitudes toward U.S. law enforcement are shaped, in part, by their experiences with governments in their countries of origin. Muslims coming from countries with low levels of institutional corruption arrive to the United States with relatively optimistic prior beliefs about the fairness of law enforcement compared to those who come from corruption-ridden countries. Home-country effects, however, fade as Muslims become more familiar with the U.S. system and update their beliefs about U.S. law enforcement. Citizens who have gone through the naturalization process have much more pessimistic views toward law enforcement overall, regardless of their country of origin. This suggests that through time and the process of naturalization, foreign-born Muslims increasingly reflect the more cynical attitudes of U.S.-born Muslims toward government institutions such as the police.

While understanding attitudes of legitimacy and fairness among citizenry is important normatively, an extensive literature suggests that beliefs about government fairness and legitimacy also have important policy implications for governments and law enforcement agencies. According to Tyler

(2009), procedural justice predicts cooperation with law enforcement, with legitimacy as the mediator. If individuals believe they are being treated unfairly, perceptions of legitimacy, and therefore cooperation, will decline (Levi 1997). Indeed, I find elsewhere that beliefs about police legitimacy and fairness among Muslim Americans have a direct and significant effect on willingness to cooperate with the police (Gillum 2018). This indicates that the large majority of the Muslim American community is no different than other segments of the American population—eager to assist the government when they believe that government representatives will uphold the rights and will not discriminate against its citizens.

REFERENCES

Abdo, Geneive. 2006. *Mecca and Main Street*. Oxford: Oxford University Press.

Apuzzo, Matt, and Adam Goldman. 2013. *Enemies Within: Inside the NYPDs Secret Spying Unit and bin Laden's Final Plot against America*. New York: Simon and Schuster.

Bakalian, Anny, and Medhi Bozorgmehr. 2009. *Backlash 9/11: Middle Eastern and Muslim Americans Respond*. Berkeley: University of California Press.

Bergen, Peter, David Sterman, Emily Schneider, and Bailey Cahall. 2014. "Do NSA's Bulk Surveillance Programs Stop Terrorists?" New America Foundation, January. Available at https://www.newamerica.org/international-security/policy-papers/do-nsas -bulk-surveillance-programs-stop-terrorists.

Blaydes, Lisa, and Drew A. Linzer. 2012. "Elite Competition, Religiosity, and Anti-Americanism in the Islamic World." *American Political Science Review* 106 (2): 225–243.

Brooks, Clem, and Jeff Manza. 2013. *Whose Rights? Counterterrorism and the Dark Side of American Public Opinion*. New York: Russell Sage Foundation.

Brunson, Rod K. 2007. "'Police Don't Like Black People': African-American Young Men's Accumulated Police Experiences." *Criminology and Public Policy* 6:71–101.

Cainkar, Louise A. 2009. *Homeland Insecurity: The Arab American and Muslim American Experience after 9/11*. New York: Russell Sage Foundation.

Cao, Liqun, James Frank, and Francis Cullen. 1996. "Race, Community Context and Confidence in the Police." *American Journal of Police* 15 (1): 3–22.

Chaundry, Ajay, Randolph Capps, Juan Pedroza, Rosa Maria Castaneda, Robert Santos, and Molly M. Scott. 2010. *Facing Our Future: Children in the Aftermath of Immigration Enforcement*. Washington, DC: Urban Institute.

Chow, Henry. 2002. "Police-Community Relations: Chinese Attitudes toward the Police in Toronto." *Canadian Ethnic Studies* 34 (2): 90–101.

CHRGJ (Center for Human Rights and Global Justice). 2011. "Targeted and Entrapped: Manufacturing the 'Homegrown Threat' in the United States." Available at https://chrgj.org/wp-content/uploads/2016/09/targetedandentrapped.pdf.

Chun, Kevin M., Pamela Balls Organista, and Gerardo Marin, eds. 2003. *Acculturation: Advances in Theory, Measurement, and Applied Research*. Washington, DC: American Psychological Association.

Correia, Mark E. 2010. "Determinants of Attitudes toward Police of Latino Immigrants and Non-immigrants." *Journal of Criminal Justice* 38 (1): 99–107.

Delhey, Jay, and Ken Newton. 2005. "Predicting Cross-National Levels of Social Trust: Global Pattern or Nordic Exceptionalism?" *European Sociological Review* 21 (4): 311–327.

De Vos, George, and Marcelo Suarez-Orozco. 1990. *Status Inequality: The Self in Culture.* Thousand Oaks, CA: Sage.

Eberhardt, Jennifer L., P. A. Goff, Valerie J. Purdie-Vaughns, and P. G. Davies. 2004. "Seeing Black: Race, Crime, and Visual Processing." *Journal of Personality and Social Psychology* 87 (6): 876–893.

Eight Years after 9/11: Confronting the Terrorist Threat to the Homeland; Hearing Before the Committee on Homeland Security and Governmental Affairs, United States Senate. 2009. 111th Congress, September 30. Statement of Robert Mueller, Director of the Federal Bureau of Investigation. Available at https://www.hsgac.senate.gov/imo/media/doc/TestimonyMueller20090930.pdf.

Finch, Brian Karl, Bohdan Kolody, and William A. Vega. 2000. "Perceived Discrimination and Depression among Mexican-Origin Adults in California." *Journal of Health and Social Behavior* 41 (3): 295–313.

Garcia, Venessa, and Liqun Cao. 2005. "Race and Satisfaction with the Police in a Small City." *Journal of Criminal Justice* 33 (2): 191–199.

Garcia-Bedolla, Lisa. 2005. *Fluid Borders: Latino Power, Identity, and Politics in Los Angeles.* Berkeley: University of California Press.

Gilliam, Franklin D., and Shanto Iyengar. 2000. "Prime Suspects: The Influence of Local Television News on the Viewing Public." *American Journal of Political Science* 43 (3): 560–573.

Gillum, Rachel. 2010. "Allies or Adversaries: Analyzing Anti-American Sentiment in Muslim-Majority Countries." Paper presented at the Midwest Political Science Association Conference, Chicago, IL, April 24.

———. 2018. *Muslim Americans in a Post-9/11 World: A Survey of Attitudes and Beliefs and Their Implications for U.S. National Security Policy.* Ann Arbor: University of Michigan Press.

Hainmueller, Jens, Dominik Hangartner, and Giuseppe Pietrantuono. 2015. "Naturalization Fosters the Long-Term Political Integration of Immigrants." *Proceedings of the National Academy of Sciences of the United States of America* 112 (41): 12651–12656.

Hurst, Yolander G., James Frank, and Sandra Lee Browning. 2000. "The Attitudes of Juveniles toward the Police: A Comparison of Black and White Youth." *Policing* 23 (1): 37–53.

Hurwitz, Jon, and Mark Peffley. 2005. "Explaining the Great Racial Divide: Perceptions of Fairness in the U.S. Criminal Justice System." *Journal of Politics* 63 (3): 762–783.

Jamal, Amaney. 2008. "Civil Liberties and the Otherization of Arab and Muslim Americans." In *Race and Arab Americans before and after 9/11: From Invisible Citizens to Visible Subjects,* edited by Amaney Jamal and Nadine Naber, 114–130. Syracuse, NY: Syracuse University Press.

Just, Aida, and Christopher J. Anderson. 2012. "Immigrants, Citizenship and Political Action in Europe." *British Journal of Political Science* 42 (3): 481–509.

Kaufman, Daniel, Art Kraay, and Massimo Mastruzzi. 2009. "Governance Matters VIII: Aggregate and Individual Governance Indicators, 1996–2008." World Bank

Development Research Group Policy Research Working Paper 4978. Available at https://openknowledge.worldbank.org/bitstream/handle/10986/4170/WPS4978 .pdf.

Kurzman, Charles. 2014. "Muslim-American Terrorism in 2013." Available at https:// sites.duke.edu/tcths/files/2013/06/Kurzman_Muslim-American_Terrorism_in _2013.pdf.

Levi, Margaret. 1997. *Consent, Dissent and Patriotism*. New York: Cambridge University Press.

Levi, Margaret, Audrey Sacks, and Tom Tyler. 2009. "Conceptualizing Legitimacy, Measuring Legitimating Beliefs." *American Behavioral Scientist* 53 (3): 354–375.

Maxwell, Rahsaan. 2008. "Assimilation, Expectations, and Attitudes: How Ethnic Minority Migrant Groups Feel about Mainstream Society." *DuBois Review* 5 (21): 387–412.

———. 2010. "Evaluating Migrant Integration: Political Attitudes across Generations in Europe." *International Migration Review* 44 (1): 25–52.

Michelson, Melissa. 2001. "Political Trust among Chicago Latinos." *Journal of Urban Affairs* 23 (3–4): 323–334.

———. 2003a. "Boricua in the Barrio: Political Trust among Puerto Ricans." *Centro: Journal of the Center for Puerto Rican Studies* 15 (1): 138–151.

———. 2003b. "The Corrosive Effect of Acculturation: How Mexican Americans Lose Political Trust." *Social Science Quarterly* 84 (4): 918–933.

———. 2007. "All Roads Lead to Rust: How Acculturation Erodes Latino Immigrant Trust in Government." *Aztlán: A Journal of Chicano Studies* 32 (2): 21–46.

Muslim Advocates. 2011. "Losing Liberty: The State of American Freedom 10 Years After the Patriot Act." Available at https://www.muslimadvocates.org/ten_years_after _patriot_act_time_to_restore_america_s_freedoms.

New America. 2017. "Terrorism in America after 9/11." Available at https://www .newamerica.org/in-depth/terrorism-in-america.

Obama, Barack. 2015. "Remarks by the President in Closing of the Summit on Countering Violent Extremism." February 18. Available at https://obamawhitehouse .archives.gov/the-press-office/2015/02/18/remarks-president-closing-summit -countering-violent-extremism.

Peek, Lori. 2011. *Behind the Backlash: Muslim Americans after 9/11*. Philadelphia: Temple University Press.

Pew Research Center. 2011. "Muslim Americans: No Signs of Growth in Alienation or Support for Extremism." August 30. Available at http://www.people-press.org/2011/ 08/30/muslim-americans-no-signs-of-growth-in-alienation-or-support-for -extremism.

———. 2013. "The Rise of Asian Americans." April 4. Available at http://www.pew socialtrends.org/2012/06/19/the-rise-of-asian-americans.

Pogrebin, Mark R., and Eric D. Poole. 1990. "Cultural Conflict and Crime in the Korean American Community." *Criminal Justice Policy Review* 4 (1): 69–78.

Roder, Antje, and Peter Muhlau. 2012. "What Determines the Trust of Immigrants in Criminal Justice Institutions in Europe?" *European Journal of Criminology* 9 (4): 370–387.

Rothstein, Bo, and Eric M. Uslaner. 2005. "All for All: Equality, Corruption, and Social Trust." *World Politics* 58 (1): 41–72.

Russell, Joseph, and Jeanne Batalova. 2012. "Refugees and Asylees in the United States." Migration Policy Institute, September 27. Available at https://www.migrationpolicy .org/article/refugees-and-asylees-united-states-3.

Sharp, Douglas, and Susie Atherton. 2007. "To Serve and Protect? The Experiences of Policing in the Community of Young People from Black and Other Ethnic Minority Groups." *British Journal of Criminology* 47 (5): 746–763.

Skogan, Wesley G. 2009. "Policing Immigrant Communities in the United States." In *Immigration, Crime and Justice*, edited by William F. McDonald, 189–203. Bingley, UK: Emerald Group.

Sunshine, Jason, and Tom Tyler. 2003. "The Role of Procedural Justice and Legitimacy in Shaping Public Support for Policing." *Law and Society Review* 37 (3): 513–548.

Tyler, Tom. 2009. "Legitimacy and Criminal Justice: The Benefits of Self-Regulation." *Ohio State Journal of Criminal Law* 7 (1): 307–359.

Tyler, Tom, and Jeffrey Fagan. 2008. "Legitimacy and Cooperation: Why Do People Help the Police Fight Crime in their Communities?" *Ohio State Journal of Criminal Law* 6:231–275.

Tyler, Tom, and R. Folger. 1980. "Distributional and Procedural Aspects of Satisfaction with Citizen-Police Encounters." *Basic and Applied Social Psychology* 1 (4): 281–292.

Tyler, Tom, and Yuen Huo. 2002. *Trust in the Law.* New York: Russell Sage.

Uslaner, Eric M. 2008. *Corruption, Inequality, and the Rule of Law: the Bulging Pocket Makes the Easy Life.* Cambridge: Cambridge University Press.

Waldinger, Roger, and Michael Lichter. 2003. *How the Other Half Works: Immigration and the Social Organization of Labor.* Los Angeles: University of California Press.

Weitzer, Ronald. 2002. "Incidents of Police Misconduct and Public Opinion." *Journal of Criminal Justice* 30 (5): 397–408.

Wortley, Scot, and Akwasi Owusu-Bempah. 2009. "Unequal before the Law: Immigrant and Racial Minority Perceptions of the Canadian Justice System." *Journal of International Migration and Integration* 10 (4): 447–473.

Wu, Yunig, Ivan Y. Sun, and Brad W. Smith. 2010. "Race, Immigration, and Policing: Chinese Immigrants' Satisfaction with Police." *Justice Quarterly* 28 (5): 745–774.

The 9/11 Mosque and Partisan Polarization

KEREM OZAN KALKAN

A s the preceding chapters show in various ways, Muslims are one of the least popular out-groups in the United States. This may seem readily explicable by the conflicts between many Muslim countries and the United States, as well as the terrorist attacks on 9/11. Such conflicts suggest that Americans would view Muslims with suspicion. But attitudes toward Muslims—both before and after 9/11—were based on more general attitudes toward minorities than on either political or security considerations (Kalkan, Layman, and Uslaner 2009). Political leaders from both parties strived to keep politics out of evaluations of Muslims, and they have largely succeeded—until recently.

Views of Muslims have become politicized since 2007. After the 9/11 terrorist attacks, President George W. Bush sought to reassure Muslims that they were respected—and cautioned other Americans not to demonize them.[1] More recently, Republican leaders have questioned the patriotism of Muslims. For example, Ben Carson repeatedly expressed during the 2016 presidential primary season that a Muslim could not become the president of the United States (Bradner 2015). There has also been a growing partisan

---

1. Bush addressed the nation after the fall of the Twin Towers in New York: "We respect your faith. It's practiced freely by many millions of Americans, and by millions more in countries that America counts as friends. Its teachings are good and peaceful, and those who commit evil in the name of Allah blaspheme the name of Allah." For the text of the speech, see http://www.presidentialrhetoric.com/speeches/09.20.01.html.

divide on attitudes toward Muslims in the mass public as well. As mentioned in Chapter 2, the signature event that led to the increased salience and politicization of attitudes toward Muslims was the proposal to build a community center and mosque, the "9/11 Mosque," near the site of the World Trade Center towers that were destroyed in the 9/11 terrorist attacks.

The debate over the 9/11 Mosque reflected attitudes toward Muslims, but virtually no opponents used explicit anti-Muslim rhetoric. Instead they focused on the community center as a potential threat from terrorists. The opposition from Republican politicians nevertheless generated political support in the 2010 elections (Hulse 2010). Political independents who opposed the 9/11 Mosque were substantially more likely to say that they would support Republican House candidates. Republican identifiers who opposed the mosque were more likely to say that they were certain to vote in 2010. And Tea Party supporters were substantially more likely to say that the mosque was a major factor in shaping their vote choice. The debate over the mosque reflected a growing partisan polarization among Americans. These partisan divisions continued to grow—and Republican politicians made more explicit attacks on Muslims.

After the attacks on the Bataclan concert hall in Paris and on a regional center in San Bernardino, California, by Muslim terrorists in November and December 2015, Republican then presidential contender Donald Trump proposed banning Muslim immigrants from the United States. At the same time, hundreds of thousands of Muslim refugees were escaping Syria into Europe, and President Barack Obama proposed admitting 25,000 of them into the United States. And many feared that at least some refugees could be terrorists. Most other Republican candidates endorsed this proposal (Reilly 2015). Even the most moderate, Ohio governor John Kasich, favored the ban and even proposed a government agency to promote "Judeo-Christian values" (Caldwell 2015). Fifty-nine percent of Republican identifiers supported the ban on Muslim immigrants (compared to 18 percent of Democrats), and 80 percent of Trump supporters in South Carolina (an early primary state) agreed with the proposal (Jensen 2016). The elite language had shifted from concern about terrorism to negativity toward Muslims more generally, which reflected partisan divisions on Islam among the public (Beinart 2015).

This chapter argues that the conflict over the 9/11 Mosque was the first shot in a growing cultural divide between Democrats and Republicans. Specifically, it was the first and most prominent incident that led to overt position taking by political parties on the issue of Muslims. Before the 9/11 Mosque, there was at least a marginal consensus among party elites that the problem was one of terrorism and *not* Islam. In other words, Republicans became increasingly likely to see Islam negatively and to accept Trump's charges that Obama was not born in the United States, to believe that the president was himself a Muslim, and to see a "clash of civilizations" between Christianity and Islam (Tesler 2015; Beinart 2015). In 2010, Republicans exploited fears of radical Islam by linking it to what had seemed to be an uncontroversial community center in Manhattan. By 2015 and 2016, the conflict over identities had moved to the center of political debate. As I show below, Pew Research Center data provide strong empirical support for this increasing mass and elite partisan divide on the issue of Muslims.

The 9/11 Mosque as an "Efficient Symbol"

The opposition to the 9/11 Mosque represents a break with previous attitudes on Muslims. While Americans have viewed Muslims less favorably than most other groups, such attitudes had largely reflected more general attitudes toward minorities rather than partisan conflicts (Kalkan, Layman, and Uslaner 2009). But views on the mosque at Ground Zero were driven more by political divisions. Only 28 percent of Americans (and just 9 percent of Republicans) supported the 9/11 Mosque. Republican leaders used this center as an "efficient symbol" of the terrorist threat (Leege et al. 2002) to mobilize their base without demonizing all Muslims. Efficient symbols are arguments using a presumably universal fear (terrorism) as a substitute for a more divisive target (Muslims). In 2010 direct attacks on Islam were still unacceptable. Opposition to the 9/11 Mosque was based on fear of Islamic extremism rather than attacks on Muslims more generally, but Republican elites and party identifiers soon came to blunt the distinction between radical Islam and Muslims. Analysis of 2010 surveys by *Washington Post*/ABC News and by *Time* magazine reveals that opposition to the center reflected increased partisan polarization on immigration and on attitudes toward Muslims in particular, especially among Tea Party supporters. Republican leaders were able to focus on this issue to mobilize votes from fellow partisans and independents in the 2010 election (see "Washington Post–ABC News Poll" 2010; Altman 2010).

Anti-Muslim sentiments are particularly strong among Tea Party supporters, suggesting that opposition to the 9/11 Mosque and criticism of Muslims more generally is responsive to an important part of the Republican constituency. Tea Party supporters were also considerably more likely to say that the mosque was important to their vote choice. It was thus a sound strategy for Republican leaders to use this efficient symbol to oppose this community center. I show that political independents who opposed the mosque were more likely to vote for Republican House candidates in the 2010 elections.

Party elites were strategic in exploiting the partisan divisions on this issue well before the 2016 presidential election primaries. According to the 2012 Convention Delegate Studies data, the average rating of Muslims among Republican Party activists was almost 30 percentage points lower than among Democratic Party activists on a 100-point feeling thermometer scale. The Republicans' negativity toward Islam is part of a more general ethnocentrism. Immigration has become a flash point for the party—with most (though not all) candidates favoring strong sanctions against undocumented immigrants. This has led, for example, to sharp rhetoric against Mexicans and other Latino immigrants, especially from Trump, and to opposition to any legislation that would lead to a path to permanent residence (or citizenship) for undocumented immigrants. While negativity toward other immigrants stems from the same ethnocentrism, Islam has been a more direct target of party candidates.

Attitudes toward Muslims in the United States and elsewhere—notably in Europe—are part of a larger ethnocentric syndrome. People who view other out-groups—notably illegal immigrants, people on welfare, gays and lesbians, blacks, Hispanics, and Jews—negatively are likely to view Muslims negatively (Gallup 2009; Kalkan, Layman, and Uslaner 2009; Kupper and Zick 2010; Sniderman and Hagendoorn 2007; Zick, Kupper, and Hovermann 2011). Anti-Muslim sentiments stem largely from the view that followers of Islam are "not like us" (not Christians). Among all minority religious, ethnic, and racial groups, Muslims are the least popular (other than atheists) (Kalkan, Layman, and Uslaner 2009).

Some Muslims (notably the very religious from the Middle East) dress and look different from Westerners; they also have different customs (notably women who cover their hair or their entire face) and thus appear to be behaviorally distinct, as well as culturally different (Kalkan, Layman, and Uslaner 2009). Unlike African Americans and Hispanics, who are predominantly Christian, Muslims seem less "like us" than do most other minorities. Many cultural conservatives tried to paint Democratic nominee Barack Obama as a "secret Muslim" in the 2008 election. In a survey conducted by the Pew Research Center in August 2010, 18 percent of respondents identified Obama's religion as Muslim. Republicans, especially in the South, were more likely to see Obama as a Muslim (Meeks 2012).

David Leege and colleagues (2002) argue that parties, especially minority parties, exploit cultural divisions in society that are efficient symbols designed to provoke divisions within the electorate by scapegoating and out-grouping unpopular minority groups through symbols and code words. I argue that the 9/11 Mosque is such a symbol. Anti-Muslim sentiments strongly predict voting behavior in 2008, even after controlling for ethnocentrism, racial resentment, political predispositions, and sociodemographic variables (Kam and Kinder 2012; Tesler and Sears 2010). It was not Islam per se that these leaders found objectionable—it was *radical* Islam. But the message was that most Muslims were radical and threatening. I find that 77 percent of Republicans (compared to 36 percent of Democrats) believed that Islam is a more violent religion than other faiths. Opposition to the mosque—and the linkage to Ground Zero—by Republican politicians mobilized such sentiments without directly attacking Muslims.

I hypothesize that partisanship will predict attitudes toward the Cordoba Community Center (the 9/11 Mosque's official name) more strongly than other potential factors. Specific negative attitudes toward Islam will be influential in explaining opposition against the center. My analysis uses a survey conducted by *Time* magazine in August 2010 to test these political explanations of the mosque controversy. The outcome variable asks respondents whether they favor or oppose the building of the Muslim community center and mosque near where the World Trade Center stood. Those who favor are coded 1, and those who oppose are coded 0. The main explanatory variable is a five-category party identification measure that ranges from "strong Republican" to "strong Democrat." To control for the ideological predispositions, the model includes two dichotomous measures—liberal and conservative—with moderates as being the comparison category.

Another set of explanatory variables includes Islam-specific measures. The first one asks the respondents whether the Islamic religion is more likely than other religions to encourage violence against nonbelievers, less likely, or about the same as most other religions. I coded those who said that Islam is more likely than other religions to encourage violence against nonbelievers 3, those who said it is less likely 1, and those who said it is the same 2. The second Islam-specific measure asks respondents whether they would say Muslims in the United States are patriotic Americans who believe in American values. Those who identified Muslims as patriotic are coded 1, and the rest are 0. The survey also asked the respondents whether they personally know any Americans who are followers of the Islamic religion. I coded the respondents who personally know Muslims 1 and the rest 0. The final Islam-specific variable asks respondents their overall prejudice about Muslims. It is a four-category variable that ranges from "very favorable" to "very unfavorable." I expect that people with more favorable views of Muslims and Islam will be more likely to support the mosque, as will people who know Muslims.

I also control for age and education of the respondents. More educated and younger people should be more favorable to the Cordoba Community Center. I recoded all variables to range from 0 to 1. This enables us to compare variables' predictive power. The estimation sample for this and all other

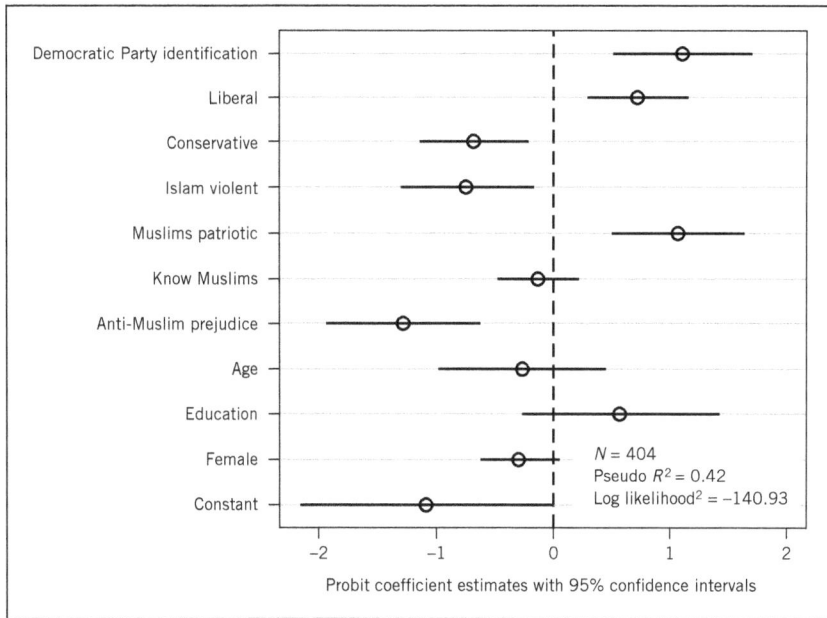

Figure 7.1 Favorability toward the Ground Zero mosque
Source: 2010 *Time* survey.

models presented includes non-Latino white respondents only.[2] Since the outcome variable is a dichotomous measure, I use probit to estimate coefficients and standard errors.

The findings are presented in Figure 7.1. The hollow circles refer to the probit coefficient estimates with 95 percent confidence interval bars around them. Positive and statistically significant coefficient estimate on party identification variable provides empirical support for our major hypothesis. Democrats and liberals are more favorable toward the 9/11 Mosque.

Since it is not intuitive to compare probit coefficient estimates substantively, I estimate predicted probabilities by setting all explanatory variables at their observed values (Hanmer and Kalkan 2013). They are presented in Table 7.1. Strong Democrats are 21 percent more likely to support the mosque than strong Republicans, a statistically significant ($p < .05$) result. Liberals are 16 percentage points more likely than moderates to exhibit favorable opinions of the 9/11 Mosque, whereas conservatives are 13 percentage points

---

2. It is fairly common in the study of intergroup attitudes to limit the estimation sample to the predominant portion of the population that harbor prejudice toward the target minority (for further details, see Sniderman and Piazza 1993 and Davis 2007).

TABLE 7.1: CHANGES IN PREDICTED PROBABILITY OF FAVORING THE GROUND ZERO MOSQUE

Explanatory variables	Change in predicted probability
Democratic Party identification	.21*
Liberal	.16*
Conservative	−.13*
Islam violent	−.16*
Muslims patriotic	.20*
Know Muslims	−.02
Anti-Muslim prejudice	−.27*
Age	−.05
Education	.11
Female	−.05

Source: August 2010 *Time* magazine survey (non-Latino whites only).
Note: The predicted probabilities are computed from the model presented in Figure 7.1. Change in predicted probability reflects the change from minimum to maximum on the explanatory variable while holding all other variables at their observed values. Standard errors are computed using the delta method.
*$p < .05$.

less likely to favor it. The changes in predicted probabilities for ideological variables are also statistically significant.

I also find empirical support for my hypotheses related to Islam-specific variables. Those who think that Islam is violent are less likely than others to favor the Cordoba Community Center. Thinking that Muslims are patriotic citizens boosts the support for the mosque at statistically significant levels. And prejudice toward Muslims leads to lower levels of favorability toward the mosque. The only Islam-specific variable that fails to reach conventional levels of statistical significance is familiarity with Muslims. Those who know Muslims are no more or less likely than those who do not to favor the building of a mosque near where the World Trade Center stood.

People who see Muslims as violent are 16 percentage points less likely to favor the mosque. Association of Muslims with patriotism increases support by 20 percentage points. The most prejudiced are 27 percent less supportive of the community center. All of these changes are statistically significant ($p < .05$). Older males who are highly educated are more likely to support the building of the mosque. However, none of the sociodemographic variables reach conventional levels of statistical significance.

Tea Party Influence in the Mosque Controversy

Republican identifiers have had more negative views of Islam than Democrats or independents, at least since 2008. The 2010 rise of the Tea Party provided a strong base for the use of the 9/11 Mosque as an efficient symbol. The Republican leaders saw their attack on the center as an election issue. Senator John Cornyn (R-TX), chair of the Republican Senatorial Campaign Committee, said that party candidates would use the mosque as an issue in their campaigns (Jackson and Vanden Brook 2010). Michael Tesler (2011) shows that attitudes toward Muslims shaped vote intentions even before the 9/11 Mosque became salient. As Republicans made the mosque a campaign issue, anti-Muslim sentiment became more salient to voters opposed to the community center.

Tea Party supporters felt more threatened by out-groups compared to other Republicans; they were also much more likely to vote and to participate in other activities (Abramowitz 2011; Jacobson 2011). And they were especially more likely to say that a candidate's position on the mosque would affect their vote choice, as I show below. Another effect of Republican politicians raising the issue of the 9/11 Mosque is that independents who opposed the center were more likely to say that they would vote Republican in the congressional elections.

My second set of hypotheses concerns the influence of Tea Party favorability on the Ground Zero mosque controversy. Attitudes toward the Tea Party movement should be as influential as other political predispositions, like party identification and ideology. To test this hypothesis, I use a survey conducted by the *Washington Post*/ABC News in August–September 2010. The outcome variable is a four-category measure that asks people whether they think the Muslim community center should or should not be built at the site of the former World Trade Center. The response options range from "strongly, should not" to "strongly, should."

The main explanatory variable is the Tea Party favorability. The survey asks people whether they have a favorable or unfavorable impression of the political movement known as the Tea Party. I coded those who had favorable opinions 1 and the rest to 0. The rest of the model variables use similar wording to that of the first survey. I control the model for party identification, ideology, Islam-specific variables, and sociodemographic features. All variables are coded to range from 0 to 1. Since the outcome variable is a four-category measure, I use ordered probit to estimate the coefficients and standard errors. And the estimation sample stays the same: non-Latino white respondents.

I present the model results in Figure 7.2. Democrats are more likely than others to favor the building of the mosque. Those who have favorable opinions about Islam are more positive toward the community center. Knowing Muslims, again, does not predict the opinions about the 9/11 Mosque at statistically significant levels. Older and more educated males are more likely than others to have favorable opinions about the mosque. According to

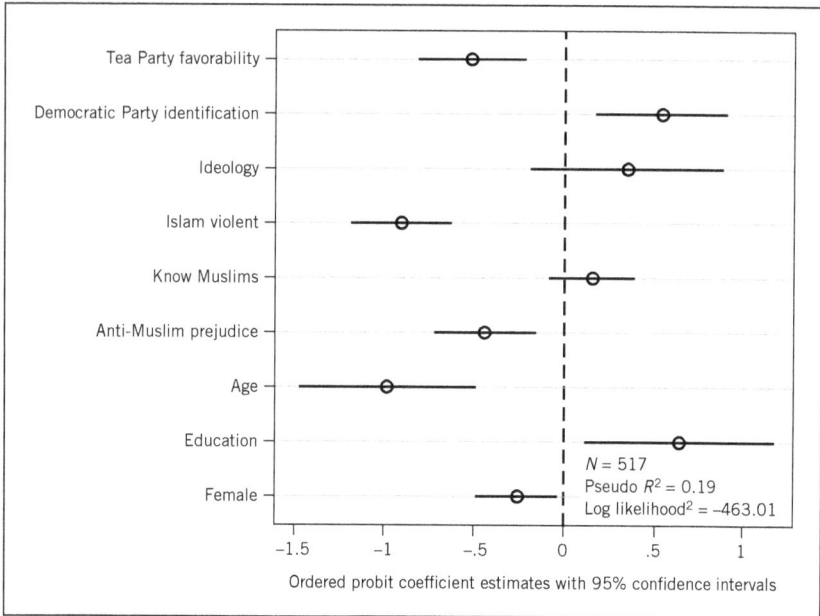

Figure 7.2 Favorability toward the Ground Zero mosque and Tea Party support
Source: 2010 *Washington Post*/ABC News survey (non-Latino whites only).

Table 7.2, favorability toward the Tea Party movement leads to an 8-point decline in support for the mosque, a statistically significant change.

I also examined whether the support for the Tea Party movement shapes whether people see the issue of the mosque as affecting their vote intentions in the midterm elections. I coded those who felt that the issue would strongly shape their vote 1 and others 0. I present the probit model estimates in Figure 7.3. Tea Party favorability is the only political variable that reaches statistical significance. Supporters of the Tea Party are 15 percent more likely to say that this issue was central to their vote choice, a significant effect. Neither party identification nor ideology reaches conventional levels of statistical significance. Believing that Islam promotes violence makes respondents 29 percentage points more likely to rely on the controversy when it comes to their voting behavior (see Table 7.3). Neither anti-Muslim attitudes more generally nor knowing Muslims is significant—perhaps because of collinearity.

A History of Partisan Divide?

In the 2001 Pew Religion survey—conducted before 9/11—there is a weak relationship between favorability of Muslim Americans and party identification (tau-c = −.127), with majorities of Democrats (71 percent) and Republi-

TABLE 7.2: CHANGES IN PREDICTED PROBABILITY OF FAVORING THE GROUND ZERO MOSQUE AND TEA PARTY FAVORABILITY

Explanatory variables	Change in predicted probability
Tea Party favorability	−.08*
Democratic Party identification	.09*
Ideology	.06
Islam violent	−.12*
Know Muslims	.02
Anti-Muslim prejudice	−.07*
Age	−.15*
Education	.10*
Female	−.05

Source: 2010 ABC News/*Washington Post* survey (non-Latino whites only).

Note: The predicted probabilities are computed from the model presented in Figure 7.2. Change in predicted probability reflects the change from minimum to maximum on the explanatory variable while holding all other variables at their observed values. Standard errors are computed using the delta method.

*p < .05.

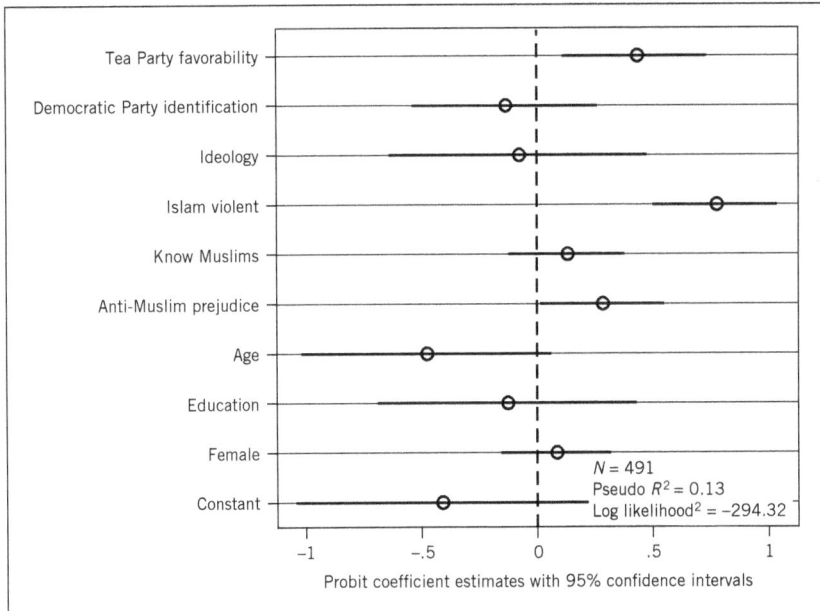

Figure 7.3 The role of the Tea Party movement in influencing whether the Ground Zero mosque issue affects vote intentions
Source: 2010 *Washington Post*/ABC News survey (non-Latino whites only).

TABLE 7.3: CHANGES IN PREDICTED PROBABILITY OF THE GROUND ZERO MOSQUE INFLUENCING THE VOTE CHOICE

Explanatory variables	Change in predicted probability
Tea Party favorability	.15*
Democratic Party identification	−.05
Ideology	−.03
Islam violent	.29*
Know Muslims	.05
Anti-Muslim prejudice	.10
Age	−.15
Education	−.05
Female	.03

Source: 2010 ABC News/*Washington Post* survey (non-Latino whites only).

Note: The predicted probabilities are computed from the model presented in Figure 7.3. Change in predicted probability reflects the change from minimum to maximum on the explanatory variable while holding all other variables at their observed values. Standard errors are computed using the delta method.
*$p < .05$.

cans (56 percent) holding favorable views. A year later, after the Twin Towers fell, the relationship of Muslim favorability and partisanship was even weaker in the 2002 Pew Religion Survey (tau-c = −.073): 58 percent of Republicans and 69 percent of Democrats had positive views of Muslims. The reassurance by President George W. Bush that Islam is a "religion of peace" sent a clear message that attitudes toward Muslims should not divide Americans (Bush 2001).

But we begin to see some partisan divisions in the 2007 Pew survey, in which 65 percent of Democrats but just 37 percent of Republicans had positive evaluations of Muslims (tau-c = −.185). By 2010, the partisan division was much stronger in the Pew survey: Democrats' positive feelings toward Muslims fell to 61 percent, but only 25 percent of GOP identifiers had similar positive evaluations (tau-c = −.286). In the 2011 University of Maryland Program on International Policy Attitudes (PIPA) survey "The American Public and the 9/11 Decade,"[3] 60 percent of Democrats had a favorable view of Muslims—and the share of Republican identifiers with such views increased to 39 percent (tau-c = −.159). There is little evidence in these figures of increased polarization of views on Muslims since the 9/11 Mosque controversy. However, attitudes toward the religion of Islam became more sharply negative—with two-thirds of Americans expressing negative views. A slight majority

3. The data, the codebook, and the report are available at http://hdl.handle.net/1903/11855.

of Democrats were unfavorable toward Islam, and 82 percent of Republicans held such views (tau-c = –.233).

Partisan divisions on attitudes toward Muslims were on the rise in the middle of the first decade of the twenty-first century. These cleavages became stronger in 2008 than in previous presidential elections—most notably as Democratic nominee Barack Hussein Obama was widely (and mistakenly) identified as a Muslim and thus as not a "real American." Republican vice-presidential candidate Sarah Palin argued that Obama "is not a man who sees America the way that you and I see America" (Beinart 2008). Attitudes became more polarized in 2010 with the rise of the Tea Party, whose supporters hold more negative views of minorities than do other Republicans (Abramowitz 2011; Jacobson 2011). The actions of Republican Party elites in opposing the 9/11 Mosque, often using harsh language, and the partisan divisions over hearings in the House of Representatives on radical Islam in 2011 send strong cues to party followers. Americans in 2011 became less favorable overall toward Muslims, and were increasingly likely to link Muslims to values that are more aligned with the 9/11 terrorists (Telhami and Kull 2011, 11–12).

While there are now various surveys on Tea Party supporters, only two—the University of Maryland PIPA survey "The American Public and the 9/11 Decade" and the Pew Political Typology 2011 survey—ask any question about Islam. In the PIPA survey, 70 percent of strong Tea Party supporters had unfavorable views of Muslims, and 89 percent had negative views of Islam as a religion (compared to 50 percent of strong Tea Party opponents). Forty-two percent of Americans agreed that the actions of the 9/11 terrorists were typical of mainstream Islam; 58 percent of Republicans (and 32 percent of Democrats) and 77 percent of strong Tea Party supporters expressed this view. In the Pew survey, about half of all respondents believe that Islam is more likely to encourage violent religion than other faiths. Almost 70 percent of Republicans hold this view, as do 78 percent of Tea Party supporters, compared to just a third of Democrats. These additional surveys support our findings that Tea Party supporters have strongly negative views of not just the 9/11 Mosque but of Muslims more generally.

I cannot link party elites directly to their supporters in the electorate. I can, however, point to polarization on the larger issue of immigration among party elites. In 2008, 22 percent of delegates to the Republican convention favored allowing illegal immigrants to stay and apply for citizenship compared to 68 percent of the delegates to the Democratic convention. The public was less polarized than the elites: 26 percent of Republican voters favored letting illegals stay compared to 50 percent of Democrats. Fifty-eight percent of Republican delegates saw illegal immigration as a serious problem in 2008 compared to 64 percent of Republican voters, 36 percent of Democratic voters, and 15 percent of Democratic delegates (*New York Times* and *CBS News* 2008, 10). By 2010, the gap among voters had spread to 78 percent for Republicans and 45 percent for Democrats (Roper Center 2010).

I see a shift in the official positions of the Republican Party over time. In 2004 the Republican Party platform stated, "As the home to millions of Muslim believers, America welcomes the valuable role of Muslim leaders in promoting peace. We recognize that acts of violence against innocents violate the fundamental tenets of the Islamic faith" (Republican Party 2004). In 2008, the platform stated, "We appreciate the loyalty of all Americans whose family roots lie in the Middle East, and we gratefully acknowledge the contributions of American Arabs and Muslims" (Republican Party 2008, 12). The 2012 platform had two references to the threat of "radical Islam" throughout the Middle East and Africa, but none to Muslim Americans (Republican Party 2012, 40, 47).

There has long been a partisan gap on attitudes toward illegal immigrants (in the American National Election Studies), but in 2008 the correlation with party identification increased from –.17 to –.22 among whites. This may not seem a great increase, but the partisan gap in thermometer ratings has steadily increased from eight points (1994) to nine (2004) to twelve (2008). The salience of illegal immigration as a "very important" voting issue increased from 37 percent to 45 percent among Republicans from 2006 to 2010 and among Independents (from 24 to 37 percent). It stayed constant (27–28 percent) among Democrats ("CBS News Polls" 2010).

On the other hand, contact builds support: 72 percent of people who know Muslims favor the 9/11 Mosque (see Pettigrew and Tropp 2011; Pew Research Center 2014, 10; Hewstone and Schmid 2014). Half of people who do not know Muslims oppose the center. And people who know Muslims have a standardized score on the community band measure that is .36 greater than people with no Muslim contacts. Especially when you know someone of a different background, you are less likely to feel threatened by her as a neighbor. But the rhetoric of politicians on the 9/11 Mosque painted Muslims as terrorists who were determined to harm America.

Reprise

The partisan division on the mosque—and on overall Muslim favorability— suggests that the controversy over the 9/11 Mosque reflects growing tensions over Islam—and perhaps minorities more generally—in American politics. Party polarization is also growing on issues affecting other minority groups—the increasing division over state laws on illegal immigration and on Tea Party–backed legislation to prevent vote fraud—or as others see it, to intimidate minority voters (Urbina 2010; Weiser and Norden 2011).

Tea Party supporters, almost all Republicans, are overwhelmingly white with above-average incomes, compared to all voters and to other supporters of the GOP (Abramowitz 2011, 20–22). They are the demographic and political opposites of the minorities that now compose much of the Democratic coalition. The increasing party polarization in American is not just a conflict over economic issues or the size of government, even as these issues have dominated public discourse. Conflicts over economic and social issues have converged in recent decades (Carsey and Layman 2006). Racial attitudes now increasingly divide Republican and Democratic partisans (Valentino and Sears 2005), and cultural issues have become more important than economic concerns in shaping vote choice in recent elections (Highton 2012). Gary Jacobson (2011) shows that attitudes toward immigration and racial resentment were strongly tied to partisanship, ideology, and vote choice in 2010.

Republican officials and candidates do not attack minorities per se but instead focus on efficient symbols such as terrorists (for Muslims), illegal immigrants (most of whom are Hispanic), and welfare recipients (African Americans are overrepresented; see Gilens 1999) and demand that all voters have a photographic identification, which could disenfranchise many African Americans and Hispanics (Weiser and Norden 2011). After the attacks by Muslim extremists in Paris and San Bernardino, Republican officials and candidates more generally shifted from attacking efficient symbols and directly linked Muslims with terrorism. By 2016 the partisan divisions on attitudes toward Muslims had become crystallized.

Opposition to the 9/11 Mosque united most Republican officials. This was reflected the increasing partisan division on Muslim favorability. In contrast to earlier surveys showing little difference between partisans on attitudes toward Muslims, the *Time* survey showed that 37 percent of white non-Hispanic Republicans had a favorable view of Muslims compared to 59 percent of Democrats. In Alabama and Mississippi almost half of Republican primary voters in 2012 believed that Obama was a Muslim, while barely more than 10 percent said that he was a Christian (see Meeks 2012). Alabama and Mississippi are states where cultural conservatives (and Tea Party members) control the Republican Party. Seeing Obama as a Muslim is seeing him as outside the American mainstream.

The politicization of xenophobia does not generally rise from the ground up. In Europe, anti-immigrant (largely anti-Muslim) sentiments became politically important only when party leaders adopted anti-immigrant rhetoric. Anti-immigrant views came to take a prominent role in Danish politics in the past two decades as political leaders thought they could gain strategic advantages by such rhetoric, while party strategists in Sweden, which has a similar culture and even more immigrants, refused to make ethnic/religious issues the basis of political conflict (Green-Pedersen and Krogstrup 2008; Rydgren 2010).

The Cordoba Community Center was not initially controversial: Initial approval was quick and overwhelming in New York City, until the handful of protests from conservative activists were taken up by national Republican leaders. These officials were clearly responding to the greater emphasis on cultural issues among the party base—notably, Tea Party supporters. The low salience of the community center until Republican leaders publicly opposed it suggests that the politicization of the 9/11 Mosque came from the top down rather than from the bottom up. I do not argue that anti-Muslim arguments came only from the elites. The negative views of Muslims among Tea Party supporters made the 9/11 Mosque controversy spill over to neighborhood mosques, which were largely not politicized. The politicization of the 9/11 Mosque depended on having a receptive audience. The end of the first decade of the twenty-first century was marked by the end of the bipartisan consensus to combat anti-Muslim sentiments.

The rise of identity politics is a central part of the growing polarization in American politics. Defining those who are not part of your coalition as the "other" is central to identity politics. Identity is also central to the new polarization in American politics. Muslims may not be alone in such characterizations of "people (not) like us." As one of the least popular minorities,[4] they have become a more direct target. As the role of identity becomes increasingly important in American politics, who counts as an American may become more contested. Americans believe that "real" Americans are white Christians (Theiss-Morse 2010), a view shared by 55 percent of Tea Party members in 2010 (Jones and Cox 2010, 31). As cultural issues become more central to American politics (Highton 2012), the divisions between in-groups and out-groups become more salient. Republicans can build winning coalitions for congressional elections without the support of minority voters (Cohn 2014). And a presumed threat from without in what may seem to be a more dangerous world can perpetuate a fragmented society.

---

4. Muslims have a mean thermometer score of 52 in the 2008 American National Election Studies. In the *Time* survey, 85 percent had a favorable view of Jews and Protestants, 81 percent of Catholics, 66 percent of Latter-Day Saints, 57 percent of atheists, and 51 percent of Muslims.

REFERENCES

Abramowitz, Alan I. 2011. "Political Polarization and the Rise of the Tea Party Movement." Paper presented at the Annual Meeting of the American Political Science Association, Seattle, September 1–4.

Altman, Alex. 2010. "Time Poll: Majority Oppose Mosque, Many Distrust Muslims." *Time*, August 19. Available at http://content.time.com/time/nation/article/0,8599, 2011799,00.html.

Beinart, Peter. 2008. "Is Barack Obama American Enough?" *Time*, October 9. Available at http://www.time.com/time/magazine/article/0,9171,1848755,00.html.

———. 2015. "The New Enemy Within," *The Atlantic*, May. Available at http://www .theatlantic.com/magazine/archive/2015/05/the-new-enemy-within/389573.

Bradner, Eric. 2015. "Ben Carson Again Explains Concerns with a Muslim President." *CNN*, September 27. Available at https://www.cnn.com/2015/09/27/politics/ben -carson-muslim-president-sharia-law/index.html.

Bush, George W. 2001. "Islam Is Peace." September 17. Available at https://georgewbush -whitehouse.archives.gov/news/releases/2001/09/20010917-11.html.

Caldwell, Leigh Ann. 2015. "Kasich Proposes New Government Agency to Promote Judeo-Christian Values." *NBC News*, November 17. Available at http://www .nbcnews.com/politics/2016-election/kasich-proposes-new-governmentagency -promote-judeo-christian-values-n465101.

Carsey, Thomas M., and Geoffrey C. Layman. 2006. "Changing Sides or Changing Minds? Party Identification and Policy Preferences in the American Electorate." *American Journal of Political Science* 50:464–477.

"CBS News Polls: 8/26/10." 2010. *CBS News*, August 30. Available at https://www .cbsnews.com/news/cbs-news-polls-8-26-10.

Cohn, Nate. 2014. "Why House Republicans Alienate Hispanics: They Don't Need Them." *New York Times*, October 24. Available at http://www.nytimes.com/2014/ 10/21/upshot/why-house-republicans-alienate-hispanics-they-dont-need-them .html.

Davis, Darren. 2007. *Negative Liberty: Public Opinion and the Terrorist Attacks on America*. New York: Russell Sage Foundation.

Gallup. 2009. *Religious Preferences in America*. Washington, DC: Gallup/Coexist Foundation.

Gilens, Martin. 1999. *Why Americans Hate Welfare*. Chicago: University of Chicago Press.

Green-Pedersen, Christoffer, and Jesper Krogstrup. 2008. "Immigration as a Political Issue in Denmark and Sweden." *European Journal of Political Research* 47:610–634.

Hanmer, Michael J., and Kerem Ozan Kalkan. 2013. "Behind the Curve: Clarifying the Best Approach to Calculating Predicted Probabilities and Marginal Effects from Limited Dependent Variable Models." *American Journal of Political Science* 57 (1): 263–277.

Hewstone, Miles, and Katharina Schmid. 2014. "Neighbourhood Ethnic Diversity and Orientations toward Muslims in Britain: The Role of Intergroup Contact." *Political Quarterly* 85 (3): 320–325.

Highton, Benjamin. 2012. "Sorting the States into Red and Blue: Culture, Economics, and the 2012 US Presidential Election in Historical Context," *The Forum* 10: 11–19.

Hulse, Carl. 2010. "G.O.P. Seizes on Mosque Issue Ahead of Elections," *New York Times*, August 16. Available at http://www.nytimes.com/2010/08/17/us/politics/17mosque.html.

Jackson, David, and Tom Vanden Brook. 2010. "NYC Mosque Will Be Election Issue, Republican Predicts." *USA Today*, August 15. Available at http://usatoday30.usatoday.com/news/washington/2010-08-16-mosque16_ST_N.htm.

Jacobson, Gary C. 2011. "The President, the Tea Party, and Voting Behavior in 2010: Insights from the Cooperative Congressional Election Study." Paper presented at the Annual Meeting of the American Political Science Association, Seattle, September 1–4.

Jensen, Tom. 2016. "Trump, Clinton Continue to Lead in SC." Public Policy Polling, February 16. Available at http://www.publicpolicypolling.com/pdf/2015/PPP_Release_SC_21616.pdf.

Jones, Robert P., and Daniel Cox. 2010. "Religion and the Tea Party in the 2010 Election: An Analysis of the Third Biennial American Values Survey." Available at http://publicreligion.org/research/2010/10/religion-tea-party-2010.

Kalkan, Kerem Ozan, Geoffrey C. Layman, and Eric M. Uslaner. 2009. "'Bands of Others?' Attitudes toward Muslims in Contemporary American Society." *Journal of Politics* 71 (3): 847–862.

Kam, Cindy D., and Donald R. Kinder. 2012. "Ethnocentrism as a Short-Term Force in the 2008 American Presidential Election." *American Journal of Political Science* 56 (2): 326–340.

Kupper, Beate, and Andreas Zick. 2010. *Religion and Prejudice in Europe: New Empirical Findings—NEF Initiative on Religion and Democracy in Europe*. London: Alliance Publishing Trust.

Leege, David C., Kenneth D. Wald, Brian S. Krueger, and Paul D. Mueller. 2002. *The Politics of Cultural Differences: Social Change and Voter Mobilization Strategies in the Post–New Deal Period*. Princeton, NJ: Princeton University Press.

Meeks, David. 2012. "Poll: Obama's a Muslim to Many GOP Voters in Alabama, Mississippi." *Los Angeles Times*, March 12. Available at http://articles.latimes.com/2012/mar/12/news/la-pn-poll-obamas-a-muslim-to-many-gop-voters-in-alabama-mississippi-20120312.

New York Times and *CBS News*. 2008. "2008 Republican National Delegate Survey." Available at http://graphics8.nytimes.com/packages/pdf/politics/20080901-poll.pdf.

Pettigrew, Thomas, and Linda Tropp. 2011. *When Groups Meet: The Dynamics of Intergroup Contact*. New York: Psychology Press.

Pew Research Center. 2014. "How Americans Feel about Religious Groups." July 16. Available at http://www.pewforum.org/2014/07/16/how-americans-feel-about-religious-groups.

Reilly, Mollie. 2015. "Republican Candidates Want to Block Syrian Refugees after Paris Attacks." *Huffington Post*, November 16. Available at http://www.huffingtonpost.com/entry/republicans-refugees-paris-attacks_us_564a1747e4b08cda3489da73.

Republican Party. 2004. "2004 Republican Party Platform: A Safer World and a More Hopeful America." Available at http://www.presidency.ucsb.edu/papers_pdf/25850.pdf.

———. 2008. "2008 Republican Platform." Available at http://www.presidency.ucsb.edu/papers_pdf/78545.pdf.

———. 2012. "We Believe in America: 2012 Republican Platform." Available at http://www.presidency.ucsb.edu/papers_pdf/101961.pdf.

Roper Center. 2010. "CBS News Poll: Economy/New Orleans/Iraq." Available at https://ropercenter.cornell.edu/CFIDE/cf/action/catalog/abstract.cfm?type=&start=&id=&archno=USCBS2010-08B&abstract=.

Rydgren, Jens. 2010. "Radical Right-Wing Populism in Denmark and Sweden: Explaining Party System Change and Stability." *SAIS Review* 30:57–71.

Sniderman, Paul M., and Louk Hagendoorn. 2007. *When Ways of Life Collide*. Princeton, NJ: Princeton University Press.

Sniderman, Paul M., and Thomas Leonard Piazza. 1993. *The Scar of Race*. Cambridge, MA: Harvard University Press.

Telhami, Shibley, and Steven Kull. 2011. "The American Public on the 9/11 Decade: A Study of American Public Opinion." Available at https://www.brookings.edu/wp-content/uploads/2016/06/0908_opinion_poll_telhami.pdf.

Tesler, Michael. 2011. "President Obama and the Influence of Anti-Muslim Sentiments in the 2010 Midterm Elections." Paper presented at the Annual Meeting of the American Political Science Association, Chicago, March 30–April 3.

———. 2015. "How Hostile Are Trump Supporters toward Muslims? This New Poll Will Tell You." *Washington Post*, December 8. Available at https://www.washingtonpost.com/news/monkey-cage/wp/2015/12/08/how-hostile-are-trump-supporters-toward-muslims-this-new-poll-will-tell-you/?utm_term=.d4727937d283.

Tesler, Michael, and David O. Sears. 2010. *Obama's Race*. Chicago: University of Chicago Press

Theiss-Morse, Elizabeth. 2010. *Who Counts as an American?* New York: Cambridge University Press.

Urbina, Peter. 2010. "Fraudulent Voting Re-emerges as a Partisan Issue." *New York Times*, October 26. Available at http://www.nytimes.com/2010/10/27/us/politics/27fraud.html.

Valentino, Nicholas A., and David O. Sears. 2005. "Old Times There Are Not Forgotten: Race and Partisan Realignment in the Contemporary South." *American Journal of Political Science* 49:672–688.

"Washington Post–ABC News Poll." 2010. Available at http://www.washingtonpost.com/wp-srv/politics/polls/postpoll_09072010.html.

Weiser, Wendy R., and Lawrence Norden. 2011. "Voting Law Changes in 2012." Brennan Center for Justice. Available at http://www.brennancenter.org/sites/default/files/legacy/Democracy/VRE/Brennan_Voting_Law_V10.pdf.

Zick, Andreas, Beatte Kupper, and Andreas Hovermann. 2011. *Intolerance, Prejudice, and Discrimination: A European Report*. Berlin: Friedrich Ebert Stiftung.

Priming Identity, Framing Community

Christians, Muslims, and Intergroup Trust

Brian R. Calfano, Oguzhan (Oz) Dincer,
Danielle M. McLaughlin, and Yusuf Sarfati

Our colleagues argue in Chapter 1 that Muslim Americans constitute perhaps the nation's most closely scrutinized minority group, with hate crimes against Muslims (and Arabs) increasing seventeen-fold in the aftermath of 9/11 (Hutchison and Rosenthal 2011). This sentiment is reinforced to varying extents in Chapters 2 through 7. Irrespective of the research question or data set used, sizeable percentages of non-Muslims view Muslims as more untrustworthy and violent than any other religious community in the United States (Panagopoulos 2006; Sides and Gross 2013). Such social intolerance is intertwined with the institutional violence directed at Muslims by government policies that receive broad public support (Naber 2008; Maira 2008). At the heart of the matter is the reality that many non-Muslim Americans simply do not trust Muslim Americans.

But affect toward Muslims does not occur in a vacuum. As Kerem Kalkan, Geoffrey Layman, and Eric Uslaner (2009) argue, how people perceive Muslims is dependent, in part, on associations that are made about Muslims in conjunction with other racial/ethnic and religious groups. Extending this argument a bit further, we use this chapter to examine the processes by which non-Muslims go about adopting attitudes that may be the antecedents for trust and positive orientation toward Muslims and other minorities. Thus, the chapter fills a gap in this volume by moving beyond continued focus on the negativity surrounding the Muslim experience in what Kalkan, Layman, and Uslaner refer to as the nation's "Judeo-Christian mainstream" (2009, 1). Instead, we examine whether religious identity does more than breach intergroup trust—we look for whether it can help build it.

The backdrop against which this study is conducted is not a positive one for Muslim Americans. Muslims are experienced as personal targets; 40 percent report personally experiencing discrimination, while 57 percent state that they know other Muslims who have (Jalalzai 2011). The Center for Race and Gender at the University of California, Berkeley, documents that Islamophobia (which the study defines as close-minded prejudice against, or hatred of, Islam and Muslims) has been on the rise in recent years. Clearly, and despite some minor fluctuation in the toplines, large swaths of the general public hold a negative view of Islam and American Muslims (Kalkan, Layman, and Uslaner 2009; Khan and Ecklund 2013; Panagopoulos 2006; Sides and Gross 2013; Lajevardi 2017; Lajevardi and Abrajano 2018), though Muslims are certainly not the only minority group, religious or racial, at which public suspicion has been directed (see Bedolla 2005; Chong and Kim 2006; Lee 2008).

Negative public views toward a particular minority are closely associated with, among other things, a lack of trust toward said minority. This linkage is found in scholarship showing that people identify more strongly with groups with which they perceive a certain degree of similarity (Doosje, Ellemers, and Spears 1995). Though group membership is different from categorizations (e.g., gender, religion, race, etc.), both groups and categories reflect an underlying basis for individual identity construction stemming from interaction with particular collectives. Where one's affinity or interest is expressed as a social group phenomenon, social identity theory sets core expectations for individual perceptions and behavior. Henri Tajfel describes social identity as "that part of an individual's self-concept which derives from [her or] his membership in a social group (or groups) together with the value and emotional significance attached to that membership" (1981, 225).

Group identities can affect an array of political outcomes (see Hutchings and Valentino 2004; Dawson 2001; Dickson and Scheve 2006). Throughout this chapter, we reference elements of social identity theory and identity self-categorization theories, which derive from the social psychology literature. Because the theories apply to slightly different circumstances in individual versus collective perception, navigating between the specifics of each theory can be challenging. To avoid this, we adopt the inherent assumptions of balanced identity theory (see Greenwald et al. 2002; Cvencek, Greenwald, and Meltzoff 2012). This approach takes the perspective that, though people have multiple identities that may be activated under certain circumstances (Chandra 2009), whichever identity they are focused on at a given time constitutes their salient sense of self (for all intents and purposes).

The balanced identity framework is important for two reasons. First, it enables us to focus on how momentary shifts in one's identity construct can affect outcomes without falling into a litany of caveats about effects from alternate identities. Though these alternate or additional identities are no less relevant to the individual overall, the balanced identity approach emphasizes identity salience at given times, with one identity having a pride of place over others. This leads to the second reason for the theory's import: identities have been found to be susceptible to cognitive priming, as have the stereotypes one holds about social minorities or out-groups (particularly along racial and religious lines) (Bargh, Chen, and Burrows 1996; Wittenbrink, Judd, and Park 1997; Gilliam and Iyengar 2000). The inherent variability suggested by the priming effect—both in terms of identity self-concept and perception of other identity groups—may provide leverage in understanding the puzzle of intergroup perceptions among different segments of the public and religion's potential role in generating perception.

Our reference to Muslim maltreatment is but one of several possible examples of how the general public in America—which is still basically Anglo and Christian in identity—perceives and treats religious and racial minorities. But there is also a litany of comparisons within minority groups that may be made, especially since there is no ex ante reason to expect that minority groups are more likely to perceive fellow minorities as people sharing a common experience (the variable influence of linked fate and related factors notwithstanding; see Sanchez and Vargas 2016). If anything, the competition between minority groups over available resources and political power may make them (and their individual members) more antagonistic than not. Hence, the basic question of intergroup trust and related perceptions—which have been General Social Survey measures since 1972 and in research long before that (see Stouffer 1955)—represent the building blocks toward potential relational betterment between groups.

Of course, fostering intergroup trust is not an easy enterprise, even when less polarizing groups than Muslims are involved. Trust can require a substantial investment of social capital, although the payoffs for successful trust building can be great. Trust and trustworthiness have the capability to reduce risk and conflict, can increase support for authorities and decision-making outcomes, and are a predictor of economic success (Arrow 1972; Thibaut and Walker 1975). It is important, therefore, to understand the determinants of trust (e.g., gender, ethnicity, religious affiliation, etc.). In fact, several experiments have demonstrated that expectations of positive reciprocity reinforce trust (Falk and Zehnder 2007; Fehr, Fischbacher, and Gächter 2002).

Background, identity, or demographic characteristics can condition one's beliefs of reciprocity and trust. And while religion might be a stumbling block to positive intergroup relations, it may also promote trust or distrust within and between communities. For example, John Orbell and colleagues (1992) found that both religious and nonreligious people believe the former to be more cooperative. But biases and stereotypes can remain powerful influences on perception and behavior, often fostering favoritism or discrimination. Dissimilarity in group affiliation (i.e., intergroup rivalry) or stereotypes attributed to certain groups (including those from different religious traditions) can induce these biases and subsequent intergroup distrust (Fiske 1998).

The results of religion's influence on behavior and trust in experimental research is mixed. Some have found little evidence of religion's effect on prosocial behavior or intergroup trust and solidarity. For example, using a public goods and bilateral trust game, Lisa Anderson, Jennifer Mellor, and Jeffrey Milyo (2010) found that religious affiliation was unrelated to prosocial behavior. Catherine Eckel and Philip Grossman (2004) conducted dictator games in which participants unilaterally decided contributions to a list of secular charities, and they discovered no significant difference in charity contributions between those attending religious services and those not. Similarly, bilateral trust games between Hindu and Muslim subjects show that neither group demonstrated preferential treatment to partners from their own group (Johansson-Stenman, Mahmud, and Martinsson 2009). Jonathan Tan (2006) reports similar results using dictator and ultimatum games with German subjects, as do Lisa Anderson and Jennifer Mellor (2009) using public goods games.

But Bradley Ruffle and Richard Sosis (2006) discovered that religious Jewish men were more cooperative than their female religious counterparts and both secular men and women. Additionally, in a separate study, the authors measured kibbutz members' trust and cooperation in a bilateral trust game. Kibbutz members cooperated more with other anonymously paired kibbutz members than with Israeli city residents (Ruffle and Sosis 2007). Similarly, scholars observed in-group favoritism by Israeli students as directed toward in-group religious students from a neighboring college (versus students from a secular university or anonymous students) (Fershtman, Gneezy, and Verboven 2005).

Meanwhile, a subset of studies using randomized priming of religious identities prior to participants engaging in trust, public goods, and dictator ultimatum games shows promising results. For example, in Brandon Randolph-Seng and Michael Nielsen's (2007) experiment, subjects primed with religious words cheated less on an honesty task. Similarly, subjects in a different study acted more prosocially by taking more charity pamphlets after being primed with religious words (using subliminal and supraliminal techniques) (Pichon, Boccato, and Saroglou 2007). And in a dictator game, participants primed with religious words acted more generously (Shariff and

Norenzayan 2007; Ahmed and Salas 2011). Overall, these findings indicate that prosocial orientation can extend beyond people's salient awareness or social desirability concerns and that religion plays a role.

In terms of trust levels, much of the literature has focused on conflict and contact between group members. According to the conflict hypothesis, diversity causes intergroup trust to decrease (La Ferrara 2002; Delhey and Newton 2005). This is because people tend to associate, socialize, and be more comfortable with people who appear similar to themselves (Delhey and Newton 2005). Conversely, the contact hypothesis expects that the more people live in an ethnically diverse society, the more likely they are to come into contact with those from other racial, ethnic, and religious groups (Putnam 2000). To be sure, intergroup contact is critical to improving any perception one group has of "the other" and is a necessity in turning diversity into trust (Hewstone et al. 2006; Stolle, Soroka, and Johnston 2008).

Yet both the conflict and contact hypotheses, taken in their most basic forms, may be too simplistic for our purposes. As Marc Hooghe and Ellen Quintelier (2013) argue, not all intergroup contact is sufficient at increasing trust—a reality that speaks to different conceptions of social capital from what Robert Putnam (1995) describes. Even the notion of "quality" contact, which attempts to differentiate the kind of interactions people have, is a highly subjective concept when measured directly on surveys. And though intergroup contact measures are useful as aggregate assessments of self-reported interactions, an endogeneity problem arises when using these measures as a predictor of trust and related perceptions. This is because, when generated using traditional survey methods, observational data offer no way to identify a temporal order between the reported intergroup contact levels and trust (or similar outcomes). In reality, one's trust level may drive the reported intergroup contact, not the other way around.

Perhaps an even greater limitation in some prior studies of intergroup trust is that researchers were not able to exact control over the cognitive considerations their survey respondents had while providing answers about their perception of other groups. In conducting an observational survey on non-Muslim opinions of Muslims and Islam, for example, the researcher does not have control over the relevant mental processes by which the respondent offers her or his answers. Though absolute control of this kind is impossible, social scientists have available tools that allow them to intentionally introduce concepts at random for respondents to consider prior to providing their question response—especially in a survey experiment design (see Gaines, Kuklinski, and Quirk 2007). This enables direct comparison between the answers provided by those who received one type of antecedent consideration and the answers of those who received another (or none at all, as the case may be).

In the context of social group and social psychology research, identity priming, which is usually achieved by randomly selecting subjects for exposure to specific identity-based questions before they encounter group-based questions in a survey, provides researchers with needed causal leverage. The researcher's intent is to make subject identity more cognitively accessible (or primed) during the survey response—an approach that has found wide use in race and ethnic identity studies (Schuman and Bobo 1988; Sniderman and Piazza 1993; Peffley, Hurwitz, and Sniderman 1997; Shih, Pittinsky, and Ambady 1999). Priming has also been used to assess subject response tendencies more generally (Sudman 1985; Willits and Ke 1995).

In recent years, scholars have added a framing element to the primed group-based identities (see Phalet, Baysu, and Verkuyten 2010). Framing highlights a specific aspect of an item or entity vis-à-vis others, and it provides a greater level of control over what a researcher can intentionally encourage participants to consider than priming alone. Such control is important when assessing group identity and its effects, as priming may actually heighten threat perception and identity consolidation against groups judged to be outside accepted bounds (see Wright and Tropp 2002; Klein, Spears, and Reicher 2007).

Importantly, the mechanisms at work in identity priming and framing can extend far beyond basic measures of intergroup trust. The self-categorization processes documented in the identity literature writ large (see Turner et al. 1987) indicate that social categories based on differences in gender, age, race, religion, sexual orientation, and similar groupings can facilitate social dominance orientations in group members (Wood and Eagly 2002). Overlaying social dominance is Herbert Blumer's (1958) theory of relative group position as the progenitor of prejudice, suggesting that feelings of social dominance may extend toward American Muslims as well.

The negative attention American Muslims receive is hardly the first case of negative reaction from socially dominant groups. For example, a long literature has focused on the public's varying levels of anti-Semitism (Selznick and Steinberg 1969; Quinley and Glock 1979; Smith 1993), which, itself, may be affected by the growing salience of interfaith tensions and the issues surrounding Israel and the Palestinians (Brustein 2003). Against the balanced identity backdrop, John Transue's (2007) work on the role of superordinate identity priming in support of broadly beneficial policy initiatives shows the promise of additional experimental research on public perceptions of Muslims and other minorities.

It is this sharing of a certain, salient identity that generates a sense of collectiveness and maintains the boundaries of imagined communities (Stoecker 1995). The premise for why people seek out and nourish group attachments is that they provide meaning and esteem. And as one's self-concept develops through experiences related to certain salient identities, activities intended to sustain these self-concepts become the norm (Snow and Anderson 1987; Hunt, Benford, and Snow 1994). These activities lead to identity seeking (see Balch and Taylor 1978), in which people with a strong sense of attachment to a particular identity look for groups that enable expression of that identity. The classic assumption in social identity theory is that groups are predisposed to establishing distinctiveness by accentuating their difference from other groups (Tajfel and Turner 1986). This boundary making between one's in-group and corresponding out-groups does not directly lead to conflict, distrust, and related outcomes, but it helps lay the foundation for them.

So how can we use experimental design to assess priming and framing effects from religion on out-group trust (including of Muslims)? We suggest a combination of religious identity priming and the framing of one's approach to out-group members that reflects the tolerant, trust-based relationships that Paul Djupe and Brian Calfano (2013) feature in their priming of religious values. Specifically, what the authors call "inclusive" value primes (e.g., the Christian admonition to "love thy neighbor") tend to move subjects toward greater out-group tolerance, whereas the opposite effect is found when "exclusive" values (e.g., "It is important to keep company with those of my faith") are employed. Here, the outcome of interest is trust, not tolerance, so our assessment helps extend Djupe and Calfano's insights.

We ask whether simple religious identity priming affects out-group trust levels when the prime is paired with a group frame that asks subjects to act on inclusive religious values by assisting minority group members. In this way, the frame takes on a superordinate aspect central in Transue's (2007) findings. We first hypothesize, based on the basic expectations of social identity theory, that priming subject religious/racial identity will lead to a decrease in expressed trust of out-groups (and religious out-groups such as Muslims in particular). Our second hypothesis is that, at the same time, and reflecting a general antipathy for out-groups, subjects receiving only the superordinate group frame will also exhibit a decrease in out-group trust. Our third hypothesis expects that, in line with the general takeaways from Djupe and Calfano's (2013) and Transue's (2007) experiments, exposure to the identity prime makes religion salient for a subject per balanced identity theory, and cognitive attention toward a battery of help-oriented questions benefitting out-groups increases a subject's expressed trust of out-groups.

These expectations are based, in part, on the notion that the primed religious identity and superordinate help frame work to encourage motived perception by subjects to see out-groups from a vested interest perspective, or what Steven Neuberg and Susan Fiske (1987) call "outcome dependency." Essentially, a motivated perceiver with a sense of vested interest will be less likely to form out-group impressions based on existing, negative stereotypes without making some additional cognitive effort. But what guides this effort is critical, as it would not be hard to imagine that cognitive considerations could rather quickly move to negative out-group evaluations in the absence of encouragement to constructively engage with the out-group. In this case, constructive encouragement comes in the form of the "help" questions (reflecting action on the "Love thy neighbor" value) to which we randomly expose select subjects. This, in part, enables a test of whether a guided cognitive effort enables preexisting impressions to be abandoned (Hilton and Darley 1991).

Design

Using a modified version of Karen Phalet, Gülseli Baysu, and Maykel Verkuyten's (2010) design, we leveraged an Internet-based questions-as-treatment experiment on a randomly selected subject of pool of Chicago adults. The goal was to (1) selectively prime either subject religious and racial identities, (2) frame subject behavior toward out-groups in a superordinate way, (3) both, or (4) none of these (depending on the group to which a subject was randomly assigned). The religious and racial priming is modeled on Maykel Verkuyten's (2005) identity battery, while the superordinate group frame is based on a modified version of Phalet, Baysu, and Verkuyten's question battery about subjects' willingness to undertake personal action on behalf of an out-group. Note that our analysis does not focus on the actual, self-reported responses that subjects provided to these identity and help questions. Instead, we examine the effect of the encountering the priming and framing treatments themselves.

Verkuyten's (2005) battery included two four-item Likert scales (one for race and one for religion). Specifically, subjects were asked whether their level of agreement about (1) regretting being a member of their religious and racial groups, (2) their level of agreement that their religious and racial groups are important to them, (3) their level of agreement with being proud of their religious and racial groups, and (4) their agreement with feeling good about being in their religious and racial groups. Meanwhile, Phalet, Baysu, and Verkuyten's (2010) battery inquired as to subject willingness to help out-group members—"How willing would you be to do the following things to help address a problem facing X in your community?"—using a series of five-item Likert scales asking about (1) signing a petition, (2) donating money, (3) demonstrating, (4) contacting public officials, (5) writing op-eds, (6) organizing community groups, (7) protesting, and (8) placing signs on behalf of one of a series of a randomly assigned out-groups: blacks, Hispanics/Latinos, whites, Muslims, Jews, Christians, or a "majority of people in your community." Response items were arranged so that subjects received only out-group options in responding to the Phalet, Baysu, and Verkuyten battery (e.g., black subjects would not be asked about performing actions on behalf of the blacks in their community). Though they have been underutilized in the political study of Muslims, experimental designs using random assignment represent the "gold standard" in social science research (Green and Gerber 2003) and are increasingly applied to the religion and politics literature (see Calfano and Djupe 2009; Djupe and Calfano 2013; Calfano, Lajevardi, and Michelson 2017; Calfano 2018).

Our Internet-based experiment was conducted on 838 randomly selected Chicago adults, and administered via Qualtrics (which uses a subject recruitment protocol similar to Knowledge Networks) in January and February 2012. Chicago was selected as a subject recruitment site given its population size and the tendency for researchers to focus more on larger coastal cities in conducting studies. At the start of the survey, subjects were asked their religious and racial/ethnic characteristics. From there, each was assigned to one of three separate treatments: 1 = religious/racial affiliation question primes only: 231 subjects, 2 = racial/religious prime + superordinate group frame (i.e., the out-group help questions; prime and frame component order were varied at random): 221 subjects, and 3 = superordinate group frame only: 194 subjects. A fourth condition, the control group (191 subjects), received neither the prime nor the frame. Treatment assignment was not statistically correlated with measures of subject age, gender, or race. Note that, in keeping with standard design of survey-embedded experiments, all subjects were asked to respond to all questions during the course of the survey. However, the survey software was programmed to provide only out-group-based questions (related to the subject's personal characteristics) for the superordinate frame.

In creating independent variables for our models, we noticed that self-identified Christians constituted the overwhelming number of subjects ($N = 640$). This is advantageous given our focus on the public's perception of Muslims and the Christian-Muslim dynamic more generally (i.e., from the standpoint of non-Muslims). Ideally, the large number of Christian subjects should also prove useful in understanding how certain racial subgroups within our Christian cohort respond to the treatments. However, in running preliminary models, we found that none of the racial subgroup variables (either base or

Christian interactions) returned statistical significance. Rather than indicate a lack of effect, these null findings might have more to do with the relatively small number of subjects within each of the racial subgroups themselves. In addition, we initially explored whether differences existed between versions of the help questions referencing specific out-groups. Finally, we found no significant effects for any of the separate variables across the seven out-group types (i.e., the race and religious groups that were different from the subject's) in the superordinate group frame. This led us to use a variable combining the separate out-groups into one superordinate group frame treatment measure.

Our dependent variables are measures of trust taken from Likert items ranging from 1 to 5, and constructed based on the answer to the following question: "Generally speaking, would you say that the groups in the table below can be trusted, or that you can't be too careful in dealing with them (where 1 means you 'can't be too careful,' and 5 means that the 'group can be trusted')?" We provided subjects a list of twenty, randomly ordered group names for them to rate using this ordinal trust measure. The groups sort orthogonally into three separate factors using polychoric rotated factor analysis. As Figure 8.1 shows, these are (1) The "Christian in-group" (rotated eigenvalue = 2.57), (2) "Non-Muslim Minority out-group" (rotated eigenvalue = 1.69), and (3) "Muslim/Arab out-group" (rotated eigenvalue = 1.48). Using these factors, we created additive indices measuring aggregate trust per subject across groups in each of the three categories. These indices are the dependent variables referenced in our tables.

Given the nonparametric nature of these data and the relatively modest size of the subject pool, extreme outliers may pose particular problems for

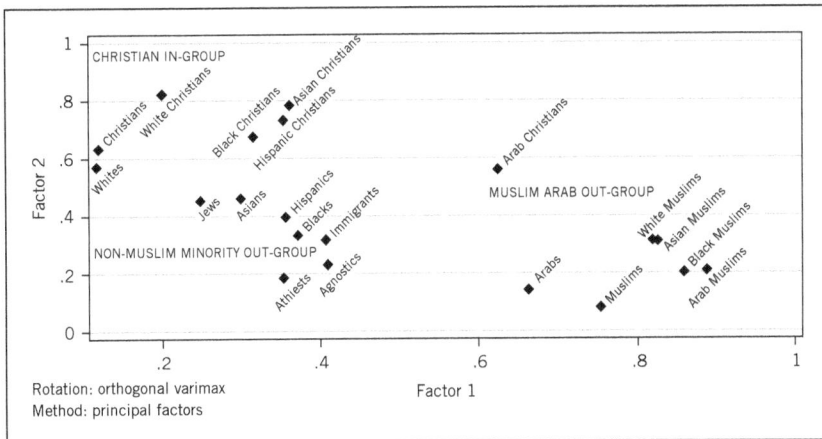

Figure 8.1 Polychoric factor loadings of group trust

model fitting. To mitigate any effects on coefficient estimation, we employ Huber-Biweights. This weighting procedure drops observations with a Cook's distance score greater than 1, and down-weights the remaining observations with large absolute residuals.

We present three series of models for analysis. The first set (in Table 8.1) features the three assigned treatment groups across the trust index scores for the three identity groupings depicted in Figure 8.1. The second set of models in Table 8.2 adds multiplicative interaction terms between the treatments and Christian subjects (owing to the overwhelming number of Christians in the subject pool). Finally, the third set of models in Table 8.3 adds a series of covariates for subject demographic characteristics. We report jackknife standard errors using 10,000 replications with replacement.

Priming and Framing Effects

Interestingly, of the three treatment variables in Table 8.1, only the superordinate group frame in the non-Muslim out-group model shows a statistically significant and positive impact on trust across all subjects (without differen-

TABLE 8.1: SUBJECT TRUST BY RANDOMIZED TREATMENT (AGGREGATED CATEGORIES)

	Christian in-group trust	Non-Muslim out-group trust	Muslim out-group trust
Religion/race prime	−.0001	−.043	.015
	(.078)	(.077)	(.087)
Religion/race prime with group frame	.060	.042	.098
	(.078)	(.078)	(.089)
Group frame	−.091	.173	−.022
	(.082)	(.082)*	(.095)*
Constant	3.66	3.39	3.03
	(.057)	(.057)	(.064)**
AIC	2.33	2.28	2.53
BIC	−4891.8	−4892.7	−4694.3
1/df deviance	.62	.61	.86
Log pseudo likelihood	−942.92	−922.12	−1019.26
N	813	814	809

Note: Iteratively reweighted generalized linear regression coefficients in two-tailed tests. Jackknife standard errors in parentheses using 10,000 replications with replacement.
$*p < .05; **p < .01.$

TABLE 8.2: SUBJECT RESPONSE BY RANDOMIZED TREATMENT: CHRISTIAN SUBJECT INTERACTIONS

	Christian in-group trust	Non-Muslim out-group trust	Muslim out-group trust	Groups are self-supporting
Religion/race prime	−.484	−.369	.015	.270
	(.182)**	(.169)*	(.087)	(.219)
Religion/race prime with group frame	−.398	−.361	.098	−.526
	(.173)*	(.174)*	(.089)	(.185)**
Group frame	−.426	−.392	−.022	−.077
	(.194)*	(.190)*	(.095)*	(.216)
Christian subject	−.225	−.643	−.450	−.083
	(.147)	(.147)**	(.169)**	(.166)
Religion/race prime × Christian subject	.604	.406	.221	−.189
	(.200)**	(.189)*	(.220)	(.243)*
Religion/race prime with group frame × Christian subject	.602	.502	.464	.493
	(.193)**	(.194)**	(.223)*	(.212)*
Group frame × Christian subject	.424	.275	.307	−.133
	(.213)*	(.210)	(.242)	(.241)
Constant	3.84	3.89	3.38	4.60
	(.134)**	(.134)**	(.152)**	(.149)**
AIC	2.28	2.25	2.58	2.61
BIC	−4888.1	−4882.7	−4648.9	−4693.3
1/df deviance	.64	.64	.89	.98
Log pseudo likelihood	−922.47	−911.15	−1036.87	−1069.1
N	814	814	809	826

Note: Iteratively reweighted generalized linear regression coefficients in two-tailed tests. Jackknife standard errors in parentheses using 10,000 replications with replacement.
*$p < .05$; **$p < .01$.

tiating Christians from non-Christians, as we do in later models). By contrast, this same superordinate group frame-only treatment has a significant and negative effect on Muslim out-group trust—suggesting that the impetus to trust minorities may be encouraged through random exposure to the superordinate cue (but only non-Muslim groups benefit from this effect). Though these data were collected in 2012, it is easy to imagine that any public tendency to separate Muslims from other minorities in determining whom to trust has increased in recent years.

Moving to the models containing interactions for Christian subjects, the four models in Table 8.2 show a striking departure from the Table 8.1. Unsurprisingly, trust in Christians increases for both the race/religion prime only and the identity prime + superordinate group frame treatment. But while Christian subjects show a significant decrease in trust of both non-Muslim and Muslim out-groups, these same subjects show a significant *increase* in trust for both sets of out-groups when exposed to the identity prime + superordinate group frame treatment (which asked "how willing would you be to you do the following things to help address a problem facing X").

Confirming both Djupe and Calfano's (2013) and Transue's (2007) premises from the third hypothesis, increased intergroup trust appears to be a function of the effect from the superordinate group frame coupled with religious/racial identity prime. The prime or frame treatment alone does not increase intergroup trust across categories as robustly as the combined prime and frame condition (the religious identity prime has significant effects only half the time). Still, it is noteworthy that the effect size and significance levels from the combined treatment are higher in trust generated for the non-Muslim minorities. This suggests that, whatever benefit Muslims receive from the identity prime and group frame combination, they remain the least trusted groups. Also note that the religion and race prime interaction with Christian subjects is a significant and positive influence on trust of non-Muslim minorities, but this treatment has no impact on Christian trust of Muslims. The simple act of priming religious identity alone does not encourage positive appraisals for Muslims among non-Muslims (and self-identifying Christians in particular).

Table 8.2 includes an additional response measure about the perception of minorities more generally to check the robustness of our treatment effects. This dependent variable asks subjects whether members of specific minority groups (e.g., whites, blacks, women, Hispanics, and Muslims) are "self-supporting," and is scaled 1–7. Focusing only on response about the minority groups, the responses show a rotated polychoric eigenvalue of 1.71. Thus, we created a "self-supporting" response index for use in Tables 8.2 and 8.3.

The treatment/interaction variable effects on this outcome in Table 8.2 are interesting in that only the prime + superordinate group frame treatment interacted with Christian subjects fosters a significant and positive increase in response that minorities are "self-supporting." In contrast, the prime + superordinate group frame treatment actually decreases Christian subject perceptions that minorities have this characteristic. Though Muslims are but

TABLE 8.3: SUBJECT RESPONSE BY RANDOMIZED TREATMENT: INTERACTION MODELS WITH COVARIATES

	Christian in-group trust	Non-Muslim out-group trust	Muslim out-group trust	Groups are self-supporting
Religion/race prime	−.510	−.322	−.118	.187
	(.179)**	(.164)	(.188)	(.215)
Religion/race prime with group frame	−.450	−.342	−.241	−.612
	(.170)**	(.167)*	(.191)	(.189)**
Group frame	−.520	−.407	−.442	−.190
	(.196)**	(.188)*	(.206)*	(.215)
Christian subject	−.201	−.607	−.385	−.185
	(.145)	(.140)**	(.161)*	(.166)
Christian × religion/ race prime	.640	.377	.215	−.150
	(.198)**	(.185)*	(.213)	(.239)
Christian × religion/ race/group frame	.707	.539	.486	.580
	(.190)**	(.187)**	(.217)*	(.216)**
Christian × group frame	.531	.314	.309	−.052
	(.213)**	(.207)	(.233)	(.239)
Subject sex	.060	.030	.083	.111
	(.055)	(.054)	(.063)	(.065)
Subject age	.025	.004	−.075	.157
	(.021)	(.020)	(.024)**	(.025)**
Subject income	.052	.076	.047	.064
	(.020)**	(.020)*	(.023)*	(.024)**
Subject U.S. citizen	.279	.108	.120	−.111
	(.174)	(.166)	(.167)	(.185)
Subject black	−.348	−.313	−.076	.366
	(.067)**	(.067)**	(.080)	(.086)**
Subject Latino	−.064	.218	.254	.391
	(.113)	(.105)*	(.123)*	(.130)**
Subject Asian	.198	−.026	.338	.248
	(.146)	(.132)	(.152)*	(.160)
Constant	3.01	3.41	3.06	3.90
	(.382)**	(.367)*	(.381)**	(.410)**
AIC	2.26	2.21	2.55	2.59
BIC	−4858.8	−4856.4	−4628.2	−4672.3
1/df deviance	.61	.61	.86	.95
Log pseudo likelihood	−902.56	−884.65	−1013.87	−1054.6
N	813	813	808	825

Note: Iteratively reweighted generalized linear regression coefficients in two-tailed tests. Jackknife standard errors in parentheses using 10,000 replications with replacement.

$*p < .05; **p < .01.$

one of the minority groups lumped into this outcome measure, the results suggest that the basic act of identity priming along racial and religious lines alone does not encourage positive views of out-groups.

The trend generally continues in the second round of models in Table 8.3, which include a series of covariates for subject race (black, Latino, Asian), age, income, citizenship status, age, and sex. Again, we see that the prime + superordinate group frame treatment has the most consistent, significant, and positive effect on out-group trust levels. Meanwhile, religious identity priming alone is effective some of the time—but not in bolstering trust of the Muslim out-group. Meanwhile, notable findings from the covariates are that older subjects are significantly less likely to say they trust Muslims, while Latino subjects are significantly more likely to say they trust both the non-Muslim and Muslim out-groups (while also viewing minorities as self-supporting). The primary treatment effects from these final three models (including the covariate adjustments) are graphed in Figures 8.2–8.4 using local polynomial smooths.

Conclusions

Using the social identity framework and balanced identity expectations more generally, our analysis draws attention to a couple of findings that advance our understanding of predictors of group perception. Specifically, we find that, while priming religious identity among Christian subjects helps

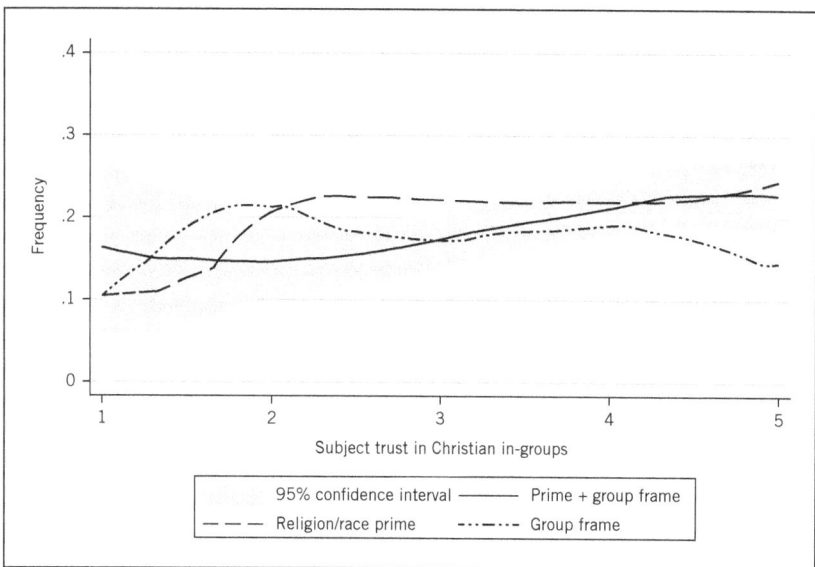

Figure 8.2 Trust in Christian in-groups by treatment

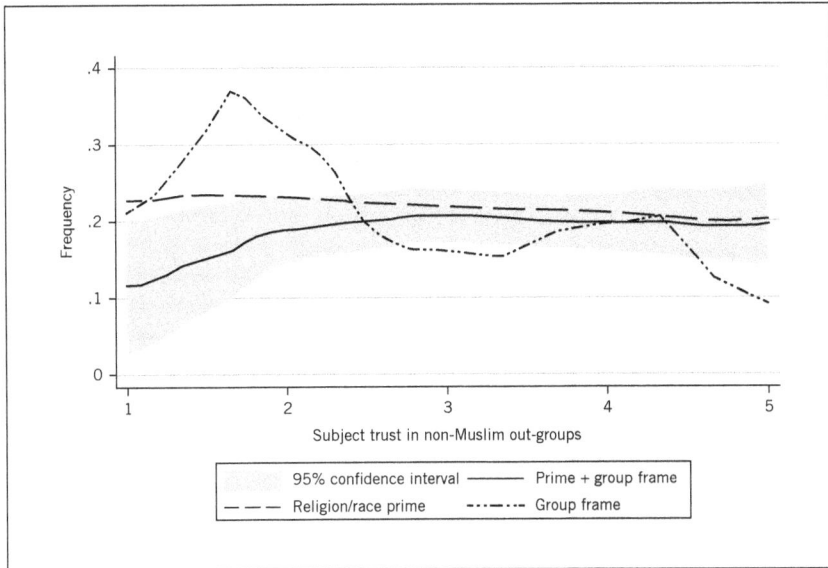

Figure 8.3 Trust in non-Muslim out-groups by treatment

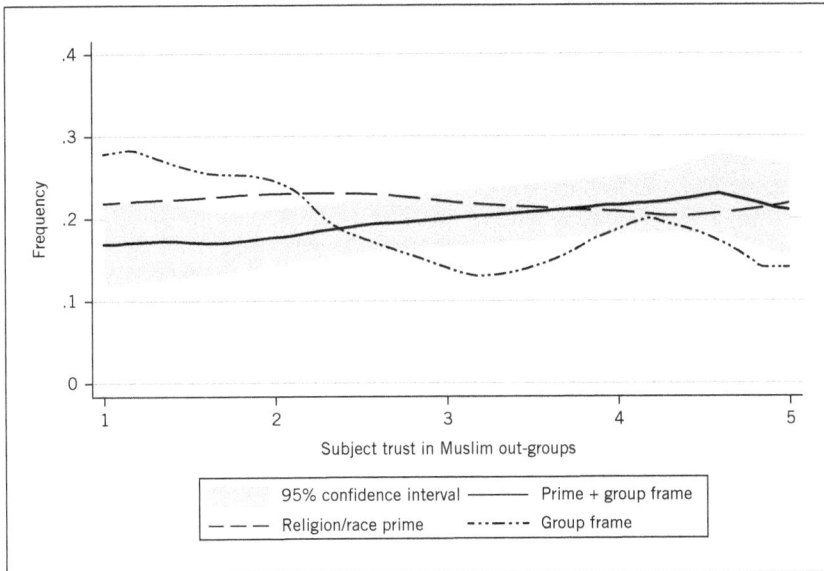

Figure 8.4 Trust in Muslim out-groups by treatment

improve trust across the board, in terms of trust of Muslims, only the priming of religion coupled with a superordinate group frame (in the form of
asking about one's willingness to help out-group members) shows consistent,
statistically significant, and positive effects on perceptions of the Muslim

out-group. Given the consistent and robust trust-inducing effects of the prime/frame treatment, we are encouraged to explore the linkage between these two mechanisms further.

With these results alone, however, we cannot effectively isolate where the effects of identity priming end and group framing begin. If the significance and effect sizes of the treatment interactions with our Christian subjects are any indication, one might argue that identity priming alone has a stronger overall effect than superordinate framing (although our approach to tapping a superordinate motive was different from Transue's [2007]). Yet because the religion prime did not always precede the group frame (the order of these components was determined at random), just how those primed with their religious identity (Christians, in this case) are moved to increase their trust of out-groups when encountering superordinate framing (and vice versa) remains an area for further investigation.

That said, these results are heartening because they show that distrust toward Muslims, whether its source is negative media representations, popular culture, or ideological orientations, can be mitigated through concerted efforts of bridge building—even if the "bridges" are merely cognitive. With specific regard to our subjects' area of residence, there are grassroots efforts in Chicago that try to build intergroup trust between Muslims and other racial and religious communities. The United Congress of Community and Religious Organizations, in which the Inter-City Muslim Action Network is a participant, is a valuable example of a multiracial, multireligious human rights alliance. Through its Lived Experiences discussion series, the organization creates a safe space where members from different religious and racial backgrounds come into contact and share experiences from different perspectives (Grant-Thomas, Sarfati, and Staats 2009). Based on the results from our experiment, we can claim that the coupling of this and similar initiatives to create opportunities for quality contact between Muslims and non-Muslims may find enhanced success if the initiatives broach the kind of religious identity prime and group frame exercise that we assessed. The benefit is a clear contribution to the ideal of a pluralistic society by enhancing the level of intergroup trust against the backdrop of increasingly incendiary reactions toward Muslims in the United States.

REFERENCES

Ahmed, Ali M., and Osvaldo Salas. 2011. "Implicit Influences of Christian Religious Representations on Dictator and Prisoner's Dilemma Game Decisions." *Journal of Socio-Economics* 40:242–246.
Anderson, Lisa R., and Jennifer M. Mellor. 2009. "Religion and Cooperation in a Public Goods Experiment." *Economics Letters* 105:58–60.

Anderson, Lisa, Jennifer Mellor, and Jeffrey Milyo. 2010. "Did the Devil Make Them Do It? The Effects of Religion in Public Goods and Trust Games." *Kyklos* 63:163–175.

Arrow, Kenneth J. 1972. "Gifts and Exchanges." *Philosophy and Public Affairs*, July, pp. 343–362.

Balch, Robert W., and David Taylor. 1978. "On Getting in Tune: Some Reflections on the Process of Making a Supernatural Contact." Paper presented at meeting of the Pacific Sociological Association, Anaheim, CA.

Bargh, J. A., M. Chen., and L. Burrows. 1996. "Automaticity of Social Behavior: Direct Effects of Trait Construct and Stereotype Activation on Action." *Journal of Personality and Social Psychology* 71:230–244.

Bedolla, Lisa Garcia. 2005. *Fluid Borders: Latino Power, Identity and Politics in Los Angeles.* Berkeley: University of California Press.

Blumer, Herbert. 1958. "Race Prejudice as a Sense of Group Position." *Pacific Sociological Review* 1 (1): 3–7.

Brustein, W. 2003. *The Roots of Hate: Anti-Semitism in Europe before the Holocaust.* New York: Cambridge University Press.

Calfano, Brian Robert. 2018. *Muslims, Identity, and American Politics.* New York: Routledge.

Calfano, Brian Robert, and Paul A. Djupe. 2009. "God Talk: Religious Cues and Electoral Support." *Political Research Quarterly* 62 (2): 329–339.

Calfano, Brian Robert, Nazita Lajevardi, and Melissa R. Michelson. 2017. "Trumped Up Challenges: Limitations, Opportunities, and the Future of Political Research on Muslim Americans." *Politics, Groups, and Identities* 5:1–17.

Chandra, K. 2009. "Making Causal Claims about the Effect of 'Ethnicity.'" In *Comparative Politics: Rationality, Culture, and Structure*, edited by M. Lichbach and A. Zuckerman, 376–412. New York: Cambridge University Press.

Chong, D., and D. Kim. 2006. "Experiences and Effects of Economic Status among Racial and Ethnic Minorities." *American Political Science Review* 100:335–351.

Cvencek, D., A. Greenwald, and A. Meltzoff. 2012. "Balanced Identity Theory: Evidence for Implicit Consistency in Social Cognition." In *Cognitive Consistency: A Fundamental Principle in Social Cognition*, edited by B. Gawronski and F. Strack, 157–177. New York: Guilford.

Dawson, M. C. 2001. *Black Visions: The Roots of Contemporary African-American Political Ideologies.* Chicago: University of Chicago Press.

Delhey, Jan, and Kenneth Newton. 2005. "Predicting Cross-national Levels of Social Trust: Global Pattern of Nordic Exceptionalism?" *European Sociological Review* 21:311–327.

Dickson, E. S., and K. Scheve. 2006. "Social Identity, Political Speech, and Electoral Competition." *Journal of Theoretical Politics* 18 (1): 5–39.

Djupe, Paul A., and Brian R. Calfano. 2013. "Divine Intervention? The Influence of Religious Value Communication on U.S. Intervention Policy." *Political Behavior* 35 (4): 643–663.

Doosje, B., N. Ellemers, and R. Spears. 1995. "Perceived Intragroup Variability as a Function of Group Status and Identification." *Journal of Experimental Social Psychology* 31:410–36.

Eckel, Catherine C., and Philip J. Grossman. 2004. "Giving to Secular Causes by the Religious and Nonreligious: An Experimental Test of the Responsiveness of Giving to Subsidies." *Nonprofit and Voluntary Sector Quarterly* 33:271–289.

Falk, Armin, and Christian Zehnder. 2007. "Discrimination and In-Group Favoritism in a Citywide Trust Experiment." Institute for Empirical Research in Economics Working Paper No. 318. Available at http://www.econ.uzh.ch/static/wp_iew/iewwp318.pdf.

Fehr, Ernst, Urs Fischbacher, and Simon Gächter. 2002. "Strong Reciprocity, Human Cooperation, and the Enforcement of Social Norms." *Human Nature* 13 (1): 1–25.

Fershtman, Chaim, Uri Gneezy, and Frank Verboven. 2005. "Discrimination and Nepotism: The Efficiency of the Anonymity Rule." *Journal of Legal Studies* 34:371–396.

Fiske, S. T. 1998. "Stereotyping, Prejudice and Discrimination." In *The Handbook of Social Psychology*, 4th ed., edited by D. T. Gilbert, S. T. Fiske, and G. Lindzey, 375–411. New York: McGraw-Hill.

Gaines, Brian J., James H. Kuklinski, and Paul J. Quirk. 2007. "The Logic of the Survey Experiment Reexamined." *Political Analysis* 15 (1): 1–20.

Gerber, Alan S., Donald P. Green, and Christopher W. Larimer. 2008. "Social Pressure and Voter Turnout: Evidence from a Large-Scale Field Experiment." *American Political Science Review* 120:33–48.

Gilliam, F. D., and Shanto Iyengar. 2000. "Prime Suspects: The Influence of Local Television News on the Viewing Public." *American Journal of Political Science* 44:560–573.

Grant-Thomas, Andrew, Yusuf Sarfati, and Cheryl Staats. 2009. *African American-Immigrant Alliance Building*. Columbus: Ohio State University Kirwan Institute for the Study of Race and Ethnicity.

Green, Donald P., and Alan S. Gerber. 2003. "The Underprovision of Experiments in Political Science." *Annals of the American Academy of Political and Social Science* 589 (1): 94–112.

Greenwald, A., M. Banaji, L. Rudman, S. Farnham, B. Nosek, and D. Mellott. 2002. "A Unified Theory of Implicit Attitudes, Stereotypes, Self-Esteem, and Self-Concept." *Journal of Personality and Social Psychology* 79:1022–1038.

Hewstone, Miles, Ed Cairns, Alberto Voci, Juergen Hamberger, and Ulrike Niens. 2006. "Intergroup Contact, Forgiveness, and Experience of 'The Troubles' in Northern Ireland." *Journal of Social Issues* 62:99–120.

Hilton, J. L., and J. M. Darley. 1991. "The Effects of Interaction Goals on Person Perception." In *Advances in Experimental Social Psychology*, edited by M. P. Zanna, 235–267. San Diego, CA: Academic Press.

Hooghe, Marc, and Ellen Quintelier. 2013. "Do All Associations Lead to Lower Levels of Ethnocentrism? A Two-Year Longitudinal Test of the Selection and Adaptation Model." *Political Behavior* 35:289–309.

Hunt, Scott A., Robert D. Benford, and David A. Snow. 1994. "Identity Fields: Framing Processes and the Social Construction of Movement Identities." In *New Social Movements: From Ideology to Identity*, edited by Enrique Larana, Hank Johnson, and Joseph R. Gusfield, 185–208. Philadelphia: Temple University Press.

Hutchings, Vincent L., and Nicholas A. Valentino. 2004. "The Centrality of Race in American Politics." *Annual Review of Political Science* 7:383–408.

Hutchison, Paul, and Harriet E. S. Rosenthal. 2011. "Prejudice against Muslims: Anxiety as a Mediator between Intergroup Contact and Attitudes, Perceived Group Variability, and Behavioural Intentions." *Ethnic and Racial Studies* 34:40–61.

Jalalzai, Farida. 2011. "Anxious and Active: Muslim Perception of Discrimination and Treatment and Its Political Consequences in the Post–September 11, 2001 United States." *Politics and Religion* 4:71–107.

Johansson-Stenman, O.L.O.F., M. Mahmud, and P. Martinsson. 2009. "Trust and Religion: Experimental Evidence from Rural Bangladesh." *Economica* 76:462–85.

Kalkan, Kerem Ozan, Geoffrey C. Layman, and Eric M. Uslaner. 2009."'Bands of Others?' Attitudes toward Muslims in Contemporary American Society." *Journal of Politics* 71 (3): 1–16.

Khan, Mussarat, and Kathryn Ecklund. 2013. "Attitudes toward Muslim Americans Post-9/11." *Journal of Muslim Mental Health* 7 (1): 1–16.

Klein, Olivier, Russell Spears, and Stephen Reicher. 2007. "Social Identity Performance: Extending the Strategic Side of SIDE." *Personality and Social Psychology Review* 11:28–45.

La Ferrara, E. 2002. "Inequality and Participation: Theory and Evidence from Rural Tanzania." *Journal of Public Economics* 85 (2): 235–273.

Lajevardi, Nazita. 2017. "A Comprehensive Study of Muslim American Discrimination by Legislators, the Media, and the Masses." Ph.D. diss., University of California, San Diego.

Lajevardi, Nazita, and Marisa A. Abrajano. 2018. "How Negative Sentiment towards Muslims Predicts Support for Trump in the 2016 Presidential Election." *Journal of Politics*, December 11. Available at https://www.journals.uchicago.edu/doi/full/10.1086/700001.

Lee, T. 2008. "Race, Immigration, and the Identity-to-Politics Link." *Annual Review of Political Science* 11:457–478.

Maira, Sunaina. 2008. "Citizenship, Dissent, Empire: South Asian Muslim Immigrant Youth." In *Being and Belonging: Muslims in the United States Since 9/11*, edited by Katherine Pratt Ewing, 15–46. New York: Russell Sage Foundation.

Naber, Nadine. 2008. "Arab Americans and U.S. Racial Formations." In *Race and Arab Americans before and after 9/11*, edited by Amaney Jamal and Nadine Naber, 1–45. Syracuse, NY: Syracuse University Press.

Neuberg, Steven L., and Susan T. Fiske. 1987. "Motivational Influences on Impression Formation: Outcome Dependency, Accuracy-Driven Attention, and Individuating Processes." *Journal of Personality and Social Psychology* 53:431–444.

Orbell, John, Marion Goldman, Matthew Mulford, and Robyn Dawes. 1992, "Religion, Context, and Constraint toward Strangers." *Rationality and Society* 4:291–307.

Panagopoulos, Costas. 2006. "The Polls-Trends: Arabs and Muslim Americans and Islam in the Aftermath of 9/11." *Public Opinion Quarterly* 70:608–624.

Peffley, Mark, Jon Hurwitz, and Paul M. Sniderman. 1997. "Racial Stereotypes and Whites' Political Views of Blacks in the Context of Welfare and Crime." *American Journal of Political Science* 1:30–60.

Phalet, Karen, Gülseli Baysu, and Maykel Verkuyten. 2010. "Political Mobilization of Dutch Muslims: Religious Identity Salience, Goal Framing, and Normative Constraints." *Journal of Social Issues* 66 (4): 759–779.

Pichon, Isabelle, G. Boccato, and V. Saroglou. 2007. "Nonconscious Influences of Religion on Prosociality: A Priming Study." *European Journal of Social Psychology* 37:1032–1045.

Putnam, Robert. 1995. "Bowling Alone: America's Declining Social Capital." *Journal of Democracy* 6:65–78.

———. 2000. *Bowling Alone*. New York: Simon and Schuster.

Quinley, Harold E., and Charles Y. Glock. 1979. *Anti-Semitism in America*. New York: Free Press.

Randolph-Seng, Brandon, and Michael E. Nielsen. 2007. "Honesty: One Effect of Primed Religious Representations." *International Journal for the Psychology of Religion* 17:303–315.

Ruffle, Bradley J., and Richard Sosis. 2006. "Cooperation and the In-Group–Out-Group Bias: A Field Test on Israeli Kibbutz Members and City Residents." *Journal of Economic Behavior and Organization* 60:147–163.

———. 2007. "Does It Pay to Pray? Costly Ritual and Cooperation." *B.E. Journal of Economic Analysis and Policy* 7 (1). Available at http://citeseerx.ist.psu.edu/viewdoc/download?doi=10.1.1.482.3899&rep=rep1&type=pdf.

Sanchez, Gabriel R., and Edward D. Vargas. 2016. "Taking a Closer Look at Group Identity: The Link between Theory and Measurement of Group Consciousness and Linked Fate." *Political Research Quarterly* 69:160–174.

Schuman, Howard, and Lawrence Bobo. 1988. "Survey-Based Experiments on White Racial Attitudes toward Residential Integration." *American Journal of Sociology* 94 (2): 273–299.

Selznick, G. S., and S. Steinberg. 1969. *The Tenacity of Prejudice: Anti-Semitism in Contemporary America*. New York: Harper and Row.

Shariff, A. F., and A. Norenzayan. 2007. "God Is Watching You: Priming God Concepts Increases Prosocial Behavior in an Anonymous Economic Game." *Psychological Science* 18:803–809.

Shih, Margaret, Todd L. Pittinsky, and Nalini Ambady. 1999. "Stereotype Susceptibility: Identity Salience and Shifts in Quantitative Performance." *Psychological Science* 10 (1): 80–83.

Sides, John, and Kimberly Gross. 2013. "Stereotypes of Muslims and Support for the War on Terror." *Journal of Politics* 75 (3): 583–598.

Sinclair, Betsy. 2012. *The Social Citizen: Peer Networks and Political Behavior*. Chicago: University of Chicago Press.

Smith, T. W. 1993. "Actual Trends or Measurement Artifacts? A Review of Three Studies of Anti-Semitism." *Public Opinion Quarterly* 57:380–393.

Sniderman, Paul M., and Thomas Piazza. 1993. *The Scar of Race*. Cambridge, MA: Harvard University Press.

Snow, David A., and Leon Anderson. 1987. "Identity Work among the Homeless: The Verbal Construction and Avowal of Personal Identities." *American Journal of Sociology* 92 (6): 1336–1371.

Stoecker, Randy. 1995. "Community, Movement, Organization: The Problem of Identity Convergence in Collective Action." *Sociological Quarterly* 36 (1): 111–130.

Stolle, Dietlind, Stuart Soroka, and Richard Johnston. 2008. "When Does Diversity Erode Trust? Neighborhood Diversity, Interpersonal Trust and the Mediating Effect of Social Interaction." *Political Studies* 56:57–75.

Stouffer, Samuel A. 1955. *Communism, Conformity, and Civil Liberties: A Cross-section of the Nation Speaks Its Mind*. New York: Doubleday.

Sudman, S. 1985. "Mail Surveys of Reluctant Professionals." *Evaluation Review* 9:349–360.

Tajfel, Henri. 1981. *Human Groups and Social Categories: Studies in Social Psychology*. Cambridge: Cambridge University Press.

Tajfel, Henri, and John C. Turner. 1986. "The Social Identity of Intergroup Behaviour." In *The Social Psychology of Intergroup Relations*, edited by S. Worchel and W. G. Austin, 7–24. Monterey, CA: Brooks/Cole.

Tan, Jonathan H. W. 2006. "Religion and Social Preferences: An Experimental Study." *Economics Letters* 90:60–67.

Thibaut, J. W., and L. Walker. 1975. *Procedural Justice: A Psychological Analysis*. Hillsdale, NJ: L. Erlbaum.

Transue, John. 2007. "Identity Salience, Identity Acceptance, and Racial Policy Attitudes: American National Identity as a Uniting Force." *American Journal of Political Science* 51:78–91.

Turner, J. C., M. A. Hogg, P. J. Oakes, S. D. Reicher, and M. S. Wetherall. 1987. *Rediscovering the Social Group: A Self-Categorization Theory*. Oxford: Blackwell.

Uslaner, Eric. 2006. "Does Diversity Drive Down Trust?" FEEM Working Paper No. 69. Available at http://ssrn.com/abstract=903051.

Verkuyten, Maykel. 2005. "Ethnic Group Identification and Group Evaluation among Minority and Majority Groups: Testing the Multiculturalism Hypothesis." *Journal of Personality and Social Psychology* 88 (1): 121–138.

Willits, Fern K., and Bin Ke. 1995. "Part-Whole Question Order Effects: Views of Rurality." *Public Opinion Quarterly* 59 (3): 392–403.

Wittenbrink, B., C. M. Judd, and B. Park. 1997. "Evidence for Racial Prejudice at the Implicit Level and Its Relationship with Questionnaire Measures." *Journal of Personality and Social Psychology* 72:262–274.

Wood, W., and A. H. Eagly. 2002. "A Cross-cultural Analysis of the Behavior of Women and Men: Implications for the Origins of Sex Difference." *Psychological Bulletin* 128:699–727.

Wright, Stephen C., and Linda R. Tropp. 2002. "Collective Action in Response to Disadvantage: Intergroup Perceptions, Social Identification, and Social Change." In *Relative Deprivation: Specification, Development, and Integration*, edited by I. Walker and H. J. Smith, 200–236. Cambridge: Cambridge University Press.

Performance Politics

Negotiating Muslim and American Identities

Brian R. Calfano, Valerie Martinez-Ebers,

Tony E. Carey Jr., and Alejandro J. Beutel

In response to public concerns over recent violent acts committed by extremists claiming to act in the name of Islam in multiple U.S. cities, some politicians have endorsed a variety of draconian measures—from heightened police surveillance at mosques and in Muslim American communities, to creating a registration database of Muslim Americans, to a total ban on Muslim immigration—that could affect the entire U.S. Muslim population (Stephenson 2016). Powering these policy prescriptions are a host of popular misconceptions and negative stereotypes, often associated with documented systematic negative media bias (e.g., Ahmed and Matthes 2016; Stone 2017; Terman 2017) regarding Islam and those who practice it.

The fact is that many non-Muslim Americans may presume that a Muslim identity is distinct and, in some cases, is in conflict with an "American" one. Multiple polls indicate that many Americans question Muslims' loyalty to the United States (Gallup 2012; Ali et al. 2011), and even some scholars claim that Muslim loyalty to the United States is far from certain (see Skerry 2011; Li 2018). It, therefore, becomes a major challenge for individuals in the Muslim community to acknowledge, much less promote, their religious identity given the popular fears and stereotypes in circulation (Kabir 2013; Zaal, Salah, and Fine 2007). And, as discussed in Chapter 3, Muslim women, in particular, face potential overt discrimination, even ridicule, when they elect to appear in public wearing burqa, hijab, and other traditional clothing of their religious culture (Sirin and Fine 2008; Kabir 2013).

So how do American Muslims negotiate their religious identity when it is perceived to be in conflict with American identity? Are there demographic differences in terms of whether they identify "first" as Muslim or American? Finally, and most importantly for the purposes of this chapter, how does the construction of survey questions regarding religious identity influence the answers that American Muslims provide to political and policy-related questions? We use this chapter to help answer these questions.

First, drawing on data from the 2007 Pew national survey of Muslims residing in the United States, we examine the relationship between group identity, gender, and race and Muslim opinions about Islam's treatment of women, evaluations of Al Qaeda, and the role that Arabs played in the 9/11 attacks. Then, we use social identity performance theory to develop expectations of how Muslim responses to survey questions about political motives and activities are influenced by framing identity choices in a manner that forces respondents to acknowledge, prioritize, and even select between their religious and national identities. We argue that when religious identity is made salient, (1) Muslims are more likely to give answers that will make them seem more similar to non-Muslims in terms of political opinions and motives, (2) Muslims are more likely to report higher levels of political activity, and (3) Muslim women are more affected by religious identity salience than men. We test these hypotheses using a 2012 national randomized survey experiment of 772 Muslims, ages eighteen to twenty-five. Our analysis contributes to the literatures on the politics of marginalized groups (including women and racialized minorities), social identity theory, and identity performance.

It may be that heightened suspicion of Muslim Americans by the non-Muslim public encourages Muslims to emphasize their American identity at the expense of their faith. Nahid Kabir, for example, finds that some Muslims, particularly women, feel they are "forcing" themselves to take on an American identity because of social pressures (2013, 100). Clearly, identifying as American has advantages over identifying as Muslim, given the social stigma involved with the latter. Yet choosing an American identity over a Muslim identity may not be borne of a sincere preference, and no study has assessed whether survey response emphasis on these two identity options may systematically affect how Muslims respond to key political questions, particularly along gender lines.

According to identity performance theory, the presence of at least two potentially conflicting social identities may motivate marginalized group members to conform to majority group (i.e., non-Muslim) standards and beliefs as reflected in society (Klein, Spears, and Reicher 2007). A commonly held public perception is that Muslims stand in opposition to "American" political and cultural values. But the existing literature emphasizes the positive effect of religious identity on Muslims' engagement in American politics, especially among women (and women's political engagement can be safely characterized as an American political value) (Jamal 2005; Jalalzai 2009; Choi, Gasim, and Patterson 2011). It would seem that American Muslims conform to identity performance expectations in acting like non-Muslims in society (at least in terms of political engagement). So how might the American and Muslim identities be in potential conflict? Though we cannot rule out other possibilities, it is reasonable to proffer that, with the degree of scrutiny Muslims encounter in American society, the conflict is not so much internal, with how Muslims view themselves, but is an externally imposed factor that pits the choices of calling oneself Muslim or American against each other.

The issue at hand regards whether effects from how scholars ask Muslims about their identity contribute to this externally imposed sense of identity conflict. If we accept that all people have sincere preferences in specifying an identity self-concept, then it is imperative for scholars to be aware of any impacts on political outcome measures driven by how identity concepts are asked about. The consequences are potentially high. Indications from Sonia Roccas and Marilynn Brewer's (2002) social identity complexity theory suggest that the subjective combination of identity elements affects group perceptions and outcomes depending on the nature of the identity combination. Marilynn Brewer and Kathleen Pierce (2005) argue that the combination of one's in-group identities may be highly congruent or cross-cutting, and that much of this determination varies by individual perspective (see also Brown and Turner 1979). It is not unreasonable, therefore, to presume that the identity response options that respondents encounter on surveys reflect a subjective combination of identity concepts that influence how they answer substantive political questions.

Though this possibility has not been directly studied in regard to Muslims, the identity denial literature examining mixed-race participants shows that limiting available identity options (which is what researchers essentially do when asking if one considers oneself "Muslim" or "American") lowers reported motivation and self-esteem while increasing pessimism (Cheryan and Monin 2005; Townsend, Markus, and Bergsieker 2009). What is more, the identity denial effect has been particularly noticeable among minority women (Barlow, Taylor, and Lambert 2000). Though the limitation of identity response to one's religion or nation of residence for Muslims is not a classic case of identity denial (as the literature describes it), the limitation creates a subjectively imposed identity choice and comparison reflecting dominant social perceptions (e.g., Muslims are not automatically considered American by many in the non-Muslim society).

In emphasizing the choice between nation and religion, available survey responses may cue a sense of threat that triggers avoidance and behavior modulation (Steele, Spencer, and Aronson 2002; Shelton, Richeson, and Vorauer 2006). Specifically, the avoidance-based impact on reported political motivation and behavior may be to reduce reports of both, particularly among women Muslims. The literature reporting an association between Muslim identity and political participation does not take these identity choice dynamics into account, which means there may be greater optimism regarding American Muslim political engagement than exists. If true, lower indicated political interest and participation among Muslims not only potentially reinforces the non-Muslim public's negative stereotypes of Muslims but may stunt the process of Muslim assimilation/incorporation into American society. Therefore, the response dynamics inherent when Muslims are asked to indicate their identity on surveys is far more than a matter of academic interest.

Identity Performance

Identity performance theory is inherent in the consideration of identity choice effects in survey response. The performance theory is rooted in the social identity literature (Tajfel and Turner 1979; Tajfel 1982), which contends that group behavior is a function of individual motives to either affirm or eschew group identification and is constrained by the degree to which the individual identifies with an in-group and the value placed on that membership. Identity performance, therefore, consists of the actions of group members to express or repress behaviors that are either positively or negatively associated with group membership. This performance serves two functions: (1) identity consolidation, which may involve affirming and strengthening in-group identification or, conversely, conforming to the dominant out-group norms, and (2) group mobilization, involving efforts to motivate group action (Klein, Spears, and Reicher 2007). We focus exclusively on the first function, identity consolidation, in this analysis.

An affirming identity consolidation performance involves engaging in behavior that supports and acknowledges the value of group membership. For example, many Muslim women living in Western nations wear traditional garments often associated, rightly or wrongly, with religious observance (e.g., hijab, niqab, and burqa) (Ahmed 1993; Dana et al. 2018) as a way to highlight their Muslim identity (Hopkins and Greenwood 2013). These garments communicate their religious identity to other Muslims and assert their primary identity to out-group (non-Muslim) members. Alternatively, identity performances can reflect an effort to conform to out-group norms (Baumeister 1982). For example, conscious of the stereotypes that they are repressed and foreign, Muslim women may choose to integrate the Islamic headdresses with modern, Westernized clothing or forego the Islamic headdress entirely in an effort to combat negative stereotypes.

American Muslims are frequently stereotyped as being violent, foreign, outside the mainstream of American values, and untrustworthy (Dorraj 2010). Thus, the expectation is that when Muslims are confronted with survey questions that relate to these traits, they will be more likely to report answers that refute stereotypes and mostly reflect dominant social and political values. The stereotype that Muslims are a uniquely violent group is often linked rhetorically to recent terrorist attacks in the United States. Although declining in recent years, this stereotype persists (see Rapoport and Berta 2018), despite evidence suggesting the greater threat that far-right violent extremism (e.g., white nationalism, antigovernment extremism, antiabortion extremism, male supremacism/violent incels) poses to domestic security (Reynolds 2004; see also Beutel 2018).[1] Those who believe Islam encourages violence point to passages of the Qur'an that they interpret as an endorsement of intolerance and hostility (Ali 2015). A significant proportion of the American public perceives Muslims as more violent than other social groups (Sides and Gross 2013). Taken together, these findings suggest that Muslim Americans may engage in identity-conforming performances when answering questions regarding violence among Muslims, particularly Islamic extremist groups.

Another stereotype of Muslims is that of being untrustworthy. Historical depictions of Muslims imply that they are hostile to the intentions of Western nations (Sides and Gross 2013). Other research suggests that negative attitudes about Muslims are fueled less by the perceived threat of violence from the group than the longstanding belief that Muslims fall outside of the cultural mainstream (Kalkan, Layman, and Uslaner 2009). Increased negative attitudes toward Muslim Americans may also be temporally associated with election cycles, leading to speculation that, along with organized net-

---

1. Alejandro Beutel's analysis identifies at least 212 post-9/11 fatalities from violence motivated by far-right ideology in the United States, compared to 103 post-9/11 "jihadist"-caused fatalities in the United States. The tally, current as of December 31, 2018, is based on data extracted from Southern Poverty Law Center 2018, Miller 2018 (which treats the October 2017 mass shooting in Las Vegas, Nevada, as an antigovernment extremist act of terrorism), and New America Foundation 2018.

works of anti-Muslim actors (Ali et al. 2011; Lean 2012; Bail 2015) often dubbed the "Islamophobia Network," political opportunism fuels post-9/11 anti-Muslim attitudes.

The identity performances of Muslim Americans are triggered by their effort to manage their religious and national identities. Most people hold multiple identities, each more or less salient depending on the value placed on the group label and the environment in which one is placed (Turner 1987; Abrams et al. 1990; Berelson, Lazarfeld, and McPhee 1954; Nelson and Kinder 1996). But it is hard to think of another contemporary example in which religious and national identities are the focus of social (and research-driven) scrutiny to the extent that they are regarding Muslim Americans. Importantly, and though some Muslim Americans are more strongly at-tached to one identity than the other, a sizeable proportion within the Mus-lim community identify with both their religious and national identities (Verkuyten 2007; Esposito 2007; Calfano 2018). In fact, many Muslims typi-cally believe that their subgroup religious distinctiveness fully complements their superordinate national identity (Hopkins 2011).

Muslim Americans utilize a range of strategies to negotiate their seem-ingly nonconvergent subgroup and superordinate identities (Roccas and Brewer 2002). One strategy is to pass or exit group membership (Tajfel 1979). But the stigma attached to passing (or exiting) one's religious identity may make this approach problematic. Instead, to reshape stereotypes held by non-Muslims, Muslim Americans may highlight how their religious and na-tional identities are aligned with the social majority (Hopkins 2011). In ef-fect, then, Muslims may seek to redefine the national identity to be inclusive of their religious identity.

Alternatively, Muslims may make efforts to signal conformity to domi-nant group standards by suppressing their religious identity as a means to avoid punitive behaviors by the dominant majority. Religious identities are often arranged in institutional or group settings (which allow them to in-form various civic and political behaviors) (Campbell and Monson 2008; Djupe and Gilbert 2009; Putnam and Campbell 2010). Yet just as not all re-ligious identities are the same, neither are their behavioral impacts. Religion, though a significant source of group attachment (see Tajfel 1982), is not an absolute, discrete, and exclusive identity boundary marker—especially where race and national origin vary within a single group (as is the case for Muslim Americans) (Brah and Phoenix 2004; Cieslik and Verkuyten 2006; Lee and Fiske 2006). Among other things, this suggests that if a Muslim deems it necessary for purposes of social or political well-being, her faith identity can be subordinated.

Gender and Muslim Identity

While the topics of Islam and gender politics have been assessed in several well-received studies (see Haddad, Smith, and Moore 2011), they have not been examined from the standpoint of whether Muslim women react differently from men to an identity framework focusing only on faith and nation of residence. Importantly, Muslim women were found to perceive the lowest amount of societal respect across all cohorts in a 2011 national survey (see Gallup 2010). This is consonant with Selcuk Sirin and Michelle Fine's (2008) finding that Muslim women experience more discrimination-related stress than Muslim men, which may be compounded by the general ambiguity about the status of women in Islamic teaching (Huddy 1994; Chaturvedi and Montoya 2013; Haifaa 1988). And given what is known from the social roles literature, the reality of how younger Muslims negotiate identity reductionism may be very different from older cohorts (Deaux and Major 1987; Bianchi, Robertson, and Milkie 2006; Diekman and Eagly 2008). Kabir takes the discussion of Muslim youth identity a step further by suggesting that some young Muslims, particularly women, feel they are "forcing" themselves to take on an American identity because of social pressures (2013, 100).

Scholars using observational data on subsets of the U.S. Muslim population have found support for both the hypothesis that Muslim women are politically active (Jamal 2005; Westfall et al. 2017) and the countervailing expectation that Muslim women are less politically engaged than their male counterparts (Read 2015), though they appear to face heightened levels of discrimination, particularly when they wear the hijab (Dana et al. 2018; Welborne et al. 2018). While Muslim women in the United States have considerable economic and political advantages over women in less developed parts of the world, there remain popular interpretations of the Qur'an, hadith, and the writings of Muslim religious jurists that advance patriarchal understandings of how female and male Muslims should act in both the private and public realms (Barazangi 2004).

While the literature is more consistent in documenting the political oppression of Muslim women in the Middle East, and while the social and cultural expectations of "American" life may provide a moderating influence on conservative applications of Islamic teachings, the Internet era has enabled the permeation of conservative and patriarchal views across borders and societies (see Calfano and Lofftus 2014). And though it is also true that oppression of women may not be related to specific facets of Islam, the correlation between these items when exposure to a limited (i.e., reductionist) set of identity categories such as "Muslim" or "American" may trigger a host of cognitive considerations of one's faith and related factors. Taken in the context of the broad literature on women in Islam, we expect that the limitation of identity choices will have a more significant and negative impact on Muslim women than men.

Hypotheses

There are a number of expectations that extend from the existing literature. The first concerns Muslim Americans' identity performance when addressing issues relevant to underlying stereotypes about the Muslim community. We examine Muslim Americans' responses when asked questions about the quality of life for Muslim women in the United States compared to other countries, how favorably or unfavorably they feel toward Al Qaeda, and whether Arabs carried out the attacks on the Twin Towers on 9/11. Each question is likely to trigger concerns about underlying stereotypes of Muslims as dangerous and foreign. When their religious identity is salient (i.e., because they have been asked how much they agree with a characterization of themselves as "Muslim" or "American"), Muslim Americans should be motivated to conform to the opinion of the dominant non-Muslim majority when posed with these political questions.

> H1: When Muslim Americans' religious identity is made salient, their answers to Muslim-related political questions will conform to the opinions of the dominant majority.

More specifically, we expect that Muslim American respondents will report the following: that Muslim women in the United States have a better quality of life than those in other countries, that they have unfavorable feelings toward Al Qaeda, and that Arabs carried out the attacks on 9/11 (each response being consonant with prevailing non-Muslim views). Second, we believe Muslim Americans will engage in similar identity performances as it relates to their political behavior. In particular, political participation reflects not only a rational calculus of the benefits of political engagement but also the psychological attachment to civic engagement. The stereotype of Muslim Americans that associates their religious identity with untrustworthiness motivates identity performances to disprove the stereotype and conform to the social norms of the dominant majority, which include high political engagement (or at least lip service to it).

> H2: When their religious identity is made salient, Muslim Americans' will report higher levels of political participation.

Last, we propose that identity performances are more likely among Muslim American women than men. Our expectation is based on existing studies that suggest Muslim women are associated with the most visible symbols of the Islamic faith and, consequently, bear the greatest social burden for stereotyping by the non-Muslim majority.

> H3: When their Muslim identity is salient, Muslim American women will be more likely to engage in identity performances than their Muslim male counterparts.

Survey Question Identity

Though it is not conclusive evidence of a question order effect, we identify three examples in data collected as part of Pew's 2007 national survey of Muslims living in the United States. While these data are somewhat old, they remain useful for illustrating the potential effects of identity items on survey response. We report the results from logit and ordered logit models in Tables 9.1 and 9.2 (later in the chapter) using Blinder-Oaxaca decomposition for nonlinear models. Though used heavily in the economics literature, this decomposition approach has been applied frequently to understand gender-based differences in a variety of outcome variables across disciplines (see Oaxaca 1973; Weich, Sloggett, and Lewis 2001; Bauer, Gohlmann, and Sinning 2007).

Our main independent variables are subject response to the questions of whether they told Pew they consider themselves "American" "first" (coded 1) or "Muslim" "first" (coded 1). We also include a series of covariates from the Pew data set, including a four-category ordinal measure of respondent age, race (dummy variables for blacks and whites—which include Arabs in Pew's data), a dummy measure for respondent sex (1 = female), a five-category ordinal measure of respondent education level, a dummy measure of respondent party identity (1 = Democrat), and a six-category ordinal measure of respondent frequency of mosque attendance.

Our outcome measures (which are described below) were asked of respondents after inquiring about which identity label they wished to identify with "first." These identity measures serve as our primary independent variables, and what we use to assess possible question order effects in these Pew data. Twenty-eight percent of Pew respondents selected the "American" identity, while 47 percent selected the "Muslim" identity, and 18 percent indicated "both equally" (and we use this response as the reference category in our models). Theoretically, and from the standpoint of identity performance expectations, a question order effect related to describing oneself as "Muslim" or "American" "first" should elicit question responses that reflect what respondents believe the higher-status out-group likely thinks or believes (i.e., what Muslim respondents perceive non-Muslims to believe about Muslims and Islam).

However, it is not clear which of the selected identities affect survey responses, and in what way. One possibility is that those who describe themselves as "American" "first" should be more likely to engage in identity performance as a way to garner increased acceptance by the higher-status, non-Muslim out-group (which is also likely to hold to an American "first" identity). But a similar rationale could be offered for those selecting their Muslim identity "first," as these respondents might be pressed to overcompensate in the eyes of the non-Muslim out-group for not prioritizing the "American" identity over their faith.

Either way, finding statistically significant effects for the identity selection questions suggests that forcing respondents to choose one identity as "first" over another may have implications for how Muslims respond to political questions that follow these identity items across surveys. In terms of gender-specific differences from the identity "first" questions, we expect that women respondents will show greater sensitivity to the identity questions than men. This is based on the notion that women are generally more vulnerable politically and economically—a status that is likely compounded by the added reality of being Muslim in America. Other things equal, this "dual-minority" status should make the identity performance motive in females more acute versus their male counterparts.

Before moving to our models, we examine gender and race-related differences in identity selection that might suggest an identity performance motive. Forty-seven percent of the 1,050 Muslim respondents that Pew surveyed were female, and, of these, 48.5 percent selected a "Muslim" identity "first," while 37.5 percent of Muslim males did the same. This difference in identity selection between females and males is significant at $p < .01$. In terms of "American" identity selection "first," 23 percent of female Pew respondents did so, versus 31.2 percent of males. This gender difference is also significant at $p < .01$.

These gender differences underscore that male Pew respondents are more likely, and perhaps feel more compelled, to select the "American" identity "first." Given that negative Muslim stereotypes dealing with terrorism usually involved males, this gender difference has an underlying logic. Interestingly, there is also a race-based difference in "first" identity selection. Among respondents Pew characterizes as "white" (33 percent of the total sample), which includes 64 percent of respondents who identify as Arab, 22.8

percent select the "Muslim" identity "first," while 42.5 percent selected the "American" identity "first," a difference significant at $p < .01$. Conversely, 33 percent of black Muslim respondents (20 percent of the total sample) select the "Muslim" identity "first" versus 26 percent selecting the "American" identity (a difference that is not statistically distinguishable from zero). That white respondents, including most of the Arabs in Pew's sample, would show a preference for the "American" identity first, is also not surprising from an identity performance standpoint, and both the gender and race differences underscore that the identity selection question may be associated with systematic differences in response to the follow-on survey items of political importance.

Our first decomposition model provides some indication of identity selection effects and focuses on perceptions of gender-based differences in Islam using the Pew question: "Do you think that the Islamic religion treats men and women equally well, or does it treat one better than the other?" Sixty-nine percent of Pew respondents said Islam treats "men and women equally well," while 23 percent said men are treated better. Two percent said women are treated better, with the remaining 6 percent of respondents offering a "don't know/refusal" reply. In terms of respondent gender breakdowns, and excluding the "don't know" responses, 50 percent of Muslim women and 50 percent of Muslim men in the Pew sample said that Islam treats men better. We recoded the Pew measure so that the "men treated better" response received a 1 as our dependent variable, with all other responses coded 0. What we find is that both "first" identities have a significant effect on response in the decomposition models, but respondent gender has a profound effect on outcomes. We report odds ratios to gauge differences in effect magnitude. Baseline odds are 1:1, which means that the opposing outcomes have equal odds of occurring. Outcomes showing negative odds are reported as a percentage of this baseline.

Turning to the results from the "Islam treats men better than women" columns in Tables 9.1 and 9.2, the odds of respondents agreeing that Islam treats men better than women are 2.70 times higher for males selecting an "American" identity "first" ($p < .01$) (Table 9.1). Meanwhile, the odds of agreement that Islam treats men better than women among males selecting their "Muslim" identity "first" is only 36 percent of the baseline odds ($p < .01$) (Table 9.1). Of the model's covariates in Table 9.1, male Democratic respondent odds of agreement are only 57 percent of the baseline odds ($p < .05$, one tailed).

As seen in Table 9.2, the odds of agreeing that Islam treats men better than women are 3.36 times higher for females selecting an "American" identity "first" ($p < .01$). The "Muslim" "first" variable is not significant in this

TABLE 9.1: THE ROLE OF IDENTITY IN MEDIATING BELIEFS ABOUT ISLAM, AL QAEDA, AND ARABS (MALE RESPONDENTS)

Muslim males	Islam treats men better than women		Favorable view of Al Qaeda		Arabs carried out 9/11 attacks	
	Odds ratio	Robust SE	Odds ratio	Robust SE	Odds ratio	Robust SE
American first	2.70	1.07***	.779	.487	1.82	1.29
Muslim first	.358	.149***	.297	.157**	.491	.306
Age	.994	.010	.978	.013*	.981	.017
Black	.501	.232	1.03	.515	2.57	.2.00
White	1.08	.388	1.84	.906	1.51	.821
Education	.900	.083	1.20	.136	1.64	.254**
Mosque attendance	1.01	.094	.922	.112	1.28	.201
Democrat	.573	.187*	.844	.343	.623	.300
Cut 1			−5.53	1.27**		
Cut 2			−3.94	1.11**		
Cut 3			−2.41	1.07**		
Raw differential	.02		−.54		−.05	
Wald Chi^2	35.3		17.3		26.9	
Prob > Chi^2	.000		.030		.001	
Pseudo R^2	.13		.08		.20	
L-pseudo. LL	120.4		−102.2		−53.9	
N	251		185		120	

Source: Pew Research Center 2007.
Note: Numbers are unstandardized logit and ordered logit models reporting odds ratios using Blinder-Oaxaca decomposition for nonlinear regression models.
$*p < .05$ (one-tailed); $**p < .05$ (two-tailed); $***p < .01$ (two-tailed).

model. Regarding the covariate effects, the odds of agreement are 1.20 times higher for female respondents indicating higher levels of mosque attendance ($p < .05$, one tailed), while the odds of agreement are 97 percent of the baseline for older female respondents ($p < .05$) and 44 percent of the baseline for white females ($p < .05$).

In making sense of these identity effects, it appears that both female and male respondents who were motivated to select an "American" "first" identity clearly engage in a type of identity performance, leading them to agree with a generally held stereotype of Islam—that it treats men better than women. However, instead of finding overcompensation among the "Muslim" "first" respondents, we see that males selecting this identity move away from agreeing with the stereotype about Islam and differences in

TABLE 9.2: THE ROLE OF IDENTITY IN MEDIATING BELIEFS ABOUT ISLAM, AL QAEDA, AND ARABS (FEMALE RESPONDENTS)

Muslim females	Islam treats men better than women		Favorable view of Al Qaeda		Arabs carried out 9/11 attacks	
	Odds ratio	Robust SE	Odds ratio	Robust SE	Odds ratio	Robust SE
American first	3.36	1.36***	.824	.434	3.81	2.24**
Muslim first	.712	.307	.451	.214*	1.54	.794
Age	.977	.011**	1.02	.013*	1.08	.018**
Black	.656	.262	5.23	3.38***	1.62	1.04
White	.440	.184**	1.49	.673	1.07	.541
Education	.959	.090	1.28	.144**	1.11	.150
Mosque attendance	1.20	.111*	1.03	.116	1.01	.142
Democrat	1.20	.382	1.35	.512	.804	.346
Cut 1			−2.33			
Cut 2			−.961	.997**		
Cut 3			.635	.874**		
Raw differential	.02		−.54	.854	−.05	
Wald Chi^2	30.1		27.3		15.4	
Prob > Chi^2	.000		.000		.052	
Pseudo R^2	.11		.10		.10	
L-pseudo. LL	126.7		−124.5		−70.5	
Omega = 1	−153.3		−.45		14.7	
N	270		230		158	

Source: Pew Research Center 2007.

Note: Unstandardized logit and ordered logit models reporting odds ratios using Blinder-Oaxaca decomposition for nonlinear regression models.

$^*p < .05$ (one-tailed); $^{**}p < .05$ (two-tailed); $^{***}p < .01$ (two-tailed).

treatment by gender. This suggests that identity performance might not extend to males who identify with their religion over their nation of residence.

The outcome variable in our second model is the response to the question: "Overall, do you have a favorable or unfavorable view of Al Qaeda?" which is reverse coded from the original Pew data and situated on a 1–4 Likert scale (excluding "don't know/refused" replies—27 percent of the sample), with 4 being "very favorable." Sixty-eight percent of Pew respondents selected the "somewhat unfavorable" or "very unfavorable" options (including 97 percent of men and 95 percent of women in the Pew sample).

Importantly, selecting one's Muslim identity "first" suggests identity performance significantly influenced the male respondents in Table 9.1. The odds of Muslim males in the Pew sample offering a favorable opinion of Al Qaeda when selecting a "Muslim" identity "first" are only 30 percent of the baseline ($p < .01$). The "American" identity is not significant in this model. Among the covariates in the male model, the odds of offering a favorable impression are 98 percent of the baseline for older respondents. Moving to the female model in Table 9.2, the odds of offering a favorable opinion of Al Qaeda when selecting a "Muslim" identity "first" is only 45 percent of the baseline ($p < .05$, one tailed). Yet there are also several significant covariate effects in the female model that show opposite effects. Black female respondents show a 5.23 increase in odds of giving a favorable opinion of Al Qaeda ($p < .01$), while females with higher levels of education have a 1.28 increase in odds of doing the same ($p < 05$). Finally, older female respondents show a 1.02 increase in odds of providing a favorable view of the group ($p < .05$, one tailed).

It is important to recognize that, apart from the September 11 attacks, Al Qaeda's role in the global geopolitical context is perceived more ambivalently than American-driven narratives that tend to be entirely negative. In the female model especially, that the "Muslim" "first" identity was a significant predictor of respondent views on Al Qaeda—and that the identity item was signed in the opposition direction of three different demographic covariates—suggests that presenting the identity selection item prior to the Al Qaeda question encouraged female respondents to engage in identity performance to a substantial degree. Whether the difference in effect for the "Muslim" "first" response was due to the type of question asked (i.e., a more politically charged question about an international terror group versus a religious-oriented question about gender treatment, as in our first model) is an intriguing possibility that we cannot further assess with these data. Regardless, the second model's results clearly show that both female and male respondents selecting their Muslim identity "first" can be motivated to engage in identity performance depending on the issue at hand.

Our third model focuses on the Pew question: "Do you believe that groups of Arabs carried out the attacks against the United States on September 11, 2001, or don't you believe this?" Forty percent of Pew respondents agreed that Arabs carried out the attacks, 28 percent said they did not believe Arabs did so, and 32 percent said "don't know/refused" to answer. Excluding these nonresponses, we coded the outcome as a binary response variable as 1 = Arabs carried out the 9/11 attacks. Eighty percent of women and 83 percent of men in the sample agreed with the statement about Arabs and the 9/11 attacks.

As seen in Table 9.1, identity selection among male respondents actually has no statistically significant effect on the outcome. Only education level appears to matter, as males with higher levels of education show an increase in odds of 1.64 of attributing the 9/11 attacks to Arabs. The story is a bit different among the female respondents, however. Females selecting the "American" identity "first" have an increase in odds of 3.81 of attributing 9/11 to Arab attackers ($p < .05$), while older females in the Pew sample show an increase in odds of 1.08 of doing the same ($p < .05$).

In examining these results collectively, it is clear that female Muslims were generally more affected by Pew's request to pick either their Muslim or American identity "first" than their male counterparts, although there were some consistent effects found among the male respondents. If anything, females in the Pew sample appear to have been affected more by selecting the "American" identity in terms of response to follow-on survey questions. Though these models do not shed light on the exact mechanism by which respondents indicate they are American or Muslim "first," they do suggest that placement of the identity questions has a significant impact on how Pew respondents answered follow-on questions of religious and political consequence.

Overall, these results indicate that the positioning of group identity questions earlier in a nationally representative survey are correlated with different responses to political questions. And though both female and male Muslims were affected by the request to select an identity "first," female respondents were more sensitive to both aspects of this limited identity construct than their male counterparts. The question now is whether this association holds up in an experimental design where the placement of identity primes is randomly assigned to survey respondents.

Priming Identity Reductionism: An Experiment

Though randomly assigned question order primes have become fairly common (Shih, Pittinsky, and Ambady 1999), this is, to our knowledge, the first questions-as-treatment design used on Muslim survey respondents. Our data come from a national question-order experiment in which treated subjects were randomly selected to receive one of two question batteries intended to prime identities. In our design, the control group received neither question battery treatment as a prime and, instead, was exposed to both sets of priming questions at the end of the survey. Our experiment was conducted in conjunction with the Muslim Public Affairs Council (MPAC), a Muslim American faith-based advocacy organization.

Owing to MPAC's representative strength and organizational credibility among young adult Muslims at the time the survey was conducted, and considering the response drawbacks of telephone surveys without robust "cell

TABLE 9.3: DEMOGRAPHIC BREAKDOWN OF 2012 SURVEY EXPERIMENT
SUBJECTS

	Frequency
Usable treatment	772
RCI prime	227
Group prime	238
Control	307
Female/male	321/308
Born in United States	629
Ethnicity ($N = 629$)	
Arab	207
Asian	281
African	41
Hispanic	15
White	85

only" sampling frames (a necessity when sampling young adults; Lavrakas et al. 2007), we elected to deliver the experiment online. A total of 772 subjects (all Muslim young adults ages eighteen to twenty-five, which was MPAC's target age range for the young adult demographic) completed the survey experiment in August 2011. While the decomposition models described in the previous section did not show significant effects when split along age lines, the question of identity reductionism on young adult Muslims remains worthwhile, especially given the sizeable percentage of Muslims under thirty in the United States (see Pew 2007; Gallup 2010). Thus, we built our experiment subject pool around a young adult cohort (see Table 9.3 for full report of subject demographic variables).

Solicitations and email links for the experiment were extended via MPAC during organization-sponsored events and online (via organizational email lists and Internet ads). No incentives (such as money or gift cards) were provided for participation. The survey was administered using Qualtrics software and featuring clear visual recognition of MPAC's cosponsorship of the survey.[2] In this way, the ostensible organizational affiliation subjects saw prior to encountering the randomized prime was in-group specific, which is quite different from the out-group affiliations that Pew and Gallup represent.

---

2. Using Qualtrics for the online survey reduces the likelihood of the same person taking the survey more than once by blocking an IP address from accessing the survey multiple times. We found three duplicate IP addresses in the response data. These were deleted prior to analysis.

In fact, including the MPAC affiliation provides a more stringent test of the identity hypothesis in that there should be less attachment anxiety affecting respondents at the survey's outset.

The Qualtrics algorithm randomized treatment assignment for each subject independent of what other subjects were assigned, and did so once a subject clicked on the survey link. Conducting random assignment at this point in the design helps reduce nonrandom attrition. The first treatment question battery featured questions about how well "Muslim" or "American" labels describe the subject. We call this the group prime. The second treatment focused on an alternate means of referencing Muslim identity by using part of a question battery created to tap psychological religious attachment—the Religious Commitment Index-10 (RCI) (see Worthington et al. 2003). We selected the RCI as an alternate treatment because its wording avoids the inherent pitting of intergroup identity labels against each other (indeed, the terms "Muslim" and "American" are not included in the question battery). Despite its advantages, however, the RCI may retain an identity performance effect because of its religion focus. Therefore, we prefer to describe both treatments as advancing identity reductionism (i.e., limiting how Muslims define themselves to their faith and/or nation of residence), but in different ways and perhaps with different effects.

The 297 subjects randomly assigned to the RCI prime received the first three of the ten RCI psychological commitment questions (using a 1–5 Likert scale, 5 = "totally true of me") toward the beginning of their survey (after a series of warm-up questions about automobiles, eating meals out, etc.). The 301 group prime subjects received questions about how much they identify as "Muslim" and "American" (using 1–4 Likert scale, 4 = "completely") in the same introductory portion of the survey. Table 9.4 provides a breakdown of the response items used in each prime.

TABLE 9.4: RCI-10 AND GROUP PRIME TREATMENTS

RCI prime		Group prime	
Scale	Questions	Scale	Questions
From "Not at all true of me" (1) to "Totally true of me" (5)	My religious beliefs lie behind my whole approach to life.	From "Not at all" (1) to "Completely" (4)	How much do you identify as American?
	I spend time trying to grow in understanding of my faith.		How much do you identify as Muslim?
	It is important to me to spend periods of time in private religious thought and reflection.		How well do you feel the two identities (American and Muslim) go together?

Note that we do not use subject response to either set of identity questions in our analysis. The 323 control group subjects received neither prime at the beginning of their survey after the warm-up questions. Since we had no preexisting demographic information about our subject pool, we did not block randomize the treatments. Instead, with our focus on gender-related effects from the identity primes, we used subject sex as covariate to account for any nonrandom attrition, and asked about subject sex as part of the warm-up question series. The 772 usable responses were from 921 subjects who completed enough of the initial survey to indicate their sex and receive the random assignment.

Unlike with our national survey data, reliable perimeter estimation for Muslims ages eighteen to twenty-five lags behind the general sample dimensions available for older Muslim cohorts. This is because the current national Muslim surveys from Gallup, Pew, Zogby, and others have not focused on the young adult Muslim cohort with any consistency. This makes it difficult to reach this portion of the Muslim population in the United States with any sense of representativeness. Therefore, we do not claim the subject pool to be representative of Muslims in this age cohort. The inherent usefulness of experimental design, however, is its isolation of direct causal effects, even when representative samples cannot be drawn. The nonparametric Cliff's Delta measure of the experiment's statistical power is –.47, which roughly corresponds to the parametric Cohen's D effect size of .80.

Randomized Identity Priming Effects

Before assessing behavior outcomes, we explore subject motivation for political action on a Political Motive Index (polychoric rotated eigenvalue = 1.39) of four items presented in the survey following exposure to either treatment. These are 1–5 Likert scale items measuring subjects' reported perceptions of whether their political activity is motivated by (1) social appeal, (2) social obligation, (3) political tension, and (4) perceptions of marginalization (Jamal 2005). Though these motives appear disparate, all loaded with a factor score of at least .65, suggesting that motivation for political activity among Muslim subjects is a multifaceted phenomenon and justifying the use of an index score.

These results are followed by analysis of effects on a Political Activities Index (polychoric rotated eigenvalue = 1.60) of five behavior-based survey items following the introduction of either treatment, and randomly alternating a question order position in the online survey with the Political Motive Index. The Activities Index is based on 1–5 Likert scale items measuring subjects' reported activity frequency of (1) engaging in protests, (2) making political donations, (3) volunteering for political campaigns, (4) contacting elected officials, and (5) discussing politics in their household (Leighley 1990; Verba, Schlozman, and Brady 1995).

Having used random assignment, we first compare response means for our entire subject sample (without covariates or subject decomposition into female and male). Comparing the average effect of the RCI prime to the group prime on the Political Motive Index ($p < .05$) shows that the group prime average of 2.4 is .22 lower than the RCI prime average (2.62) and .19 lower than the control (2.59) ($p < .08$). There is no significant difference between the RCI prime and control means.

Experimental effects are always prone to nonrandom attrition among subjects. To account for this, we use the female subject covariate to tighten effect bound estimates (see Lee 2009). Using the covariate-adjustment, we find that, compared to control subjects, those assigned to the group prime have a lowered Political Motive Index of between .22 (upper bound) and .33 (lower bound) ($p < .05$). The tightened effect bounds were not significant for the RCI prime. Overall, the group prime effect on the Motive Index suggests that, when confronted with these "American" and "Muslim" identity items, subjects become less willing to consider and/or express underlying motivations for their political behavior. This suggests a clear psychological effect on Muslim survey response that deserves additional focus in subsequent research.

Moving to the Political Activities Index, we see that, as expected, the group prime decreases the average reported political activity of subjects assigned to that treatment by .40 (1.71) versus the control (2.1) ($p < .05$). Meanwhile, the group prime subjects have a lower Index score of .20 vs. the RCI prime subjects (1.91) ($p < .05$). The difference of .29 between the RCI prime and control subjects is also significant ($p < .05$). This suggests that, as we anticipated, the RCI represents a type of identity reductionism that affects reported political outcomes but has a less negative impact on subject indication of political activity than the group prime. When tightening the effect bounds to account for attrition, we see that the Political Activity Index decreases between .26 (upper bound) and .33 (lower bound) for the group prime when using the female subject covariate ($p < .05$). As with the Motive Index, the tightened effect bounds were not significant for the RCI prime.

To test the effect of these competing primes on subject political motives and activity with covariates, we use another series of Blinder-Oaxaca decompositions featuring a series of racial/ethnic, partisan, and citizenship controls (in addition to the treatment primes themselves). Given the nonparametric nature of our subject pool, we report bootstrap standard errors using one hundred thousand replications in Table 9.5.

Overall, the effect direction and significance are the same as in the mean comparisons, although there is some difference in magnitude with the in-

TABLE 9.5: POLITICAL MOTIVE INDEX AND POLITICAL ACTIVITY INDEX DECOMPOSITION COEFFICIENTS

	Coefficient	Bootstrap SE
Political Motive Index		
Group prime		
Female	−.21	.09**
Male	−.13	.17
RCI prime		
Female	.03	.10
Male	.04	.18
Democrat		
Female	.01	.01
Male	.06	.02**
African		
Female	−.39	.25
Male	−.08	.33
Arab		
Female	−.20	.22
Male	−.17	.31
U.S.-born		
Female	−.33	.16*
Male	.18	.26
Constant		
Female	3.08	.42**
Male	2.11	.29**
N (female/male)	321/308	
Prob. > F	.000	
Adj. R^2	.03	
Char. Omega = 1	.06	
Char. Omega = 0	.08	
Raw differential	.10	
Bootstrap replications	100,000	
Political Activity Index		
Group prime		
Female	−.22	.09**
Male	−.16	.15
RCI prime		
Female	.16	.09
Male	.20	.19
Democrat		
Female	.02	.01*
Male	.03	.02

(continued)

TABLE 9.5 (CONTINUED)

	Coefficient	Bootstrap SE
African		
Female	−.27	.21
Male	.01	.29
Arab		
Female	−.04	.28
Male	−.25	.20
U.S.-born		
Female	−.45	.14**
Male	−.45	.32
Constant		
Female	2.06	.42*
Male	2.44	.24*
N (female/male)	321/308	
Prob. > F	.000	
Adj. R^2	.05	
Char. Omega = 1	.10	
Char. Omega = 0	.12	
Raw differential	.14	
Bootstrap replications	100,000	

Note: Unstandardized linear regression coefficients in two-tailed tests. Models run using Blinder-Oaxaca decomposition of the mean outcome differential for linear and nonlinear models.
*$p < .05$; **$p < .01$.

cluded covariates. Specifically, female subjects assigned to the group prime have their Political Motive Index score lowered by .21 ($p < .05$). For males, this effect is not statistically significant. The RCI prime is not significant for either female or male subjects. The decomposition results for the Political Activity Index shows that female subjects assigned to the group prime have their index score lowered by .22 ($p < .01$). For males, this effect is not statistically significant. As for the Motive Index models, the RCI prime is not significant for either female or male subjects. Clearly, use and placement of identity questions asking Muslims to indicate how much their religious or national identities apply to them depresses indicated political activity in their survey response (and, indirectly at least, undermines Muslim signaling of the political engagement norm discussed at the start of this chapter).

Conclusions

Our work contributes to the survey prime literature (Katz and Hass 1988; Iyengar and Kinder 1989; Podsakoff et al. 2003), but our goal is not to disparage insights drawn from prior observational studies (including Pew and Gallup). Instead, it has been to test the expectation that, when identity is cued in a manner that limits Muslim identity to faith and/or nation of residence, subjects are more likely to provide what they consider to be acceptable answers in an identity performance directed at dominant out-groups. Results from our national survey data show an association between a limited set of identity choices and survey response about respondents' views of Islam, Al Qaeda, and the 9/11 attacks. Meanwhile, findings from our national survey experiment show decreases in both self-reported motivation for political activity and reported political behavior for subjects exposed to the group prime.

Both sets of results are consonant with the notion that Muslims are sensitive to cues embedded in question and response wording, and that these cues elicit identity performance effects. Ironically, the experimental effect from the group prime actually inhibited identity performance by lowering self-reported political behavior levels. We also theorized that vulnerable respondents, specifically women and young adults, are more likely to engage in identity performance. Our findings strongly support our expectations for women but less so for young adults. Given that this is the first quantitative political study on Muslim young adults in the United States, additional research on the political behavior and expectations of this age cohort versus older Muslims is needed.

Of all the outcome measures in our assessment, the reduction of self-reported political activity is arguably the most concerning because it relates directly to participation and democratic representation of minority group interests. While it is impossible to verify from these data whether the reported decline in political activity actually occurs in the real world, even the suggestion of this relationship via survey response does not bode well for Muslim prospects of full integration into American society. These concerns are especially pronounced for Muslim women, who appear much more sensitive than their male counterparts to "Muslim" and "American" conceptions of identity.

Importantly, the use of a limited set of identities in survey response has implications beyond Muslim Americans. This possibility is especially relevant in light of Donald Trump's continued use of white identity political rhetoric and his intent to implement explicitly white nationalist policy preferences in the form of proposals such as the border wall with Mexico and the suspension of immigration from Muslim-majority nation-states. It will also be important to measure how identity performance among various minority and historically disenfranchised groups is affected by the increased activity of pre- and post-Trump election identity-based movements, such as Black

Lives Matter and the Women's March, and the broader rising public opposition to President Trump's rhetoric and policy proposals (Cox, Lienesch, and Jones 2017; Telhami 2017).

Overall, then, researchers should at least consider how their approach to surveying minority group identity might influence self-reported response. Our assessment shows that even subtly suggested expectations about identity (i.e., offering just two identity response options) might create performance expectations and response bias. But avoiding identity-related bias may be not as simple as placing identity-related questions at the end of survey instruments. Even basic screening questions along religious and/or ethnic lines may have effects similar to what we discovered for Muslims, yet these items are of necessity at the beginning of the question queue if surveyors are to efficiently examine specific population groups. Another potential issue is the response validity of a more open-ended approach to identity characterization. Though there is a need to be sure that reported identity characterizations are a sincere choice, a stream-of-consciousness reply (for example) to identity questions is not feasible either.

Then there is the question of whether identity reductionism affects survey response for a particular survey. While we found confirmatory evidence for this effect, it does not mean that every survey suffers from similar response bias. Our general point is that surveyors should be sure to know whether, and to what extent, minority group responses are affected by the identity characterizations in question response options. At the least, conducting a question order effect check for a full survey report would be in order. The benefit will be greater accuracy in assessing the role that group identity plays in individual political behavior, especially as America undergoes a substantial diversification trend.

REFERENCES

Abrams, Dominic, Margaret Wetherell, Sandra Cochrane, and Michael A. Hogg. 1990. "Knowing What to Think by Knowing Who You Are: Self-Categorization and the Nature of Norm Formation, Conformity, and Group Polarization." *British Journal of Psychology* 29 (2): 97–119.

Ahmed, L. 1993. *Women and Gender in Islam.* New Haven, CT: Yale University Press.

Ahmed, S., and S. Matthes. 2016. "Media Representations of Muslims and Islam from 2000 to 2015: A Meta-analysis." *International Communication Gazette* 79:219–244.

Ali, Ayaan Hirsi. 2015. "Islam Is a Religion of Violence." *Foreign Policy*, November 9. Available at http://www.foreignpolicy.com/2015/11/09/islam-is-a-religion-of -violence-ayaan-hirsi-ali-debate-islamic-state.

Ali, Wajahat, Eli Clifton, Matthew Duss, Lee Fang, Scott Keyes, and Faiz Shakir. 2011. "Fear, Inc.: The Roots of the Islamophobia Network in America." Available at http:// www.americanprogress.org/issues/2011/08/pdf/islamophobia.pdf.

Bail, Christopher. 2015. "The Fringe Effect: Civil Society Organizations and the Evolution of Media Discourse about Islam since the September 11th Attacks." *American Sociological Review* 77:855–879.

Barazangi, Nimat Hafez. 2004. "Understanding Muslim Women's Self-Identity and Resistance to Feminism and Participatory Action Research." In *Traveling Companions: Feminisms, Teaching, and Action Research*, edited by M. Brydon-Miller, P. Maguire, and A. McIntyre, 21–39. Westport, CT: Praeger.

Barlow, Kelly M., Donald M. Taylor, and Wallace E. Lambert. 2000. "Ethnicity in America and Feeling 'American.'" *Journal of Psychology* 134:581–600.

Bauer, Thomas, Silja Gohlmann, and Mathias Sinning. 2007. "Gender Differences in Smoking Behavior." *Health Economics* 16:895–909.

Baumeister, Roy F. 1982. "A Self-Presentational View of Social Phenomena." *Psychological Bulletin* 91 (1): 3–26.

Berelson, Bernard, Paul Lazarfeld, and William N. McPhee. 1954. *A Study of Opinion Formation in a Presidential Campaign.* Chicago: University of Chicago Press.

Beutel, Alejandro J. 2018. "The Radical Right and Weapons of Mass Destruction—an Enduring Threat to the American Homeland." *Intelligence Report*, February 20. Available at https://www.splcenter.org/fighting-hate/intelligence-report/2018/radical-right-and-weapons-mass-destruction-%E2%80%94-enduring-threat-american-homeland.

Bianchi, Suzanne M., John P. Robinson, and Melissa A. Milkie. 2006. *Changing Rhythms of American Family Life.* New York: Sage.

Brah, A., and A. Phoenix. 2004. "Ain't I a Woman? Revisiting Intersectionality." *Journal of International Women's Studies* 5:75–86.

Brewer, Marilynn B., and Kathleen P. Pierce. 2005. "Social Identity Complexity and Outgroup Tolerance." *Personality and Social Psychology Bulletin* 31:428–437.

Brown, Rupert J., and John C. Turner. 1979. "The Criss-Cross Categorization Effect in Intergroup Discrimination." *British Journal of Social and Clinical Psychology* 18:371–383.

Calfano, Brian Robert. 2018. *Muslims, Identity, and American Politics.* New York: Routledge.

Calfano, Brian Robert, and Lynne Alise Lofftus. 2014. "Islam and Interpretive Ingenuities." In *Assessing MENA Political Reform Post–Arab Spring: Mediators and Microfoundations*, edited by Brian Robert Calfano, 57–94. Lanham, MD: Lexington Books.

Campbell, David E., and Joseph Quin Monson. 2008. "The Religion Card: Gay Marriage and the 2004 Presidential Election." *Public Opinion Quarterly* 72:399–419.

Chaturvedi, Nelian S., and Orlando Montoya. 2013. "Democracy, Oil, or Religion? Expanding Women's Rights in the Muslim World." *Politics and Religion* 6:1–22.

Cheryan, Sapna, and Benoit Monin. 2005. "'Where Are You *Really* From?' Asian Americans and Identity Denial." *Journal of Personality and Social Psychology* 89:717–730.

Choi, Jangsup, Gamal Gasim, and Dennis Patterson. 2011. "Identity, Issues, and Religious Commitment and Participation: Explaining Turnout among Mosque-Attending Muslim Americans." *Studies in Ethnicity and Nationalism* 11:343–364.

Cieslik, A., and M. Verkuyten. 2006. "National, Ethnic, and Religious Identities: Hybridity and the Case of the Polish Tatars." *National Identities* 8:77–93.

Cox, Daniel, Rachel Lienesch, and Robert P. Jones. 2017. "Who Sees Discrimination? Attitudes on Sexual Orientation, Gender Identity, Race, and Immigration Status."

Public Religion Research Institute, June 21. Available at https://www.prri.org/research/americans-views-discrimination-immigrants-blacks-lgbt-sex-marriage-immigration-reform.

Dana, Karam, Nazita Lajevardi, Kassra A. R. Oskooii, and Hannah L. Walker. 2018. "Veiled Politics: Experiences with Discrimination among Muslim Americans." *Politics and Religion*, June 13. Available at https://www.cambridge.org/core/journals/politics-and-religion/article/veiled-politics-experiences-with-discrimination-among-muslim-americans/A8D7933C40A9AF8016E56AD256D350DE.

Deaux, Kay, and Brenda Major. 1987. "Putting Gender into Context: An Interactive Model of Gender-Related Behavior." *Psychological Review* 94:369–389.

Diekman, Amanda B., and Alice H. Eagly. 2008. "Of Men, Women, and Motivation." In *Handbook of Motivation Science*, edited by James Y. Shah and Wendi L. Gardner, 434–447. New York: Guilford.

Dorraj, Manochehr. 2010. "Islamophobia, the Muslim Stereotype, and the Muslim-American Political Experience." In *Perspectives on Race, Ethnicity, and Religion: Identity Politics in America*, edited by V. Martinez-Ebers and M. Dorraj, 188–203. New York: Oxford University Press.

Djupe, Paul A., and Christopher P. Gilbert. 2009. *The Political Influence of Churches*. Cambridge: Cambridge University Press.

Esposito, John. 2007. "America's Muslims: Issues of Identity, Religious Diversity, and Pluralism." In *Democracy and the New Religious Pluralism*, edited by Thomas Banchoff, 133–150. New York: Oxford University Press.

Gallup. 2010. "Measuring the State of Muslim-West Relations: Assessing the 'New Beginning.'" Available at http://www.gallup.com/poll/144959/measuring-state-muslim-west-relations.aspx.

———. 2012. "Islamophobia: Understanding Anti-Muslim Sentiment in the West." Available at http://www.gallup.com/poll/157082/islamophobia-understanding-anti-muslim-sentiment-west.aspx.

Haddad, Yvonne Yazbeck, Jane I. Smith, and Kathleen M. Moore. 2011. *Muslim Women in America: The Challenge of Islamic Identity Today*. New York: Oxford University Press.

Haifaa, A. Jawad. 1988. *The Rights of Women in Islam: An Authentic Approach*. New York: St. Martin's.

Hopkins, N. 2011. "Dual Identities and Their Recognition: Minority Group Members' Perspectives." *Political Psychology* 32:251–270.

Hopkins, Nick, and Ronni Michelle Greenwood. 2013. "*Hijab*, Visibility and the Performance of Identity." *European Journal of Social Psychology* 43:438–447.

Huddy, Leonie. 1994. "The Political Significance of Voters' Gender Stereotypes." *Research in Micropolitics* 4:169–193.

Iyengar, Shinto, and Donald Kinder. 1989. *News That Matter: Television and Public Opinion*. Chicago: University of Chicago Press.

Jalalzai, Farida. 2009. "The Politics of Muslims in America." *Politics and Religion* 2:163–199.

Jamal, Amaney. 2005. "The Political Participation and Engagement of Muslim Americans: Mosque Involvement and Group Consciousness." *American Politics Research* 33:521–544.

Kabir, Nahid. A. 2013. *Young American Muslims: Dynamics of Identity*. Edinburgh, UK: Edinburgh University Press.

Kalkan, Kerem Ozan, Geoffrey C. Layman, and Eric M. Uslaner. 2009. "'Bands of Others?' Attitudes toward Muslims in Contemporary American Society." *Journal of Politics* 71:847–862.

Katz, Irwin, and Glenn R. Hass. 1988. "Racial Ambivalence and American Value Conflict: Correlational and Priming Studies of Dual Cognitive Structures." *Journal of Personality and Social Psychology* 55:893–905.

Klein, Oliver, Russell Spears, and Stephen Reicher. 2007. "Social Identity Performance: Extending the Strategic Side of SIDE." *Personality and Social Psychology Review* 11 (1): 1–18.

Lavrakas, Paul J., Charles D. Shuttles, Charlotte Steeh, and Howard Fienberg. 2007. "The State of Surveying Cell Phone Numbers in the United States: 2007 and Beyond." *Public Opinion Quarterly* 71 (5): 840–854.

Lean, Nathan. 2013. *The Islamophobia Industry: How the Right Manufactures Fear of Muslims.* New York: Pluto.

Lee, David S. 2009. "Training, Wages, and Sample Selection: Estimating Sharp Bounds on Treatment Effects." *Review of Economic Studies* 76:1071–1102.

Lee, Tiane L., and Susan T. Fiske. 2006. "Not an Outgroup, Not Yet an Ingroup: Immigrants in the Stereotype Content Model." *International Journal of Intercultural Relations* 30:751–768.

Leighley, Jan E. 1990. "Social Interaction and Contextual Influences on Political Participation." *American Politics Research* 4:459–475.

Li, Ruiqian. 2018. *Muddled Loyalty: A Study of Islamic Centers in Boston Area.* Master's thesis, Boston College. Available at http://hdl.handle.net/2345/bc-ir:108026.

Miller, Erin. 2018. "Global Terrorism Database Coding Notes: Las Vegas, 2017." National Consortium for the Study of Terrorism and Responses to Terrorism (START), December 7. Available at https://www.start.umd.edu/news/global-terrorism -database-coding-notes-las-vegas-2017.

Nelson, Thomas E., and Donald R. Kinder. 1996. "Issue Framing and Group Centrism in American Public Opinion." *Journal of Politics* 58 (4): 1055–1078.

New America Foundation. 2018. "Terrorism in America after 9/11." Available at https:// web.archive.org/web/20181231211445/https://www.newamerica.org/in-depth/ terrorism-in-america/what-threat-united-states-today.

Oaxaca, Ronald L. 1973. "Male-Female Wage Differentials in Urban Labor Markets." *International Economic Review* 14:693–709.

Pew Research Center. 2007. "Muslim Americans: Middle Class and Mostly Mainstream." Available at http://www.pewresearch.org/2007/05/22/muslim-americans-middle -class-and-mostly-mainstream.

Podsakoff, Philip M., Scott B. MacKenzie, Jeong-Yeon Lee, and Nathan P. Podsakoff. 2003. "Common Method Biases in Behavioral Research: A Critical Review of the Literature and Recommended Remedies." *Journal of Applied Psychology* 88:879–903.

Putnam, Robert D., and David E. Campbell. 2010. *American Grace: How Religion Divides and Unites Us.* New York: Simon and Schuster.

Rapoport, Robyn, and Kyle Berta. 2018. "Methodology Report: American Fears Survey, July 2108." Available at https://www.chapman.edu/wilkinson/research-centers/ babbie-center/_files/fear-2018/fear-V-methodology-report-ssrs.pdf.

Read, Jen'nan Ghazal. 2015. "Gender, Religious Identity, and Civic Engagement among Arab Muslims in the United States." *Sociology of Religion* 76:30–48.

Reynolds, Michael. 2004. "Homegrown Terror." *Bulletin of Atomic Scientists* 60:48–57.

Roccas, Sonia, and Marilynn Brewer. 2002. "Social Identity Complexity." *Personality and Social Psychology Review* 6:88–106.

Shelton, J. Nicole, Jennifer A. Richeson, and Jacquie D. Vorauer. 2006. "Threatened Identities and Interethnic Interactions." *European Review of Social Psychology* 17:321–358.

Shih, Margaret, Todd L. Pittinsky, and Nalini Ambady. 1999. "Stereotype Susceptibility: Identity Salience and Shifts in Quantitative Performance." *Psychological Science* 10 (1): 80–83.

Sides, John, and Kimberly Gross. 2013. "Stereotypes of Muslims and Support for the War on Terror." *Journal of Politics* 75:583–598.

Sirin, Selcuk R., and Michelle Fine. 2008. *Muslim American Youth: Understanding Hyphenated Identities through Multiple Methods.* New York: New York University Press.

Skerry, Peter. 2011. "The Muslim-American Muddle." *National Affairs* 37 (Fall): 14–37.

Southern Poverty Law Center. 2018. "Terror from the Right." Available at https://web .archive.org/web/20181224183236/https://www.splcenter.org/20180723/terror -right.

Steele, Claude M., Steven J. Spencer, and Joshua Aronson. 2002. "Contending with Group Image: The Psychology of Stereotype and Social Identity Threat." *Advances in Experimental Social Psychology* 34:379–440.

Stephenson, Emily. 2016. "Trump Calls for Surveillance at Mosques." *Huffington Post,* June 16. Available at http://www.huffingtonpost.com/entry/trump-calls-for -surveillance-of-mosques_us_5761b09fe4b0df4d586f0858.

Stone, Meighan. 2017. "Snake and Stranger: Media Coverage of Muslims and Refugee Policy." Harvard University Shorenstein Center on Media, Politics and Public Policy, June. Available at https://shorensteincenter.org/wp-content/uploads/2017/ 06/Media-Coverage-Muslims-Meighan-Stone.pdf?x78124.

Tajfel, Henri. 1979. "Individuals and Groups in Social Psychology." *British Journal of Social and Clinical Psychology* 18:183–190.

———. 1982. "Social Psychology of Intergroup Relations." *Annual Review of Psychology* 33:1–39.

Tajfel, Henri, and J. C. Turner. 1979. "An Integrative Theory of Intergroup Conflict." In *The Social Psychology of Intergroup Relations,* edited by W. G. Austen and S. Worschel, 33–47. Chicago: Nelson-Hall.

Telhami, Shibley. 2017. "How Trump Changed Americans' View of Islam—for the Better." Brookings Institution, January 28. Available at https://www.brookings.edu/ blog/markaz/2017/01/28/how-trump-changed-americans-view-of-islam-for-the -better.

Terman, R. 2017. "Islamophobia and Media Portrayals of Muslim Women: A Computational Text Analysis of U.S. News Coverage." *International Studies Quarterly* 61:489–502.

Townsend, Sarah S. M., Hazel R. Markus, and Hilary B. Bergsieker. 2009. "My Choice, Your Categories: The Denial of Multiracial Identities." *Journal of Social Issues* 65:185–204.

Turner, John C. 1987. *Rediscovering the Social Group: A Self-Categorization Theory.* New York: Blackwell.

Verba, Sidney, Kay Lehman Schlozman, and Henry E. Brady. 1995. *Voice and Equality: Civic Voluntarism in American Politics.* Cambridge, MA: Harvard University Press.

Verkuyten, Maykel. 2007. "Religious Group Identification and Inter-religious Relations." *Group Processes and Intergroup Relations* 10 (3): 341–357.

Weich, Scott, A. Sloggett, and Glyn Lewis. 2001. "Social Roles and the Gender Difference in Rates of the Common Mental Disorders in Britain: A 7-Year, Population-Based Cohort Study." *Psychological Medicine* 31:1055–1064.

Welborne, Bozena C., Aubrey L. Westfall, Özge Çelik Russell, and Sarah A. Tobin. 2018. *The Politics of the Headscarf in the United States.* Ithaca, NY: Cornell University Press.

Westfall, Aubrey, Özge Çelik Russell, Bozena Welborne, and Sarah Tobin. 2017. "Islamic Headcovering and Political Engagement: The Power of Social Networks." *Politics and Religion* 10 (1): 3–30.

Worthington, Everett L., Jr., Nathaniel G. Wade, Terry L. Hight, Michael E. McCullough, James T. Berry, Jennifer S. Ripley, Jack W. Berry, Michelle M. Schmitt, and Kevin H. Bursley. 2003. "The Religious Commitment Inventory-10: Development, Refinement, and Validation of a Brief Scale for Research and Counseling." *Journal of Counseling Psychology* 50 (1): 84–96.

Zaal, Mayida, Tahani Salah, and Michelle Fine. 2007. "The Weight of the Hyphen: Freedom, Fusion and Responsibility Embodied by Young Muslim-American Women during a Time of Surveillance." *Applied Development Science* 11:164–177.

Gauging Political Tolerance through a List Experiment

Findings from a Survey of Muslim Americans

YOUSSEF CHOUHOUD

Political theorists have long viewed intolerance as deleterious to democracy. From John Locke's call to abandon the imposition of religious conformity to J. S. Mill's advocacy for a "marketplace of ideas," the liberal foundations of tolerance in the public sphere are well established. Yet, despite being a cornerstone of liberal democracy, political tolerance remains a particularly difficult norm to inculcate. This is perhaps due to the gulf between its significance and its incidence that, for over sixty years, scholars have plumbed.

Despite this extensive inquiry, some blind spots remain in this literature. For example, the dozens of studies stemming from Samuel Stouffer's (1955) seminal work on political tolerance thus far have largely neglected the influence of minority status—and the particular experiences and worldviews that accompany it—in augmenting tolerance judgments. There are important differences between majority and minority citizens across various domains of public opinion (Kinder and Winter 2001; Kinder and Kam 2009; Peffley and Hurwitz 2010), and there is no reason to think that intolerance should constitute an exception to this tendency. Yet analyses of political intolerance almost exclusively draw on data from representative samples of the population at large (most often the General Social Survey), or otherwise random samples meant to approximate majoritarian attributes (e.g., religious affiliation [Eisenstein 2006]).

Additionally, within discrete categories of determinants, certain variables have not received their due attention. This is the case with studies gauging the ways in which religion influences tolerance judgments. Although scholars have evaluated the role of religious commitment, doctrinal belief, and practice, they have altogether overlooked the particularly relevant matter of views on salvation. That is, they have yet to consider whether *theological* intolerance maps to *political* intolerance. Although this link is more readily associated with, for instance, Early Modern Europe—an age when theological and literal battle lines were virtually one and the same—the issue may still be relevant today given the global resurgence of religion (Berger 1999). Indeed, despite the institutional decoupling of faith and politics, the perception that an uncompromising religious outlook negatively affects social order continues to hold sway (Huntington 1993).

This chapter tackles this topic, in part by employing a survey instrument novel to the study of political tolerance: the list experiment. Surveying respondents from a low-incidence population poses myriad challenges (Berry, Chouhoud, and Junn 2018). Given the added effort it takes to populate these samples, extra care should be taken to ensure the resultant data's validity. To this end, when social desirability may be a concern, shielded response techniques provide a means to guard against this potential source of bias by broaching sensitive topics in an unobtrusive way.

The subject of the current study is an especially salient minority: American Muslims. The opinions of this group hold particular utility for tolerance research given that liberalism not only institutionalizes the political rights of minorities but also assumes that these minorities reciprocally respect the rights of other groups in society. This latter expectation highlights a more pragmatic reason to examine this population. Namely, with anti-Muslim sentiment in the United States relatively high and periodically spiking in accordance with intermittent controversies (e.g., the so-called Ground Zero mosque),[1] investigating the attitudes of American Muslims themselves could shed light on the factors influencing negative appraisals of this community. Indeed, animosity and intolerance toward this religious minority (which previous chapters in this book elaborate on) may be motivated in part by a belief that Muslims in America are particularly dogmatic and wish to impose their worldview rather than allow all perspectives to be heard. The movement to ban any recourse to sharia in several state legislatures across the country, for example, speaks to the perception that Islam promotes a

---

1. One meta-analysis of polling data in America since 9/11 demonstrates that in the years following the terrorist attacks, highly unfavorable attitudes toward Muslims began to slightly subside only to climb once more beginning in 2010, around the time of the Park51 controversy, eventually reaching levels at or above those of late 2001 (Kurzman 2014).

legal and political system that seeks to supersede existing U.S. laws and government (Cesari 2013).

Analyzing original survey data coupled with an embedded list experiment shows two key findings: (1) American Muslim political intolerance is not discernibly triggered by generally disagreeable ideas (that is, those that are antireligion) but is focused, instead, on groups specifically espousing intolerance toward Muslims and Islam; and (2) theological intolerance, operationalized as exclusivist views toward salvation, exerts a significant and negative effect on political tolerance levels, but this disposition does not render one immune from the positive effects of education and acculturation. In practical terms, these findings undermine the contention that American Muslims are invariably intolerant and highlight the need for more empirically grounded examinations of this community's beliefs and actions. Methodologically, this study outlines a means to leverage the added internal validity of list experiments while sacrificing relatively little in terms of data richness. Additionally, the results point to salvific exclusivity constituting a meaningful standalone measure of religiosity, though more research is needed to determine the breadth of its useful application to tolerance studies.

Political Tolerance: Development and Determinants

The modern study of political tolerance arguably began with the seminal work of Samuel Stouffer (1955), who aimed to empirically examine whether liberal norms actually held sway within the American public. More specifically, conducting his research in the midst of the McCarthy-led Red Scare, Stouffer sought to gauge whether Americans' attitudes were in line with the country's widespread political repression. The overall sentiment in his analysis was unequivocal: Americans were more than willing to limit the rights and freedoms of groups (not just communists but also socialists and atheists) whose beliefs challenged their own.

Stouffer's work spawned a vast body of research outlining the determinants of political tolerance (commonly conceptualized as the degree to which one is willing to "put up with" groups they highly dislike [Sullivan, Piereson, and Marcus 1982]). Scholars have examined whether elites are systematically more tolerant than the mass public (Jackman 1972; McClosky and Brill-Scheuer 1983), alternatively confirmed or refuted Stouffer's prediction that tolerance levels in America would increase over time (J. Davis 1975; Nunn, Crockett, and Williams 1978; Sullivan, Piereson, and Marcus 1982; Mondak and Sanders 2003), and delineated a range of individual and contextual determinants of intolerance. Among this last set of studies, those elaborating the role of minority status and religiosity inform much of the following analysis.

Minority Status

Little attention has been paid to the role minority status may play as a determinant of political tolerance. One notable exception is Darren Davis (1995), who conducted the only systematic analysis of the nature of intolerance among African Americans. His findings call into question the perception that, because of cultural and socioeconomic disparities, blacks in America are predisposed to authoritarian beliefs (Dahl 1956; Lipset 1960). Specifically, Davis concludes that black intolerance is heightened when it comes to the Ku Klux Klan while registering no discernable difference from typical levels of intolerance exhibited by nonblacks toward "everyday racists" (1995, 12). This suggests that, at least among one racial minority in the United States, intolerance is not a blanket and involuntary reaction stemming from cultural proclivities, but a conscious decision to secure the group from hatred and violence.

Other tolerance studies that comparably focus on minority groups in America are rare. Most of these works were largely occasioned by specific episodes. For example, James Gibson and Richard Bingham (1984) examine American Jews' tolerance in light of an infamous legal dispute involving neo-Nazis in Skokie, Illinois. Likewise, Gibson (1987) analyzes the lead-up to a Ku Klux Klan rally in Houston, Texas, to gauge homosexuals' political tolerance. Similarly, although they do not intensely examine a single incident, Paul Djupe and Brian Calfano nonetheless open their study of American Muslims by sketching a dispute in which the Miami-Dade Transportation Authority removed ads deemed "offensive to Islam" from their buses (2012, 516). Given its clear substantive relevance, this latter study deserves further consideration.

To date, Djupe and Calfano (2012) have conducted the only academic study of tolerance—and one of the relatively few on public opinion, more generally—focused on American Muslims. As such, their findings naturally carry a lot of weight. This makes it all the more notable (and normatively troubling) that their findings relate a mostly negative tale. Specifically, after prompting their sample of American Muslims to consider the views of someone who (in the abstract) is against Christianity and Islam, respectively, Djupe and Calfano report a marked dearth of tolerant responses. Only about 30 percent of respondents chose the civil libertarian option in any of the three anti-Christian scenarios, while even fewer were tolerant of the same actions when directed against Islam: 20 percent would acquiesce to an anti-Muslim speech in their community, 9 percent would allow a person against Islam to teach at a university, and 6 percent would permit a book critical of Muslims in their local public library. What is more, the authors find that both "mosque attendance" and "Koran literalism" predict greater intolerance. These latter results point to a second set of relevant determinants.

Religiosity

From the earliest studies and for decades thereafter, scholars have consistently found a link between religious conviction and intolerance. Stouffer's (1955) original results initially suggested that regular churchgoers were generally less tolerant that those who infrequently attended services or did not attend at all. Subsequent research added more nuance to this relationship by examining additional dimensions of religious life, yet the underlying notion of "more religious" mapping to "more intolerant" remained overwhelmingly stable (Nunn, Crockett, and Williams 1978; Sullivan, Piereson, and Marcus 1982; McClosky and Brill-Scheuer 1983).

Despite these steady results, not all scholars are convinced of the resolutely negative link between religion and tolerance. Beverly Busch (1998) contends that prior findings, given their reliance on a fixed-group tolerance battery (carried over from Stouffer 1955) and blunt gauges of religiosity, are mainly measurement artifacts rather than genuine representations of underlying attitudes. Marie Eisenstein (2006) similarly opts for content-controlled (or "least-liked") political tolerance measures[2] (Sullivan, Piereson, and Marcus 1982) and couples her analysis with better specified religion variables. She concludes, after additionally applying oft-neglected psychological variables into her sequential equation model, that neither doctrinal orthodoxy nor religious commitment has a direct effect on political tolerance.[3] Adding still more nuance to this association, Ryan Burge (2013) finds that increased church attendance positively correlates with tolerance, while biblical literalism has a strongly negative influence on tolerant responses. Thus, while the preponderance of evidence still suggests that religiosity (variably defined)

---

2. See the "Data and Methods" section later in the chapter for elaboration on the difference between the fixed-group and content-controlled measures of political tolerance.

3. Notably, however, Eisenstein (2006) does find an indirect effect for these two variables. Specifically, doctrinal orthodoxy increased threat perception, which in turn decreased tolerance, whereas religious commitment negatively influenced secure personality, the latter being a positive predictor of tolerance.

exerts a negative effect on tolerance (Gibson 2010), this link is neither as airtight nor as comprehensive as once believed.

Hypotheses

In light of these extant findings and the current political and social atmosphere in America, two hypotheses guide the following analysis. The first examines whether American Muslim political intolerance is narrowly or broadly distributed. On the one hand, majoritarian accounts of political intolerance in America find it to be generally high but pluralistic in nature, rather than singling out a particular group (Sullivan, Pierson, and Marcus 1982; Gibson 2007). On the other hand, Darren Davis (1995) finds that African American intolerance is acutely directed toward the Ku Klux Klan and theorizes that this is a conscious decision motivated by the particular threat that the group poses. This concentration of African American intolerance is put in stark relief when compared to the comparatively much more tolerant responses toward other disliked groups, including unspecified racists.

I contend that American Muslim intolerance is similarly focused on Islamophobic groups (that is, those groups that are specifically anti-Muslim in their actions and speech) rather than on groups broadly against religion. This claim is generally in accordance with Davis's (1995) theory while somewhat diverging from Djupe and Calfano's (2012) results. The hypothesis, however, is not meant to equate the legacy of the Ku Klux Klan with modern-day Islamophobia—clearly the former has had a much more devastating and lasting impact on its target group. Yet, at the same time, one should not discount the very real threats that Muslims face on account of their faith. Indeed, in keeping with the rising trend in anti-Muslim sentiment (Kurzman 2014), hate crimes targeting Muslims have spiked in recent years to near record highs (Spross 2012). Islamophobic groups, therefore, should elicit a more intense perception of threat from American Muslims than antireligionists (that is, those groups broadly against religion).

> H1: American Muslim intolerance is significantly higher toward Islamophobic groups compared to antireligionists.

While the first hypothesis highlighted considerations particular to American Muslims, the second hypothesis outlines an association with a potentially more general application. Specifically, although religiosity has featured prominently in numerous tolerance studies, scholars have yet to examine whether theological intolerance, conceptualized as exclusivist views on salvation, heightens political intolerance. Speaking to this potential link, Jean-Jacques Rousseau ([1763] 1987) asserts, "It is impossible to live in peace with those one believes to be damned. . . . Whenever theological intolerance is allowed, it is impossible for it not to have some civil effect." Though not as absolute in his conviction, John Rawls, generally a champion of religious freedom, nonetheless anticipates that exclusivist visions of salvation will decline in popularity as individuals holding various comprehensive doctrines strive toward an overlapping consensus: "It is difficult, if not impossible, to believe in the damnation of those with whom we have, with trust and confidence, long and fruitfully cooperated in maintaining a just society" (1993, cited in Fadel 2013, 36). Taken together, these two quotes establish the expectation that (1) theological intolerance correlates with political intolerance, and (2) those who hold an exclusivist view of salvation are resistant to the forces that typically augment tolerance (namely, education and socialization).

H2a: Salvific exclusivity is associated with higher political intolerance.

H2b: Education level and nativity do not attenuate the negative effect of theological intolerance on political intolerance.

Data and Methods

To test the preceding hypotheses, I analyze original survey data from a sample of American Muslims recruited online from April 26 to May 30, 2014. The link to this survey was distributed through representatives of major American Muslim organizations and websites across America through email and social media across the political and ideological spectrum.[4] Additional solicitation of participants occurred through the enlistment of diverse religious and community leaders to advertise the survey to their respective networks.[5] As an incentive, each participant was given an opportunity to enter their email in a drawing for one of twenty Amazon.com gift cards valued at ten dollars each.[6]

---

4. These include, inter alia, the Muslim Public Affairs Council, the Council on American-Islamic Relations, Muslim for Progressive Values, and MuslimMatters.org.

5. These include, inter alia, Suhaib Webb, a popular imam based out of Boston at the time of the survey; Wajahat Ali, a journalist and (again, at the time) television host with Al Jazeera America; Mona Eltahawy, a well-known feminist activist and journalist; and Rabia Chaudry, a civic leader, lawyer, and columnist.

6. The online form for the drawing was separate from the main survey, and multiple assurances were given to the participants that their email addresses were in no way linked to their responses.

A total of 465 eligible respondents were ultimately obtained through this process.[7] This chain-referral recruitment technique mirrored the objective of respondent-driven sampling (RDS),[8] though admittedly lacked the latter's statistical inference as the link through which participants reached the survey was not tracked. Nonetheless, the final sample's demographic breakdown compares favorably to a nationally representative sample of American Muslims (Pew Research Center 2011) on certain dimensions, particularly those associated with religiosity, while diverging on others (see this chapter's appendix for a comparison).

To gauge political tolerance, I employ a survey instrument novel to this domain of public opinion research: a list experiment. Given the difficulties of sampling American Muslims, this shielded response technique helps ensure that the effort is worthwhile by improving the study's internal validity. Before elaborating this method, it is worth reviewing the predominant political tolerance measures in the discipline.

To date, scholars have relied on two primary means of measuring political tolerance. With the "fixed-group" method, each respondent in a survey is asked a battery of questions about the civil liberties they would be willing to extend to each of several groups (usually no more than five) from a static set. With the "content-controlled" method, respondents are first asked to identify their "least-liked" group[9] from a list (or write in their own choice if the list does not include their relevant group) and are subsequently asked roughly the same battery of questions as in the fixed-group method.

Combining aspects of both these measurement techniques, the list experiment I employed gauges American Muslim intolerance toward antireligionists, on the one hand, and Islamophobic/anti-Muslim groups, on the other. The logic behind list experiments is fairly straightforward. First, a subset of the sample is randomly assigned into a baseline condition, presented with a list of items specific to that condition, and then asked how many of those items they would choose in response to a particular prompt. In this case, the items are groups that elicit various levels of antipathy, and the corresponding prompts gauge respondents' willingness to extend these

---

7. This final tally corresponds to the total number of individuals who completed the survey and met the two fundamental criteria of being an American citizen and self-identifying as a Muslim.

8. More specifically, the goal of RDS is to attenuate the bias in an initial convenience sample by reaching a sufficiently broad cross-section of the target population in successive sampling waves (Heckathorn 1997).

9. Scholars will often also ask respondents to apply the political tolerance battery to their second or even third least-liked group for additional layers of comparison (e.g., Sullivan, Piereson, and Marcus 1982; Gibson 2013).

groups civil liberties as well as the degree of threat they perceive from these groups.

Second, a treatment condition presents the same question (or set of questions) along with the same choice of items as the baseline group, but with the addition of the researcher's item of interest (in this case, the group for which we want to measure political tolerance and threat perception toward). Subsequently, a difference-in-means test between the baseline and treatment conditions provides an unbiased estimate of the percentage of the sample population that would truthfully choose that item of interest if presented as a direct question. For example, if the question asked how many of the listed groups a respondent would oppose giving a speech in their neighborhood, and the mean number of groups chosen in the baseline condition was 2.10, comparing that result with the mean of the treatment condition, say, 2.55, allows us to estimate that 45 percent of the sample population would be unwilling to allow members of the group added as an extra item in the treatment condition to give a public speech.

List experiments are generally employed to ascertain revealed preferences when stated preferences can potentially be swayed by a social desirability norm, such as in the case of ascertaining racist attitudes, or when the survey design may be affecting the responses. In the first instance, American Muslims may be hesitant to express their willingness to limit another's civil liberties in light of, on the one hand, the atmosphere of suspicion toward their own democratic bona fides and, on the other hand, the suspicion that they themselves may have toward anyone collecting data on their community. The large number of survey participants who, despite the study's unobtrusive research design, nonetheless chose the "prefer not to answer" response option speaks to this concern.[10]

Survey effects may similarly come into play when surveying this population. Despite sound sampling strategy and standard question wording, for example, Djupe and Calfano (2012) nonetheless record a rather high percentage of Muslims willing to remove an anti-Islam book from their public library (96 percent). Typically, this prompt elicits close to the least amount of intolerance among respondents (see, e.g., Djupe, Lewis, and Jelen 2016). Thus, in addition to blunting the effect of asking sensitive questions, employing a list experiment also guards against potentially skewed results from nonobvious survey effects.

---

10. Notably, over 50 of the 465 eligible respondents in the final sample opted for that response on one of the four questions used to construct the political tolerance scale used in the multivariate regression on the pooled data below and thus were excluded from that analysis.

After an initial screening to determine if participants met the minimum requirements to take the survey (see note 8), respondents were randomized into one of four groups corresponding to a single baseline condition and three treatment conditions. Each respondent was presented with a list corresponding to his or her treatment and asked to indicate how many of the groups on that list (not which specific ones) should have their civil liberties limited in the manner described. Three of the four questions mirrored those in Djupe and Calfano's (2012) study (asking whether respondents would support a ban on members of the group teaching in a college, a ban on them giving a speech in their neighborhood, or the removal from the local public library of a book written by one of their members) with an additional query asking how many of the groups a respondent would support banning from running for public office. A question gauging sociotropic threat rounds out the list experiment portion of the questionnaire, wherein respondents are asked to indicate how many of the groups they believe are a threat to their way of life. Threat perception is one of the most consistent predictors of political intolerance (e.g., Sullivan, Piereson, and Marcus 1982; Marcus et al. 1995; Gibson and Gouws 2003; Davis and Silver 2004; Sniderman, Hagendoorn, and Prior 2004) and is a staple measure in any tailored tolerance study (i.e., one that does not rely exclusively on existing survey data).

This five-question list experiment was presented to each of the four randomized conditions with the variation being in the enumerated items respondents could choose from. In the *baseline* condition, the list included only the four control items: Nazis, the Ku Klux Klan, Christian fundamentalists, and homosexual rights activists. The *AR treatment* condition included each of the four items from the baseline group, with the addition of "anti-religionists." The *AM treatment* condition included the four control items, plus "Islamophobic/anti-Muslim groups." Finally, the *dual treatment* condition, which serves largely as a robustness check, included the four control items with the addition of both "anti-religionists" and "Islamophobic/anti-Muslim groups." The questions in the tolerance battery are as follows.

- How many of the above groups would you support banning their members from teaching at your local college?
- How many of the above groups would you support banning their members from giving a public speech in your community?
- How many of the above groups would you support removing a book written by one of their members from your local public library?
- How many of the above groups would you support banning their members from running for office in your local district?

Christian Fundamentalists
Homosexual Rights Activists
Nazis
Ku Klux Klan
[Anti-Religionists]
[Islamophobic / Anti-Muslim Groups]

How many of the above groups do you believe are a threat to your way of life?
  ○ 0 ○ 1 ○ 2 ○ 3 ○ 4 ○ [5] ○ [6] ○ Prefer not to answer

Figure 10.1 Example of a list experiment question

Figure 10.1 provides an example of the survey prompt corresponding to the list experiment portion (in this case, gauging sociotropic threat, or threats to one's way of life), with treatment-specific options in brackets.

Alongside the experimental component, the survey included several direct measures of key demographic and religion variables. In addition to questions about age, sex (female), race/ethnicity, and education, the questionnaire also asked whether respondents were either born in the United States or immigrated prior to their primary education (coded as born in America). The theoretical rationale for this variable's inclusion is that one would expect democratic norms, among them political tolerance, to be more ingrained in those individuals whose upbringing in America began from an early age.

The questionnaire's religiosity battery gauged mosque attendance, influence of Islam on the respondent's life, and frequency of prayer, drawing on the standard dimensions of behavior, belief, and belonging (with adjustments made to fit the phrasing within an Islamic frame).[11] A measurement of belief in Qur'an literalism similarly accords with the usual factors tested in tolerance studies but goes beyond the typical dichotomous rendering. Specifically, the question offers the respondent a choice to maintain the text is the literal word of God while acknowledging that some of the content is metaphoric, in addition to the standard options of, on the one hand, the text being literal in origin and interpretation and, on the other hand, the text being a book of history written by men.

The survey also includes a novel measure of religiosity, salvific exclusivity, which assesses the degree to which a respondent holds exclusionary views of the afterlife. Drawing on Mohammad Khalil's (2012) tripartite ty-

---

11. So as not to assume away bias through the possible priming of religious identity, the survey randomly assigned respondents to receive the religiosity battery either before or after the experimental component gauging political tolerance. Subsequent analysis demonstrated that the question order exerted no discernable influence on the responses.

pology of exclusivist, inclusivist, and pluralist interpretations of the hereafter in classical Islamic thought, four options (in addition to "prefer not to answer") were presented to respondents: (1) "Islam is the only religion that leads to Heaven"; (2) "Islam is the only religion that leads to Heaven, yet non-Muslims may be eligible for salvation if they did not receive the message of Islam or received only a distorted version"; (3) "Believers of any Abrahamic faith are equally eligible to enter Heaven, but not those who practice other faiths or disbelieve in God"; and (4) "All are equally eligible for salvation, regardless of belief." The resulting data thus allows the first empirical mapping of theological intolerance to political intolerance. Naturally, this particular operationalization is constructed with the target sample in mind; however, a more general version can be fashioned for broader application.

Results and Discussion

Analysis of these data supports the hypothesis that American Muslims distinguish between the targeted hatred of Islamophobic groups and the general disagreeableness of antireligionists. Comparing pooled political intolerance counts (i.e., the total number of groups that a respondent chose for each of the four scenarios presented to them) in Table 10.1 evidences that antireligionists do not trigger a statistically distinguishable level of political intolerance from the control group, while the Islamophobic treatment is statistically significant and meaningfully different in magnitude compared to both the control group and the AR treatment condition. Although no population percentage estimates can be derived from these aggregated results, the comparison is nonetheless indicative of the general finding throughout the remaining analyses.

The disaggregated data in Table 10.2 highlight the domains in which intolerance manifests most acutely. The most glaring finding is that none of

TABLE 10.1: POLITICAL INTOLERANCE SCORE (DIFFERENCE IN MEANS VERSUS BASELINE)

	AR treatment 7.30 (max = 20) (n = 99)	AM treatment 8.88 (max = 20) (n = 102)
Baseline 6.98 (max = 16) (n = 95)	0.32 (0.77)	1.90** (0.74)
AR treatment 7.30 (max = 20) (n = 99)	—	1.58* (0.85)

Note: Standard errors are in parentheses.
*$p < 0.05$; **$p < 0.01$.

TABLE 10.2: PERCENTAGE INTOLERANCE (DIFFERENCE IN MEANS VERSUS
BASELINE)

	Toward antireligionists	Toward Islamophobes
Give speech	25%	63%**
	(0.23)	(0.23)
Teach at local college	−5%	78%***
	(0.19)	(0.19)
Run for office	19%	33%†
	(0.23)	(0.23)
Book in library	−6%	15%
	(0.23)	(0.24)

Note: Standard errors are in parentheses. The baseline and both treatment groups each had approximately
  100 observations.
†$p < 0.10$; *$p < 0.05$; **$p < 0.01$; ***$p < 0.001$.

the prompts within the AR treatment elicited a statistically distinguishable
response from the baseline treatment. These results lend tentative support to
my hypothesis that those against religion, generally, do not trigger inordi-
nately high intolerant attitudes among American Muslims.[12] Indeed, in the
cumulative General Social Survey (GSS) data from 1972–2006, the questions
gauging tolerance toward antireligionists yield comparable or even higher
totals: speech, 29 percent; teach, 49 percent; book, 33 percent.

The results for the AM treatment tell an entirely different story. The only
prompt that fails to yield statistical significance is the one asking respondents about the removal of a book from the public library. With regard to
the other tolerance measures, 63 percent of the population sample are willing to support banning Islamophobic groups from giving a speech in their
neighborhood, with 78 percent willing to ban them from teaching at their
local college. These high figures could be due to the belief that limiting the
civil liberties of anti-Muslim groups would provide added security from targeted hatred, in general, and protect children from the ramifications of that
hatred, in particular. The prompt on banning groups from running for office, however, obtains neither the same magnitude nor the same level of statistical significance as either the speech or teaching scenarios. On its face,
this result seems somewhat counterintuitive; however, prior research has
shown that the degree to which one believes the target group can actually
wield power in the political system does not condition tolerance judgments
(e.g., Gibson and Gouws 2003).

---

12. This supporting evidence is tempered by the less-than-ideal sample sizes,
which lead to the strictly speaking uninterruptable results in the teach and book
prompts.

TABLE 10.3: PERCENTAGE THREATENED (DIFFERENCE IN MEANS VERSUS
BASELINE)

	Toward antireligionists	Toward Islamophobes
Sociotropic threat	29%[†]	59%***
	(0.20)	(0.20)

Note: Standard errors are in parentheses. The baseline and both treatment groups each had approximately
100 observations.
†*p* < 0.10; **p* < 0.05; ***p* < 0.01; ****p* < 0.001.

Turning to the analysis of threat perception, Table 10.3 shows that 59 percent of the population sample finds Islamophobic groups threatening to their way of life compared to 29 percent who feel this way about antireligionists. This latter finding speaks to the general validity of this approach in that it allows for greater confidence that what is being measured throughout this experiment is the actual treatment effect rather than the intent to treat.

Multivariate regression analysis of the pooled data highlights additional noteworthy results. Such an analysis is uncommon for list experiments, which often focus exclusively on point estimates for the item of interest rather than a general disposition common to all the list items, given that this underlying attitude is often meaningless. For example, in studies measuring latent racism, the shared strand between the item testing this attitude and the control items is, trivially, things that the respondent does not care for. In the present study, however, the control items along with the items of interest collectively tap political intolerance, thereby providing the basis for a scaled variable.

For ease of interpretation, the key variables of interest—political tolerance and sociotropic threat—are all rescaled from 0 to 1 as a function of the total count for each respondent given the total possible count available for their treatment condition.[13] Figure 10.2 further subsets the data on tolerance into quartiles, demonstrating a fairly stable distribution from the lowest to highest levels of intolerance. Prior to analysis, the sample was weighted (using iterated proportional fitting, also known as "raking") to the Pew Research Center (2011) percentages for age, gender, and education. The resulting weights ranged from .19 to 5.08.

Figure 10.3 displays political intolerance as a function of threat, demographics, and religiosity. In line with prior research, the effect of sociotropic threat is statistically and substantively the most significant predictor of intolerant judgments. Those born in America are more tolerant than foreign-born American Muslims, which, coupled with the effect of education,

---

13. Poisson regressions were run with the raw count data for these two scales with identical results in terms of statistical significance.

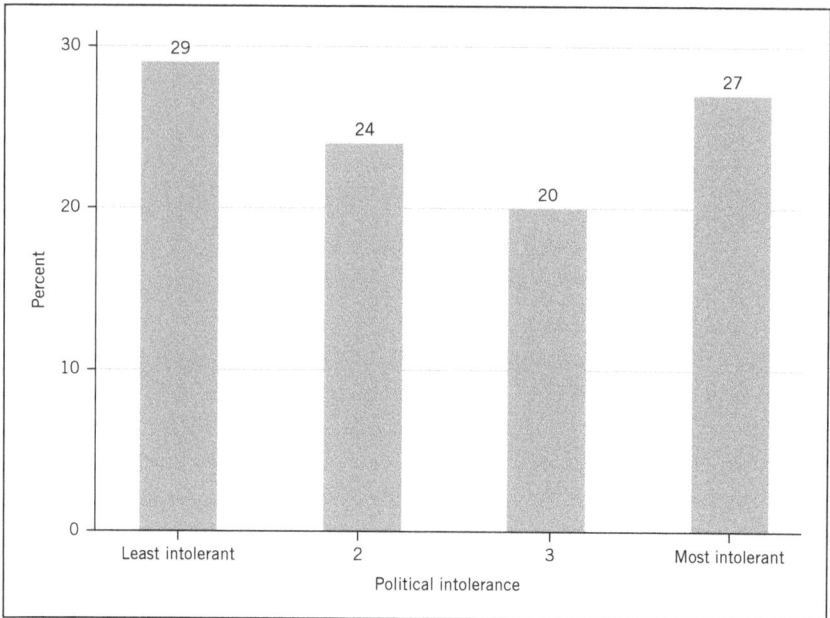

Figure 10.2 Distribution of political intolerance

suggests that respondents with more exposure to America's civil libertarian norms tend to exhibit those ideals attitudinally. Somewhat surprisingly, none of the religiosity variables exert a discernible impact on a respondent's level of political tolerance, save for salvific exclusivity: those with exclusivist views on salvation are more intolerant than those subscribing to pluralistic interpretations of the afterlife.

Given that exclusivist views on salvation seem to push respondents toward intolerance, are those who hold such beliefs less susceptible to the factors that typically pull individuals toward more tolerant attitudes? It does not appear so. Figure 10.4 plots the predicted probability that respondents would be in the "most intolerant" quartile as a function of holding either pluralist or exclusivist beliefs in salvation. Although pluralists start at a little over 20 percent likelihood and exclusivists at a little over 50 percent, these probabilities diminish for each group with each added level of education. Similarly, as Figure 10.5 shows, those respondents born in the United States have a lower likelihood than their foreign-born counterparts (all else equal) to provide highly intolerant judgments. Indeed, this result is likely conservative as the survey included only American citizens and not more recent immigrants. Thus, the negative effect of holding salvifically exclusive views does not seem to be uniquely intractable. This finding further undermines

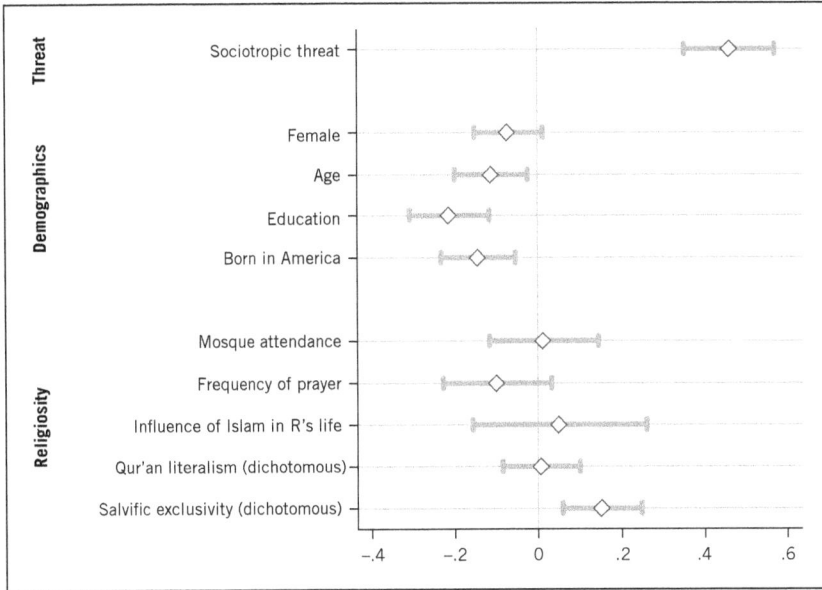

Figure 10.3 Determinants of American Muslim political intolerance (weighted)
Note: Numbers are OLS regression coefficients (with 95 percent confidence intervals). Race/ethnicity and treatment assignment are included in the analysis but excluded from the model.

the contention that American Muslims are, on account of their faith, particularly dogmatic or antidemocratic.

Conclusion

This study sought to expand the paucity of empirical literature on minority political tolerance. The experimental data support the hypothesis that American Muslims intolerance is targeted rather than invariable; groups that are explicitly anti-Muslim elicit intolerance to a significantly higher degree than unspecified antireligionists. Multivariate analysis of the observational data further elaborates the role of key determinants in this dynamic. In particular, I demonstrate the utility of theological intolerance as a meaningful predictor of political intolerance, while also highlighting that the negative effect of exclusivist belief in salvation is far from insurmountable. These findings thus suggest that future studies examining the influence of religiosity on tolerance should incorporate salvific exclusivity in their empirical models.

On a more practical level, the preceding analysis undermines Islamophobic contentions that Muslims in America are broadly and deeply intolerant, and thus not adopting (or adapting to) liberal democratic norms. More

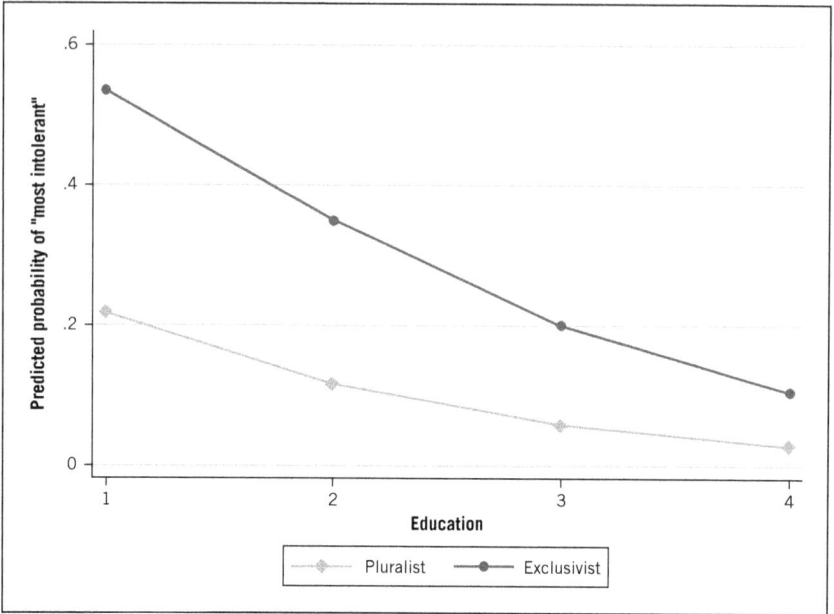

Figure 10.4 Marginal effects of salvific exclusivity by education

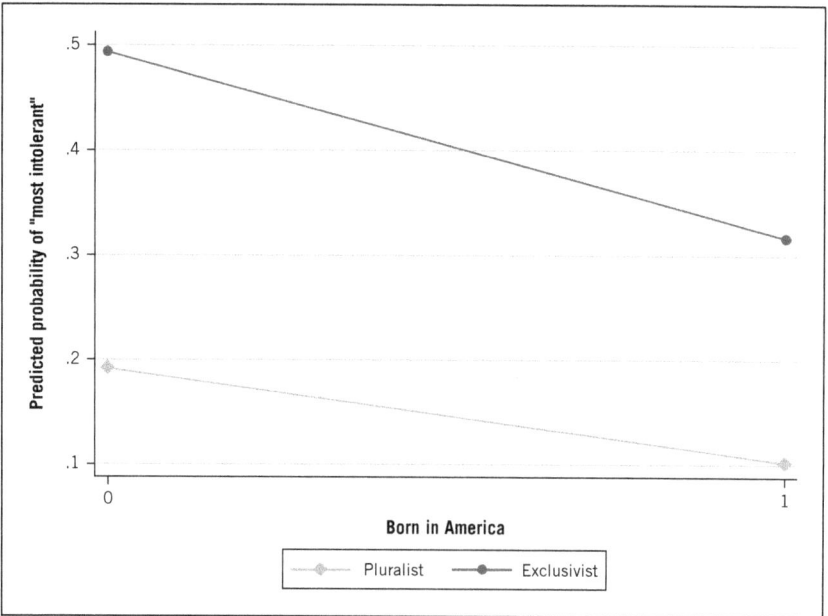

Figure 10.5 Marginal effects of salvific exclusivity by nativity

generally, this study underscores the need for further research on the attitudes and behaviors of minority groups in America. In the absence of such systematic examinations, it is clear that isolated anecdotes and unfounded accusations will continue to cloud our understanding of these increasingly vulnerable populations.

Appendix

TABLE 10A.1: SAMPLE COMPARISON

Demographic and religious measures	Pew 2011 (%)	Current study (%)
Female	45	61
Born in the United States	37	79*
Sunni	65	84
Nonwhite	70	60
College graduate	15	40
Age 18–29	36	50
Age 40–54	18	16
Offers five daily prayers	48	48
Attends mosque at least weekly	47	48

* The survey question for this variable asked not only whether the respondent was born in the United States but also whether he or she immigrated to America before age five. Thus, this figure is likely inflated. Moreover, the survey excluded those who were not American citizens. This criterion, given that 30 percent of foreign-born Muslims in America are not naturalized citizens (Pew 2011), also likely skewed the tally in the current study.

REFERENCES

Berger, Peter, ed. 1999. *The Desecularization of the World: The Resurgence of Religion in World Politics*. Grand Rapids, MI: William B. Eerdmans.

Berry, Justin, Youssef Chouhoud, and Jane Junn. 2018. "Reaching beyond Low-Hanging Fruit: Surveying Low Incidence Populations." In *The Oxford Handbook of Polling and Survey Methods*, edited by Lonna Rae Atkeson and R. Michael Alvarez, 181–206. New York: Oxford University Press.

Burge, Ryan. 2013. "Using Matching to Investigate the Relationship between Religion and Tolerance." *Politics and Religion* 6 (2): 264–281.

Busch, Beverly G. 1998. "Faith, Truth, and Tolerance: Religion and Political Tolerance in the United States." Ph.D. diss., University of Nebraska.

Cesari, Jocelyne. 2013. *Why the West Fears Islam: An Exploration of Muslims in Liberal Democracies*. New York: Palgrave Macmillan.

Dahl, Robert A. 1956. *A Preface to Democratic Theory*. Chicago: University of Chicago Press.

Davis, Darren W. 1995. "Exploring Black Political Intolerance." *Political Behavior* 17 (1): 1–22.

Davis, Darren W., and Brian D. Silver. 2004. "Civil Liberties vs. Security: Public Opinion in the Context of the Terrorist Attacks on America." *American Journal of Political Science* 48 (1): 28–46.

Davis, James A. 1975. "Communism, Conformity, Cohorts, and Categories: American Tolerance in 1954 and 1972–73." *American Journal of Sociology* 81 (3): 491–513.

Djupe, Paul A., and Brian R. Calfano. 2012. "American Muslim Investment in Civil Society Political Discussion, Disagreement, and Tolerance." *Political Research Quarterly* 65 (3): 516–528.

Djupe, Paul A., Andrew R. Lewis, and Ted G. Jelen. 2016. "Rights, Reflection, and Reciprocity: Implications of the Same-Sex Marriage Debate for Tolerance and the Political Process." *Politics and Religion* 9 (3): 630–648.

Eisenstein, Marie A. 2006. "Rethinking the Relationship between Religion and Political Tolerance in the US." *Political Behavior* 28 (4): 327–348.

Fadel, Mohammad. 2013. "'No Salvation Outside Islam': Muslim Modernists, Democratic Politics, and Islamic Theological Exclusivism." In *Between Heaven and Hell: Islam, Salvation, and the Fate of Others*, edited by Mohammad Hassan Khalil, 35–63. New York: Oxford University Press.

Gibson, James L. 1987. "Homosexuals and the Ku Klux Klan: A Contextual Analysis of Political Tolerance." *Western Political Quarterly* 40 (3): 427–448.

———. 2007. "Political Intolerance in the Context of Democratic Theory." In *Oxford Handbook of Political Behavior*, edited by Russell J. Dalton and Hans-Dieter Klingemann, 323–341. Oxford: Oxford University Press.

———. 2010. "The Political Consequences of Religiosity: Does Religion Always Cause Political Intolerance?" In *Religion and Democracy in the United States: Danger or Opportunity?* edited by Alan Wolfe and Ira Katznelson, 147–175. New York: Russell Sage Foundation.

———. 2013. "Measuring Political Tolerance and General Support for Pro–Civil Liberties Policies Notes, Evidence, and Cautions." *Public Opinion Quarterly* 77 (S1): 45–68.

Gibson, James L., and Richard D. Bingham. 1984. "Skokie, Nazis, and the Elitist Theory of Democracy." *Political Research Quarterly* 37 (1): 32–47.

Gibson, James L., and Amanda Gouws. 2003. *Overcoming Intolerance in South Africa: Experiments in Democratic Persuasion*. New York: Cambridge University Press.

Heckathorn, Douglas D. 1997. "Respondent-Driven Sampling: A New Approach to the Study of Hidden Populations." *Social Problems* 44 (2): 174–199.

Huntington, Samuel P. 1993. "The Clash of Civilizations?" *Foreign Affairs* 72 (3): 22–49.

Jackman, Robert W. 1972. "Political Elites, Mass Publics, and Support for Democratic Principles." *Journal of Politics* 34 (3): 753–773.

Khalil, Mohammad Hassan. 2012. *Islam and the Fate of Others: The Salvation Question*. New York: Oxford University Press.

Kinder, Donald R., and Cindy D. Kam. 2009. *Us against Them: Ethnocentric Foundations of American Opinion*. Chicago: University of Chicago Press.

Kinder, Donald R., and Nicholas Winter. 2001. "Exploring the Racial Divide: Blacks, Whites, and Opinion on National Policy." *American Journal of Political Science* 45 (2): 439–456.

Kurzman, Charles. 2014. "Anti-Muslim Sentiment Rising in the U.S.: What Is Happening to Religious Tolerance?" *ISLAMiCommentary*, February 13. Available at https://web.archive.org/web/20170214045922/https://islamicommentary.org/2014/02/anti-muslim-sentiment-rising-in-the-u-s-what-is-happening-to-religious-tolerance.

Lipset, Seymour Martin. 1960. *Political Man: The Social Bases of Politics*. Garden City, NY: Doubleday.

Marcus, George E., John L. Sullivan, Elizabeth Theiss-Morse, and Sandra L. Wood. 1995. *With Malice toward Some: How People Make Civil Liberties Judgments*. New York: Cambridge University Press.

McClosky, Herbert, and Alida Brill-Scheuer. 1983. *Dimensions of Tolerance: What Americans Believe about Civil Liberties*. New York: Russell Sage Foundation.

Mondak, Jeffery J., and Mitchell S. Sanders. 2003. "Tolerance and Intolerance, 1976–1998." *American Journal of Political Science* 47 (3): 492–502.

Nunn, Clyde Z., Harry J. Crockett, and Allen J. Williams. 1978. *Tolerance for Nonconformity*. San Francisco: Jossey-Bass.

Peffley, Mark, and Jon Hurwitz. 2010. *Justice in America: The Separate Realities of Blacks and Whites*. Cambridge: Cambridge University Press.

Pew Research Center. 2011. "Muslim Americans: No Signs of Growth in Alienation or Support for Extremism." Available at http://www.pewforum.org/2011/08/30/muslim-americans-no-signs-of-growth-in-alienation-or-support-for-extremism.

Rawls, John. 1993. *Political Liberalism*. New York: Columbia University Press.

Rousseau, Jean-Jacques. (1763) 1987. *On the Social Contract*. Reprint. Indianapolis, IN: Hackett.

Sniderman, Paul M., Louk Hagendoorn, and Markus Prior. 2004. "Predisposing Factors and Situational Triggers: Exclusionary Reactions to Immigrant Minorities." *American Political Science Review* 98 (1): 35–49.

Spross, Jeff. 2012. "Hate Crimes against Muslims Remain Near Decade High." *ThinkProgress*, December 10. Available at https://thinkprogress.org/hate-crimes-against-muslims-remain-near-decade-high-77842ae7136e.

Stouffer, Samuel Andrew. 1955. *Communism, Conformity, and Civil Liberties: A Cross-Section of the Nation Speaks Its Mind*. New York: Doubleday.

Sullivan, John Lawrence, James Piereson, and George E. Marcus. 1982. *Political Tolerance and American Democracy*. Chicago: University of Chicago Press.

Best Practices for Gathering Public Opinion Data among Muslim Americans

Matt A. Barreto and

Karam Dana

C learly, a great deal is being said *about* American Muslims. They are the subject of considerable debate on cable news shows, presidential campaign speeches, hearings in Congress, and scholarly volumes such as this one. New social science research is examining attitudes toward and about Muslim Americans (Kalkan, Layman, and Uslaner 2009; Panagopoulos 2006; Collingwood, Lajevardi, and Oskooii 2018; Lajevardi and Abrajano 2018), as well as media coverage regarding Muslims (Lajevardi 2017; Nacos and Torres-Reyna 2007). The General Social Survey (GSS) and American National Elections Study (ANES) both have added new survey questions to gauge how Americans perceive and feel about Muslims. While this research is important, there remains little original data collection *among* Muslim Americans that provides their perspective on American politics and society (Calfano, Lajevardi, and Michelson 2017).

In this chapter we offer different methodologies that can be used to gather public opinion survey data among Muslims in the United States and what the challenges and opportunities are with different approaches. Ultimately, we conclude that social scientists can and should collect more public opinion data from American Muslims so that their viewpoints can be included in the national debate about diversity and democracy. To this end, we focus on large-*n* quantitative public opinion data as a methodological approach for understanding Muslim American social and political incorporation.

Public opinion and political behavior have been longstanding areas of significant consequence and interest to social scientists. The primary reason for using survey research is simple: if you want to know how Americans feel about politics, just ask them. Early on, pollsters learned that you could measure a great deal about voter attitudes, and possibly even predict election results through large quantitative surveys of the public. Over the past decades, the science of public opinion surveying has expanded greatly, with expertise developed in how to accurately collect and analyze survey data (see Lasswell 1941; Alpert 1956; Groves et al. 2011). When surveys are implemented accurately, results generated from a sample of the population can be inferred to the larger population from which the sample is drawn, given the appropriate sampling error, or confidence interval that must always be accounted for (Cassell, Särndal, and Wretman 1977; Graubard and Korn 1996). However, implementing an accurate survey for small or hard-to-reach populations can be much more difficult. Yet we want to push social scientists to do exactly this—to interview and survey American Muslims because their voice is important in contemporary political debates and because survey research continues to play an important role across the social sciences.

The most important starting point for sound survey research is to acquire an accurate sample frame from which to draw the eventual sample of people interviewed. If the sample is reflective of the larger population, and the survey is administered randomly and with minimal bias, the results of the eventual survey results can be considered as statistically reliable estimate (Scheaffer et al. 2011; Groves 2004). For this reason, we argue it is critical that scholars of politics, sociology, and religion extend their survey data collection to include Muslim Americans. Yet getting this desirable "accurate sample" is undoubtedly much trickier with a population like American Muslims.

Approaches to Gathering Survey Data

After decades of less rigorous sampling practices, survey research practitioners coalesced behind an approach called simple random sampling (SRS). The basic idea behind SRS is that every possible subject to be interviewed (the universe) is put into a pool, and respondents are recruited for interview in a blind and completely random fashion. This approach should ensure the sample is reflective of the overall universe in question and findings can be generalized to the larger population. Indeed, the federal government regularly relies on survey methodology in its collection of data and statistics.

In fact, the Office of Management and Budget has a division called the Federal Committee on Statistical Methodology that has reviewed best practices in survey research and recommended random digit dial (RDD) as a method to avoid noncoverage bias because it samples all known telephone numbers (Federal Committee on Statistical Methodology 1990). According to Michael Link, formerly a research scientist for the Centers for Disease Control and Prevention, and colleagues, "For more than three decades, RDD telephone surveys have been the predominant method for conducting surveys of the general public" (Link et al. 2005). When it comes to telephone surveys, RDD is a great approach, except when the researcher is trying to target a specific subpopulation, which may be small or geographically isolated. In the case of American Muslims, randomly dialing every single phone number in America, hoping to reach the 2 percent or so of the population who identify as Muslim, is a bad idea. We need a more efficient approach, one that is culturally sensitive and aware of the issues surrounding the population sampled.

In the domain of telephone surveys, some have opted for "listed samples" of potential Muslim households and then randomly dialing those lists. Unfortunately, there is not currently a well-maintained and accurate list of Muslim households for survey sampling. Or maybe this is fortunate in the Trump era, in which some anti-Muslim politicians might try to access such a list for negative or exclusionary purposes. Either way, listed samples for Muslim Americans present a challenge for researchers. Some have attempted to use "surname sampling" to identify commonly occurring Muslim last names and then randomly dialed those. On the one hand, this approach could mark an improvement over household listed samples that are surely incomplete. On the other, it is extremely difficult to identify surname sample for African American Muslims, who may or may not have obvious-looking religious surnames.

Further, it is unknown what the coverage rate would be for such a surname approach because the U.S. Census does not ask religion on the decennial questionnaire. For Hispanics and Asian Americans, it is possible to match surnames given on the census to the actual race/ethnicity box checked on the same form, and government researchers have supplied accurate lists of commonly occurring Hispanic and Asian surnames. For American Muslims, there is no known list to check surnames against religious identity, making it very difficult to determine the coverage rate. Still, we think there is some potential in surname sampling, and we discuss some opportunities in the concluding section.

Interviewer Effects and Bias

While collecting public opinion data through telephone surveys is widely used, it is also known that sometimes respondents modify their answers based on who is asking the questions. This line of research, generally called *race of interviewer effects*, finds that both white and minority respondents might alter their true opinion and give a more socially desirable answer when being interviewed by someone they perceive as not sharing their views (Cotter, Cohen, and Coulter 1982). For example, Darren Davis (1997b) finds that African Americans are less likely to tell white interviewers that racism is a problem, and research among Latinos finds that Mexican Americans moderate their answers when speaking to white interviewers (Reese et al. 1986). With respect to American Muslims, there is strong reason to believe that telephone surveys could induce social desirability and race of interviewer effects given the political climate surrounding this community. When a stranger on the other end of the telephone asks questions about perceptions of equality in America, or discrimination against Muslims, it is likely the average Muslim respondent may not feel a sense of trust with the interviewer and volunteer less than honest opinions. Indeed, one finding of K. A. Oskooii's (2016) research on Muslim Americans and discrimination is that respondents report significantly less discrimination against their community in a telephone survey than they do in a self-administered survey. This potential reality was also seen in Brian Calfano and colleagues' experiment in Chapter 9, in which the terms "American" and "Muslim" were randomly assigned for subjects to encounter prior to being asked a series of political questions.

As scholars embark on any interviewer-administered research among Muslim Americans, we urge them to take the necessary precautions to make the survey experience as open and comfortable as possible (Nederhof 1985). The surveillance of the American Muslim community is real and this has the potential for spillover into social science research. Within the last year, news accounts documented the FBI and other government agencies conducting surveillance in Muslim American communities (Sethi 2016; Hackman 2016). Therefore, we should not be surprised if American Muslims continue to view random strangers calling them on the telephone to ask them political questions with great suspicion.

If telephone interviewing is going to be used, researchers should attempt to include as many Muslim Americans in their interviewer pool as possible. To some extent, this will be essential for bilingual interviewing in Arabic, Farsi, Urdu, Hindi, or other languages. But beyond language, it is important to establish trust. In addition to a diverse interviewing staff, researchers should insist on considerable training with interviewers to express the importance of trust and why some subjects might be suspicious. Guidelines provided by universities' human subjects divisions and institutional review boards (IRBs) are important to provide potential respondents with information regarding what the survey is about, what the data will be used for, and who is sponsoring the research. Subjects need to be informed and comfortable with the research if we expect them to provide their time and their true opinions.

While challenges related to sampling and implementation can arise, we think one promising approach for data collection with the American Muslim community is in the self-administered interview settings, such as in-person or perhaps via the Internet. Indeed extensive research has demonstrated that self-administered interviews can reduce social desirability bias for sensitive questions, or for populations seen "at-risk" (Tourangeau, Rips, and Rasinski 2000; Kreuter, Presser, and Tourangeau 2009). Today, Internet-based surveys, which have the advantage of being self-administered, are one of the most popular formats, thereby increasing the likelihood that online surveys could be useful in the study of American Muslims. In a typical self-administered study, potential respondents in an existing "panel" are invited to participate in a survey in exchange for points or credits that they can accumulate for prizes or rewards.

Yet while Internet-based surveys have much promise in helping us reach a large population in a self-administered format, research on race and class suggests that the digital divide continues to represent a challenge (Servon 2002; Mossberger, Wu, and Jimenez 2016). In particular, we urge caution in the use of existing online panels from different online survey vendors when it comes to the American Muslim population. The sample size is likely to be quite small and not necessarily representative of the larger population of interest. Online snowball sampling may actually provide a stronger approach than online panels for hard-to-reach populations. While it violates the assumption of random selection, snowball sampling through online sources such as Facebook, Twitter, Instagram, and other large social media venues provides the opportunity for fresh sample, and with a large enough sample size, it may also approach generalizability (Kosinkski et al. 2015).

As email databases become more common and more accessible, it is possible that researchers can use a combination of surname sampling and self-administered Internet mode to reach a reliable population of American Muslims, though this method has not been fully tested to date. Still, with millions of email addresses available to market research outlets, there is no reason social scientists cannot access these email databases and filter by surname to target likely Muslim individuals for invitation to participate in a survey.

Of course, while new methods and approaches are exciting, older methodologies may still have something to offer. Such is the case in our study in which onsite, in-person, self-administered survey research proved successful. Below, we describe the process we undertook for the Muslim American Public Opinion Survey (MAPOS) in 2006–2008 as a possible research methodology for collecting public opinion data among American Muslims.

In-Person, Self-Administered Survey Research: Lessons from MAPOS

To help address the lack of data on American Muslims, and to delve into the issues of religion and social and political incorporation, we implemented a unique public opinion survey of Muslim Americans. Scholars familiar with the study of American Muslims know that very few empirical data sets exist regarding Muslims in America. And among the MAPS/Zogby and Pew Research Center polls that do exist, few contain the more traditional political science– or sociology-oriented survey questions that researchers are often interested in analyzing. At the same time, some media polls lack the full range of demographic and other control variables that are needed to model cause and effect in observational data. Thus, we fielded an original survey of Muslims Americans in twenty-two locations across the United States. The sample represents a diverse cross-section of American cities and the Muslim population, including twenty-two interview sites in the East, West, and Midwest, as well as the major Muslim population centers in the United States. Our sample includes large numbers of Arab, Asian, and U.S.-born respondents, making it quite representative of the overall U.S. Muslim population.

Before we moved forward with the full study, we started with a pilot project in Seattle, Washington (where we were both based at the time at the University of Washington). Pilot studies in our scholarly backyard were an ideal way to test and fine-tune new research methodologies before we moved to a larger scale. In the case of our Seattle pilot study, we selected a crowd-based sampling strategy for our in-person self-administered survey. There is a rich literature on sampling respondents in large crowds, whether it is sporting events (Tapp and Clowes 2002) or protest marches. Of considerable note, Stefaan Walgrave and Joris Verhulst (2011) provide a comprehensive review of crowd-based survey methods and conclude with a list of best practices to yield a reliable sample. We implemented our first study at the 2007 Eid-al-Fitr at the Seattle Convention Center and completed 135 interviews with American Muslims in a single setting.

We used three practices that we consider essential to gaining a robust sample. First, we had a large team of research assistants spread throughout the convention center grounds to increase the probability that any attendee of the Eid could be potentially interviewed. Second, we put a strong emphasis on cultural awareness and accuracy. We made sure that each survey team included one male and one female to recruit potential subjects, that all members of our survey team were themselves Muslim Americans (many of them were also bilingual), and that the surveyors were all dressed according to community customs and practices. Third, we insisted on random selection of respondents whereby our survey takers counted passers-by and recruited every third person to take the survey. By being spread throughout the large event at multiple locations and using skip pattern to select respondents, we retained some elements of random selection into the study.

Cultural sensitivity and awareness was perhaps our most important element in implementing the pilot study. Before the day of Eid, we had extensive discussions with the local organizing committee to let them know about our study and what our goals were, and to ensure that our research footprint would be as unobtrusive as possible. We shared copies of the survey instrument with the organizing committee, as well as our IRB approval forms, and made assurances that participation was completely voluntary and anonymous. While we did not have a letter of support for our first pilot study, we learned through the data collection that some participants wondered if it was okay for us to be there collecting data, and as a result we added this component when we expanded our study nationally. Having a letter of support from the organizing committee of the Eid proved important in other locations when and if a question arose about the validity and intentions of our survey, and we were able to share copies of this letter with any participant who had questions.

A further part of the cultural competence was to have gender-segregated participant recruitment. Female survey takers approached potential female respondents and vice versa for males. While a majority of our respondents may have been accepting of mixed-gender surveying, we did not want to make any assumptions and wanted to provide the most comfortable environment for respondents.

Self-Administered Questionnaire

One advantage that our survey had over previous data collection efforts among American Muslims is that respondents were recruited face-to-face, and subjects then self-administered the survey. Specifically, research assistants[1] handed out clipboards to participants who completed the survey in their own privacy. By contrast, and given concerns in the American Muslim community over surveillance, telephone surveys may introduce considerable social acquiescence and social desirability bias. Having fellow Muslim American research assistants recruit participants was very helpful, and allowing subjects to self-complete the survey provided even more trust. As we

---

1. Research assistants were themselves Muslim, predominantly second generation, most fluent in a second language (Arabic or Urdu) and were balanced between men and women. All research assistants attending two training sessions, and participated in a pilot survey to ensure consistency and professionalism.

note above, considerable research has demonstrated that attitudes on sensitive topics are more truthfully given in private self-administered surveys (Krysan 1998) and that minorities are likely to moderate their attitudes when being interviewed by nonwhites, the typical method in telephone surveys (Krysan and Couper 2003; Davis 1997).

The survey consisted of a single sheet of cardstock paper with questions on both the front and back. Respondents were given the clipboard and pencil and asked to fill in bubbles corresponding to their answers, and then returned the survey to an envelope so that the research assistants never saw their responses. This provided respondents with substantial privacy in completing their survey. Research assistants had copies of the survey available in English, Arabic, Farsi, and Urdu and could supply a non-English version of the survey to respondents as needed.

Site Selection

On the basis of the success of the Seattle pilot study, we expanded the data collection effort nationally. Naturally, drawing a sample of Muslims in the United States is not easy or efficient given their relatively small population. To address this concern, the survey was implemented at twenty-two randomly selected locations across eleven U.S. cities in eight states. Our goal was to make sure we included large population centers with sizable Muslim communities, including Dearborn-Detroit, Los Angeles, Chicago, Dallas, and Washington, DC, as well as locations with emerging and growing Muslim communities such as Raleigh-Durham, North Carolina, and Oklahoma City. Given our preference for crowd sampling, we needed to identify events that were likely to produce a large and representative sample of American Muslims. In Seattle, we sampled during an Eid celebration, and this provided an ideal cross-section.

In the Islamic faith, there are two Eid prayers and holidays, both marked by the lunar calendar: Eid-al-Adha and Eid-al-Fitr. While both are religious holidays, they are also larger than just religion and are cultural celebrations. Though not the religious equivalent, some compare them to Christmas and Easter in the Christian faith. That is, while they certainly have religious orientations, they draw participation from a wide spectrum of those along the religiosity scale. Within the Christian faith, it is not just deeply religious people who attend office Christmas parties, or Christmas Eve dinner with friends and family. And Sunday afternoon Easter brunch is certainly not restricted to only the most devout followers of Christianity. Indeed, a very large and diverse set of Christians participate in Christmas and Easter celebrations, and in a similar experience, a very large and diverse set of

TABLE 11.1: DEMOGRAPHIC CHARACTERISTICS OF MAPOS AND
PEW SURVEY

	MAPOS	Pew 2007
U.S.-born	38%	35%
Foreign-born	62%	65%
Noncitizen	28%	23%
Arab	51%	40%
Asian	22%	20%
Black	11%	26%
White	8%	11%
Sunni	61%	50%
Shi'a	18%	16%
N	1,410	1,050

American Muslims participate in Eid. What's more, because there is such a large attendance, traditional mosques are often not used for Eid prayer services, and, instead, organizing committees often opt for the city's convention center or county fairgrounds as a site. This provides an ideal location and opportunity for sampling a large number of participants at a single location in a single day.

To supplement the Eid surveys, interviews were gathered at a mix of religious and nonreligious locations from Islamic community centers (Basatneh 2016). While the Eid celebrations have the advantage of large crowds, the downside is that they only take place twice per year. If scholars are interested in collecting additional data, we suggest a similar crowd-sampling approach at Islamic centers, either during Jum'ah prayers on Friday or at other advertised events during the week. In total, 1,410 surveys were completed across the eleven locations, and the general demographics of our sample closely match those reported in the 2007 Pew survey of Muslim Americans.[2] Table 11.1 displays descriptive statistics on the immigrant and racial backgrounds of respondents in our sample.

Is the Sample "Too Muslim"?

Given that our sample is drawn—in part—from religious centers and community festivals, the reader may question if there is any inherent bias. We are

2. The Pew survey was conducted by telephone and went into the field at roughly the same time as our survey; however, the Pew survey does not include questions about perceived compatibility between Islam and American politics.

confident in our sample selection for two specific reasons. First, our sample demonstrates a range of religious diversity. While attending the mosque and the prayer of Eid are descriptively religious practices, they are also cultural and social practices, just as attending Sunday church services or Christmas mass are both religious and cultural events for Christian Americans. In response to a question about the importance of religion in their daily life, 50 percent stated religion was very important, 38 percent stated it was somewhat important, and 12 percent stated not too important. Likewise, when asked how involved they were with their local mosque, 26 percent said very active, 40 percent said somewhat, 20 percent said not much, and 13 percent said not at all active. Given the variation on these two key variables, we are quite confident that our sample provides the appropriate mix of religiously oriented Muslims and, at the same time, provides a spectrum of religiosity that ranges from very low to very high.

We also included questions to assess how closely respondents practiced or followed Islam. For example, we asked respondents to select which option is *not* a month in the Islamic calendar—Rabi al-thalith, Rajab, Shawwal, or Sha'ban—and 89 percent correctly identified Rabi al-thalith (but 11 percent wrongly selected another option). We also asked respondents whether they participated in *sadaqah* to an individual or organization in the past year, which is voluntary charity giving and considered as proof of one's faith. As Table 11.2 reveals, 69 percent of our sample overall said they had given *sadaqah*, and 31 percent did not. So, across a variety of measures, our data seem to point to a well-balanced and diverse sample of American Muslims and not a sample that is skewed too heavily religious.

Second, Muslims are a religious group by definition. Distinct from Hispanics, who are considered an ethnic group, or African Americans, who are

TABLE 11.2: RELIGIOUS CHARACTERISTICS OF MAPOS SAMPLE

Characteristic	Percentage
Religion very important	50
Religion somewhat important	38
Religion not too important	12
Very active in mosque	26
Somewhat active in mosque	40
Not too active in mosque	20
Not at all active in mosque	13
Correctly identifies Islamic months	89
Incorrectly identifies Islamic months	11
Participated in *sadaqah*	69
Did not participate in *sadaqah*	31

a racial group, American Muslims are most commonly described as a religious group, and we can therefore expect to encounter them in religious settings. Similar to American Jews, Muslims also express a wide spectrum of responses in the observance of their religion from orthodox and especially devout to those who are entirely secular but still consider themselves Muslim (or Jewish). At the point as which someone completely deidentifies with their religion and does not consider themselves Muslim, we should not expect to find them in a data set of Muslims. Rather, surveys and studies of communities from the Middle East, North Africa, or South Asia may be more appropriate. But if we as scholars are interested in the public opinions, social attitudes, and political behavior of Muslim Americans, then we think it is wholly appropriate to focus on those who self-identify as Muslim.

Where Do We Go from Here?

A positive development in the social sciences since 9/11 has been the increase in interest in Muslim Americans—and not just what other Americans think about them but also how American Muslims themselves view the political landscape. Indeed, a group of more than fifty political scientists, scholars, and practitioners met at Menlo College in California in December 2016 to discuss prospects for new research and further public opinion data among Muslim Americans. We think this is an exciting time to be studying this community and hope that more social scientists will jump in and collect data among Muslim communities here in the United States. We have offered some caveats and questions about how to carefully collect data that we hope will spur a debate about best practices. In particular, researchers need to be culturally aware and sensitive to issues of trust in the American Muslim community. Using Muslim American research assistants when possible is a critical step in gaining public confidence when implementing research studies. Concerns over social desirability can be alleviated with self-administered surveys that respondents can answer with privacy, either online or at an in-person setting. One proposal we have set forth is crowd-based sampling of American Muslims at Eid prayer celebrations, or other prayer services or events at Islamic centers. We think approaching Muslims on their turf, so to speak, will ease concerns and provide a more welcoming environment for answering researchers' questions.

REFERENCES

Alpert, Harry. 1956. "Public Opinion Research as Science." *Public Opinion Quarterly* 20 (3): 493–500.

Basatneh, Alaa. 2016. "Three Things Your Muslim Friends Wish You Knew about Eid Al-Fitr." *Splinter*, July 6. Available at http://fusion.net/story/321325/eid-al-fitr -explained.

Calfano, Brian Robert, Nazita Lajevardi, and Melissa R. Michelson. 2017. "Trumped Up Challenges: Limitations, Opportunities, and the Future of Political Research on Muslim Americans." *Politics, Groups, and Identities*, October 17. Available at https:// www.tandfonline.com/doi/full/10.1080/21565503.2017.1386573.

Cassel, Claes-Magnus, Carl-Erik Särndal, and Jan Hakan Wretman. 1977. *Foundations of Inference in Survey Sampling*. New York: John Wiley.

Collingwood, Loren, Nazita Lajevardi, and Kassra A. R. Oskooii. 2018. "A Change of Heart? Why Individual-Level Public Opinion Shifted against Trump's 'Muslim Ban.'" *Political Behavior* 40 (4): 1–38.

Cotter, Patrick R., Jeffrey Cohen, and Philip B. Coulter. 1982. "Race-of-Interviewer Effects in Telephone Interviews." *Public Opinion Quarterly* 46 (2): 278–284.

Davis, Darren W. 1997a. "The Direction of Race of Interviewer Effects among African-Americans: Donning the Black Mask." *American Journal of Political Science* 41 (1): 309–322.

———. 1997b. "Nonrandom Measurement Error and Race of Interviewer Effects among African Americans." *Public Opinion Quarterly* 61 (1): 183–207.

Federal Committee on Statistical Methodology. 1990. "Survey Coverage." Statistical Policy Working Paper 17. Available at https://nces.ed.gov/FCSM/pdf/spwp17.pdf.

Graubard, Barry I., and Edward L. Korn. 1996. "Survey Inference for Subpopulations." *American Journal of Epidemiology* 144 (1): 102–106.

Groves, Robert M. 2004. *Survey Errors and Survey Costs*. New York: John Wiley.

Groves, Robert M., Floyd J. Fowler Jr., Mick P. Couper, James M. Lepkowski, Eleanor Singer, and Roger Tourangeau. 2011. *Survey Methodology*. New York: John Wiley.

Hackman, Rose. 2016. "American, Muslim, and under Constant Watch: The Emotional Toll of Surveillance." *The Guardian*, March 27. Available at https://www.theguardian .com/us-news/2016/mar/27/american-muslim-surveillance-the-emotional-toll.

Kalkan, Kerem Ozan, Geoffrey C. Layman, and Eric M. Uslaner. 2009. "'Bands of Others?' Attitudes toward Muslims in Contemporary American Society." *Journal of Politics* 71 (3): 847–862.

Kosinski, Michal, Sandra C. Matz, Samuel D. Gosling, Vesselin Popov, and David Stillwell. 2015. "Facebook as a Research Tool for the Social Sciences: Opportunities, Challenges, Ethical Considerations, and Practical Guidelines." *American Psychologist* 70 (6): 543–556.

Kreuter, Frauke, Stanley Presser, and Roger Tourangeau. 2009. "Social Desirability Bias in CATI, IVR, and Web Surveys: The Effects of Mode and Question Sensitivity." *Public Opinion Quarterly* 72 (5): 847–865.

Krysan, M. 1998. "Privacy and the Expression of White Racial Attitudes: A Comparison across Three Contexts." *Public Opinion Quarterly* 62:506–544.

Krysan, M., and M. P. Couper. 2003. "Race in the Live and the Virtual Interview: Racial Deference, Social Desirability, and Activation Effects in Attitude Surveys." *Social Psychology Quarterly* 66 (4): 364–383.

Lajevardi, Nazita. 2017. "A Comprehensive Study of Muslim American Discrimination by Legislators, the Media, and the Masses." Ph.D. diss., University of California, San Diego.

Lajevardi, Nazita, and Marisa A. Abrajano. 2018. "How Negative Sentiment towards Muslims Predicts Support for Trump in the 2016 Presidential Election." *Journal of*

Politics, December 11. Available at https://www.journals.uchicago.edu/doi/full/10 .1086/700001.

Lasswell, Harold. 1941. *Democracy through Public Opinion*. Menasha, WI: Banta.

Link, Michael W., Michael P. Battaglia, Martin R. Frankel, Larry Osborn, Ali H. Mokdad. 2005. "Address-Based versus Random-Digit Dial Sampling: Comparison of Data Quality from BRFSS Mail and Telephone Surveys." Available at http://citeseerx .ist.psu.edu/viewdoc/download;jsessionid=09C892F8ABB2E00E12E2393A65 CD0D3E?doi=10.1.1.159.4675&rep=rep1&type=pdf.

Mossberger, Karen, Yonghong Wu, and Benedict S. Jimenez. 2017. "Developments and Challenges in E-Participation in Major US Cities." In *Routledge Handbook on Information Technology in Government*, edited by Y. C. Chen and M. J. Ahn, 219–238. New York: Taylor and Francis.

Nacos, Brigitte L., and Oscar Torres-Reyna. 2007. *Fueling Our fears: Stereotyping, Media Coverage, and Public Opinion of Muslim Americans*. Lanham, MD: Rowman and Littlefield.

Nederhof, A. J. 1985. "Methods of Coping with Social Desirability Bias: A Review." *European Journal of Social Psychology* 15 (3): 263–280.

Oskooii, K. A. 2016. "How Discrimination Impacts Sociopolitical Behavior: A Multidimensional Perspective." *Political Psychology* 37 (5): 613–640.

Panagopoulos, Costas. 2006. "The Polls-Trends: Arab and Muslim Americans and Islam in the Aftermath of 9/11." *Public Opinion Quarterly* 70:608–624.

Reese, Stephen D., Wayne A. Danielson, Pamela J. Shoemaker, Tsan-Kuo Chang, and Huei-Ling Hsu. 1986. "Ethnicity-of-Interviewer Effects among Mexican-Americans and Anglos." *Public Opinion Quarterly* 50 (4): 563–572.

Scheaffer, Richard L., William Mendenhall III, R. Lyman Ott, and Kenneth G. Gerow. 2011. *Elementary Survey Sampling*. 7th ed. Boston: Brooks/Cole.

Servon, Lisa J. 2002. "Redefining the Digital Divide." In *Bridging the Digital Divide: Technology, Community, and Public Policy*, 1–23. Oxford, UK: Blackwell.

Sethi, Arjun Singh. 2016. "The FBI Needs to Stop Spying on Muslim-Americans." *Politico Magazine*, March 29. Available at http://www.politico.com/magazine/story/ 2016/03/muslim-american-surveillance-fbi-spying-213773.

Tapp, Alan, and Jeff Clowes. 2002. "From 'Carefree Casuals' to 'Professional Wanderers': Segmentation Possibilities for Football Supporters." *European Journal of Marketing* 36 (11–12): 1248–1269.

Tourangeau, Roger, Lance J. Rips, and Kenneth Rasinski. 2000. *The Psychology of Survey Response*. Cambridge: Cambridge University Press.

Walgrave, S., and J. Verhulst. 2011. "Selection and Response Bias in Protest Surveys." *Mobilization: An International Quarterly* 16 (2): 203–222.

Conclusions and New Directions for the Study of American Muslims

BRIAN R. CALFANO AND

NAZITA LAJEVARDI

T he preceding chapters show that the experiences of American Muslims almost two decades after the 9/11 attacks continue to be typified by a combination of public suspicion, discrimination, and complex identity-based effects. Scholars are only now finding ways to assess the effects of these experiences through techniques like random assignment in experiments. The 2016 Trump election has reminded students of identity politics and related subjects that the maltreatment of minority groups—even those that have seen some progress in their social status relative to the majority—is ripe for reoccurrence without much warning. Though it is impossible to predict exactly where the effects of Trump's anti-Muslim rhetoric (and attendant reaction by those sharing his worldview) will lead, it is safe to suggest that any earlier attempts by leaders of both major political parties to encourage Americans to discount negative stereotypes of Muslims have been stunted.

This volume's purpose has been to offer a series of research-oriented snapshots of American Muslims in the years before the Trump presidency and at the start of the Trump era in American politics. We said in the introductory chapter that our reading of the extant literature suggests several existing themes. The first is that Muslims in America are scrutinized by out-group non-Muslims and the assumptions that many in government and the general public make about Islam and extremism. The second is that Muslims represent a diverse collection of ethnic, racial, national, and religious subgroups that have been increasingly packaged into a single panethnic

Muslim identity in the years since 9/11. Third, and most importantly, the literature contains a collection of findings about Muslim political beliefs and behavior that show them to hold a mix of political views, to both broach and shy away from political activity at various times, and to adopt many democratic norms, including tolerance of political and religious difference. Left unanswered in the literature are concrete predictions about how Muslims might behave as a political identity group, and the new approaches that scholars should take in studying Muslims in America.

In helping advance the first and third themes, findings in previous chapters discover that American Muslims have been driven to political action partially as a result of Trump's political ascendency, that female Muslims have borne a particularly difficult burden as anti-Muslim rhetoric has sharpened, and that the manner in which Muslim identity is represented in statistical surveys can have a substantial impact on how Muslims respond to key political questions that researchers ask. In regard to the second theme, the chapters highlight that also important are the reputations (perceived or otherwise) of the individuals and entities running these surveys. Given the polarized political environment (made even more so by Trump's rhetoric), reputations may affect both how Muslims represent themselves to surveyors and, just as importantly, how the public perceives insights coming from survey data.

Though we do not draw conclusive findings about an overarching theory of Muslim political behavior, we find it reasonable to suggest that Muslims in America will continue their drift toward Democratic candidates and will maintain political engagement to support candidates and policies that advance civil liberties and related causes. This political participation will be driven in large measure by the continuing threats Muslims perceive and experience in the American sociopolitical context. In addition, and in terms of approaches to the future study of Muslims, the science of generating representative samples of American Muslims represents a challenging task that even well-resourced survey firms such as Pew, Gallup, Lucid, and Survey Sampling International have trouble navigating.

Then there is the additional question of how we go about consolidating what we know as scholars about American Muslims in the contemporary political context. To date, most of the insights generated about this group were achieved through various forms of observational research (both qualitative and quantitative). But today, Muslim Americans are more difficult to survey than ever because of fears of increasing surveillance (Lambert 2016). We should, therefore, be skeptical about the role of social desirability bias even when they consent to being included in surveys.

Together, the chapters in this volume represent an advance in the literature by advocating for the inclusion of randomized treatments in experimental design frameworks as a way to establish direct causal chains between variables of interest. But there is certainly more work to be done in understanding American Muslims and their political circumstances in the Trump era. We walk through considerations of next steps for scholars and other interested parties in this final chapter.

Twin Pillars of Importance: Identity and Experimental Design

To start, we see great utility in expanding the use of experimental design in the study of empirical puzzles involving Muslims. The recommended focus on experimental design is not simply a reflection of a growing methodological trend within political science, however. It is, instead, a comment on the reality that much of what interests scholars about Muslim American experiences in the Trump era regards individual and collective identity. Furthermore, the outcomes of greatest import to scholars (and many other observers for that matter) regard how American Muslims exercise their citizenship and related political rights in the Trump era. Thus, the outcome variables of concern include all forms of political behavior but also encompass perceptions of other social groups and how Muslims see themselves in relation to the larger society in which they live and work. Independent (or causal) variables of theoretical concern include Muslim beliefs and forms of self-concept (i.e., identity).

At the basis of the identity literature is the recurring theme that the nature of one's self-concept is hardly a constant. Not only may one hold different and highly distinct identities; these identities may substantially affect how one is perceived by social out-groups. Identities may affect what members of important in-groups think about individuals as well. One example is the possibility that Muslims face criticism from fellow Muslims when their individual levels of religious devoutness are doubted. Specifically, Muslims who are perceived as looking and acting "too American" may encounter backlash from fellow Muslims with heightened Muslim identity and religiosity. At the same time, these Muslims may find rejection from the non-Muslim-dominated groups they attempt to join and in which they want to be recognized as members. In this way, identity is both a personal choice and a matter of collective acceptance, a process that American Muslims do not have an automatic or reliable way of navigating.

The randomization in experimental design would help gain leverage on the effects of Muslim identity on an array of identity-based outcome measures. Based on the arguments and ideas contained in the previous chapters, there are several outcomes that would advance our understanding of Muslim political life, particularly as it regards citizenship in the Trump era of American politics.

The first of these questions regards the interplay between Muslim religious devoutness and their adoption of "American" identity and values. The question here is not about whether Muslims think and act "American"—we know enough at this point to affirm that they do. Rather, the issue for examination more regards the salience of different religious beliefs and practices and the study of how those items affect attitudes and behavior related to their country of residence. One simple way to do this in an experimental context is to use a questions-as-treatment design to randomly position the standard religious devoutness questions ahead of key dependent measures for treated subjects, while nontreated subjects are exposed to the devoutness items at the end of the survey. The goal would be to gauge whether cognitively highlighting one's self-reported devoutness activity (e.g., prayers, attending mosque, etc.) has a systematic impact on how respondents reply to political variables later in the survey question order. Interestingly, and despite the very simple nature of this design, it has not (to our knowledge) ever been executed on a sample of American Muslims. The closest existing study is Chapter 9 (in which Muslim subjects were randomly primed with items on the Religious Commitment Inventory index), but the authors use the inventory index as an alternate way to prime Muslim identity rather than for the specific purpose of heightening one's sense of religious commitment.

In expanding on the work in Chapter 9, an obvious area of focus would be to see whether reminding Muslims of their specific degree of devoutness, measured in a multitude of ways to capture the inherent diversity of religiosity, affects a series of participatory behaviors and political opinions. Another design option would be to use vignettes in a survey experiment to randomly expose subjects to examples of Muslims displaying different levels of devoutness in an effort to see how these affect patriotic behaviors (such as flying the American flag or celebrating the Fourth of July). To be sure, the point of focusing on these outcomes is not because we would expect Muslims to be less patriotic than the general public—all else equal. Instead, and in the heightened context of scrutiny that the Trump presidency has leveled against the Muslim community, it would be important for scholars to see whether and how Muslims respond to anti-Muslim tone that has gained resurgence in recent years. It might be that Muslims with higher levels of religious commitment and a sense of linked fate exhibit substantially different responses to the hostile sociopolitical context than others in the Muslim community, but this is but one of several possible outcomes on the subject.

A related research question best addressed in an experimental context regards assessment of how exposure to different characterizations of Islamic teaching affects how Muslims perceive and respond to their citizenship roles. Elites are a critical link in generating mass opinion, including among religious publics. With some differences in religious institutional structure versus Christianity, those considered elites in the Muslim community may have a core role to play in shaping Muslim opinion and behavior. Experimental designs where characterizations of Islamic teaching (e.g., ideas that tend to be considered Islamist versus modernist) are attributed to different types of elites may gain purchase on the puzzle of what drives Muslim political views and behavior.

And there is much material from which scholars might draw in this type of assessment. Though stereotypes akin to Samuel Huntington's (1993) negative characterization of Islam abound, there is also a rich tradition of reimagining how Islam and Islamic teaching intersects with secular politics and society that began with Edward Said's *Orientalism* (1979) and the pushback against patronizing depictions of the east as inferior to the west. Tariq Ramadan's focus on "critical Islam" (2009, 144), in which the faith's principles are considered part of a continuing dialogue between other faiths, science, and society, suggests that how individual Muslims conceive of Islam and its intersection with American politics and their role as citizens may be both variable and malleable (see Tampio 2013). There is also the Islamic concept of *shura,* which provides a rationale for the Muslim public to exercise both activity in the political realm as well as empower themselves with knowledge about how public policies affect their communities (Calfano and Lofftus 2014). What would be interesting is to determine whether these concepts—as referenced through different types of elites that American Muslims would come into contact with (including imams, community leaders, politicians, etc.)—affect Muslim political beliefs and behavior against the backdrop of Trump-era scrutiny. In this type of design, subjects could be randomly assigned to different ways of framing Islamic teaching in the context of a survey experiment (with elite-based statements offering the teaching frames as in mock newspaper or related media articles), and with follow-on questions serving as the outcome variables.

An example would be to randomly assign frames of Islamic teaching regarding how Muslims should respond as citizens when confronting discrimination. The teaching frames could include reference to the need for Muslims becoming more active in American civic life as a result of encountering pushback from sectors of the non-Muslim public. This could be contrasted with an assigned frame calling for Muslims to close ranks and direct activity to their religious communities. Essentially, Islam, like most religions, contains enough sacred teaching to allow for both types of frames to be considered credible in the eyes of subjects. Scholars should consider the implications of these different teaching frames for how they might affect Muslim opinions and behavior as citizens.

While key aspects of Muslim identity concern religious devoutness and elite-based expression of Islamic concepts, culture is another core aspect. Many Muslim Americans do not practice their faith often but identify as Muslim because the religious context represents the culture in which they were raised. This culture (much like that of people who claim they were "raised Catholic" but infrequently practice their faith or follow its teachings) concerns both societal norms and political sensibilities. For example, being culturally Muslim can often translate into an understanding and embrace of norm-driven considerations about romance (such as dating and marriage), dietary restrictions, gender, and age. This Muslim cultural influence also often manifests in sympathy with Palestinians on the Palestinian-Israeli debate. Each of these issues have implications for how American Muslims view their citizenship status, political participation, and views on foreign policy, particularly with the added dimensions of the Trump presidency in the mix.

A design focus on cultural reference elements would be useful for scholars. For example, a second set of experiments could follow something akin to the survey-based experiments described above that randomly introduce subjects to statements about these cultural norms. There would also be the option of assigning competing cultural ideas embedded in survey-based treatments to assess whether specific conceptions of gender relations (e.g., traditional versus progressive) affect stated views about political participation, efficacy, patriotism, and a host of related items. It would also be interesting to determine whether both competing cultural statements, as well as references to religious devoutness, have differing impacts on Muslim response on questions about citizenship and related items.

Yet another facet to exploring Muslim identity is to build on Brian Calfano's (2018) findings showing that American Muslims are not necessarily sanguine about the identity labels "American" and "Muslim." As Chapter 9 discusses, survey researchers have asked a variation on the identity question about whether one considers herself Muslim or American "first" in several survey iterations over the last ten years. The potential effect on survey response as a result of this quite limited set of identity choices notwithstanding, scholars should consider whether experimental design featuring different combinations of identity labels (e.g., "Muslim" and "businessperson" or "Muslim" and "artist," etc.) show impacts on survey response to critical political outcome questions. One expectation from this line of inquiry would be that Muslims respond enthusiastically to characterizations of their identity outside the usual American-Muslim trade-off given the Trump-era scrutiny and stereotyping faced, and with these alternate identity characterizations instilling a sense of pride or similar emotion that may encourage greater social and political engagement.

The practical implications of such a finding would be that the seeming innocuous identity characterization that focuses almost entirely on one's religion or national residence—as if those are the only two identities that matter to Muslims—should give way to greater sensitivity as to the diversity of how Muslims in the United States self-conceptualize. As the burgeoning political science literature on the topic shows, the random assignment of treatments in the context of "real world" activities represents an advance on the lab or survey-based treatments often used in social science experiments. The use of field experimentation on Muslim publics is only now beginning to take form, with no published work from this methodology yet available.

We recommend that scholars consider whether adapting any of the above treatment mechanisms intended as survey-embedded treatments might also (or instead) be used in a field design. With the growing flexibility that scholars now have in deploying media-based research designs—including and especially Internet-based methods for delivering treatments and recording responses in unobtrusive (i.e., non-survey-based ways), the literature on American Muslims may be used to extend understanding of different research agendas throughout political science more generally. One such extension would be a modification of Alan Gerber, Donald Green, and Christopher Larimer's (2008) social pressure experiment in which an increase in voter turnout was observed for those living in precincts randomly assigned to receive mailers indicating that whether or not they show up at the polls would be publicized to neighbors.

Ideally, and given the scrutiny that Muslims face at the start of the Trump era, scholars would avoid applying pressure to Muslims in any type of academic study. Instead, the mechanism could involve something akin to social support, whereby randomly selected subjects encounter some type of social encouragement message, perhaps attributed to in-group Muslims or out-group non-Muslims (or even both in a combined treatment of some type). The idea would be to see whether Muslim engagement in political and civic life is improved through encouragement from different social groups. These messages could be distributed across different social media platforms of which subgroups of the Muslim public are known to frequent. If the funding is available, these messages could also be spread using broadcast media. Partnering with advocacy-based groups within the Muslim community may also be helpful in cultivating projects of this type (although researchers should be sure that project goals are mutually beneficial). Of course, as with any of the ideas offered in this chapter, these are merely starting points for more careful and in-depth design choices we hope scholars pursue.

Finding Paths Forward: Collaboration and Collective Action

Now comes the more challenging part: figuring out the best ways to bring these designs to fruition. The reality is that many scholars have already hatched research ideas similar to what we propose above, but have lacked the resources sufficient to field studies of the necessary size and representativeness to satisfy publication demands of the discipline's top research outlets. Indeed, we are aware of several "small n" studies featuring Muslim subjects that have not seen publication mainly because they face certain rejection at journals where reviewers raise concerns about population representativeness. In some cases, these problems stem from the use of observational data in which random assignment is not used. This makes the studies more vulnerable to questions about population representativeness in that there are no direct causal claims to be made from the independent variables featured. But it is also true that many reviewers for political science journals expect subject pools to have a passing resemblance to the population they purport to address (political science is certainly not psychology in this regard).

These realities leave scholars with a few choices. On the one hand, they could continue to toil with small n studies, perhaps leveraging a critical mass of these designs into a single article. Scholars might also seek a change of reviewer perspective. For example, and by coincidence, much of the identity literature is found in social psychology outlets where unrepresentative samples are the overwhelming norm. Rather than attempt to convince skeptical political science reviewers that findings from an unbalanced sample of Muslims has generalizability to the larger Muslim population, perhaps a change of journal venue is an appropriate response. It is not difficult to envision that several identity experiments described in the preceding section could be written from a social psychology perspective, thereby finding homes in quality journals.

But not every research question lends itself to this type of change, and not every scholar can afford to publish in outlets outside her discipline. In cases where political scientists need to publish research on American Muslims in high-impact political science outlets, the path to progress on this front requires cooperation between both scholars and the major survey research organizations that regularly conduct national-level studies on this community. In the absence of U.S. Census data on religion or on Middle

Eastern backgrounds (topics that the census does not inquire about), organizations like Pew and Gallup have the resources and infrastructure to conduct the most representative surveys of the Muslim community.

Unfortunately, the findings generated by these well-funded studies are quite limited and often offer textbook examples in desirability response bias (e.g., 96 percent of American Muslims questioned about violence against civilians in Pew's 2011 survey say they are opposed to the practice versus the 76 percent of evangelical Christians who offer opposition to the practice in a separate Pew survey). Far too often, political scientists who regularly conduct similar surveys on American Muslims are kept at arm's length from these data collection efforts. Chapter 9 explores how question order effects can also be a challenge for these surveys, especially where identity-based effects are concerned.

It, therefore, would be a logical step for the large research firms to strengthen the validity and usefulness of their data by collaborating with academics outside of their individual shops. The goal would be to marry the relatively representative samples that Pew, Gallup, and related firms generate with the insights derived from randomized experiments that provide ways to test for the direct effects of question wording on response. And the potential impact is more than academic in nature. To the extent that both the public and policy makers develop perceptions of American Muslims from the results offered in these surveys, the approach taken in asking about Muslim beliefs and behaviors can certainly benefit from a closer collaboration between the large survey firms and academic researchers interested in the topic.

The survey firms may also be helpful in collecting survey data in tandem with the field experiment designs discussed above. The approach of randomizing treatments through media platforms—including social and broadcast media—and then conducting follow-on observational surveys to track any treatment-based effects, seem like quite useful options in merging the efforts of survey firms and experimentally based researchers to address questions about American Muslims.

As briefly touched on, researchers may also explore the potential benefits of partnering with Muslim advocacy organizations in conducting research projects of mutual interest and benefit. To the extent that organizations have access to resources—including community members who can both help guide and participate in studies—a research collaboration may be useful for scholars. For their part, the organizations would end up with access to data and analysis that they might not have been able to collect otherwise.

Finally, successful advancement of the political science literature on American Muslims will require greater levels of cooperation between scholars themselves. To now, research collaboration has been limited. Scholars whose work is featured in this volume are well known for their research partnerships on the topics discussed, but even these collaborations are limited in what they can achieve. Our view is that the community of scholars studying American Muslims in the Trump era is best served by pooling their insights and resources in consortium-like efforts. The combined perceptions and expertise of a community of researchers studying American Muslims from the general standpoints articulated in this chapter and book will do much to develop the necessary critical mass in applying for large grants, designing more insightful research projects, and finding new pathways to generate linkages between their projects and research questions of interest beyond political science.

The pieces in this book raise an important area that scholarship has not yet ventured into: providing policy recommendations for how to restore ease among the Muslim American community. To be sure, the next phase of research on Muslim Americans will be replete with sensitivity toward their fears of threat and physical harm. This reality underscores the methodological challenges of understanding how they are affected by discrimination. Even preliminary studies that have been conducted on Muslim Americans to evaluate their responses to societal and political discrimination have faced problems. All of this is enough to create pause and ask ourselves whether it is ethical to place them under more stress by understanding their responses to discrimination. We consider it highly likely that American Muslims would like to be left alone and return to an era of invisibility. In today's day and age when they are persistently subject to discrimination and violence by ordinary citizens, this is not surprising or irrational. But for well-meaning researchers who would like to understand the mechanisms underlying Muslim Americans' responses to discrimination, we must be careful not to leave a harmful footprint on this already marginalized community.

The Trump era is a challenge and opportunity for both American Muslims and those who study this community. Perhaps the challenges—typified by overt scrutiny and stereotyping—are more obvious, but opportunities do abound. These include, but are hardly limited to, deeper understanding of the mechanisms behind Muslim identity and citizenship in America. At this point, we cannot know what the next four, eight, or twelve years will bring for both Muslims and non-Muslims in America. What we do have confidence saying, however, is that any progress made in advancing the collective status of American Muslims since the September 11 attacks faces a grave threat from both the Trump presidency and the social forces its policy and rhetoric have unleashed. To be sure, the news on this front is not all negative. There are many in the non-Muslim community who reject the incendiary rhetoric offered by Trump and his surrogates, including many Republicans and party leaders. At the same time, the relative educational and economic resources that many in the Muslim community enjoy help blunt negative impacts from the current political climate. Still, it is not at all certain that the basic dynamics that threaten the social, political, and identity status of American Muslims will ever truly subside. Indeed, Muslim life in the United States might be a case of contested citizenship, even long after the Trump political era has passed.

REFERENCES

Calfano, Brian Robert. 2018. *Muslims, Identity, and American Politics*. New York: Routledge.

Calfano, Brian Robert, and Lynne Alise Lofftus. 2014. "Islam and Interpretive Ingenuities." In *Assessing MENA Political Reform, Post-Arab Spring*, edited by Brian Robert Calfano, 57–94. Lanham, MD: Lexington Books.

Gerber, Alan S., Donald P. Green, and Christopher W. Larimer. 2008. "Social Pressure and Voter Turnout: Evidence from a Large-Scale Field Experiment." *American Political Science Review* 102:33–48.

Huntington, Samuel P. 1993. "The Clash of Civilizations?" *Foreign Affairs* 72 (3): 22–49.

Lambert, Lisa. 2016. "Polling Calls to U.S. Muslims Raise Surveillance Fears." *Reuters*, November 23. Available at http://www.reuters.com/article/us-usa-muslims-idUSKBN13I2PK.

Ramadan, Tariq. 2009. *Radical Reform: Islamic Ethics and Liberation*. New York: Oxford University Press.

Said, Edward. 1979. *Orientalism*. New York: Vintage.

Tampio, Nicholas. 2013. "Promoting Critical Islam: Controversy, Civil Society, and Revolution." *Politics and Religion* 6:823–843.

Contributors

Matt A. Barreto is a professor of political science and Chicana/o studies at the University of California, Los Angeles, and the cofounder of the research and polling firm Latino Decisions. His research examines the political participation of racial and ethnic minorities in the United States, and his work has been published in the *American Political Science Review*, *Political Research Quarterly*, *Social Science Quarterly*, and *Public Opinion Quarterly*, among many other peer-reviewed journals. In 2010 Barreto implemented the first-ever weekly tracking poll of Latino voters during the 2010 election, which Latino Decisions continued in 2012. Along with collaborators, he has also overseen large, multistate election eve polls, battleground tracking polls, extensive message testing research, and countless focus groups. In 2015 Barreto was hired by a national presidential campaign to run polling and focus groups of Latino voters.

Alejandro J. Beutel is a senior research analyst at Southern Poverty Law Center's (SPLC) Intelligence Project, where he monitors U.S. far-right extremism and hate. Prior to SPLC, from 2015 to 2017 Beutel was a researcher for Countering Violent Extremism at the University of Maryland's National Consortium for the Study of Terrorism and Responses to Terrorism (START). In 2014 he was a Policy and Research Engagement Fellow at the Institute for Social Policy and Understanding (ISPU), an applied research think tank specializing in the study and promotion of evidence-based development strategies for positive civic, social, and political engagement outcomes for American Muslim communities. From 2009 to 2012 Beutel was also a policy analyst at the Muslim Public Affairs Council, an advocacy-based organization based in Los Angeles and Washington, D.C.

Brian R. Calfano is an assistant professor of political science and journalism at the University of Cincinnati and the author of more than fifty academic journal articles and books. Calfano's fields of specialization are religion and politics, political behavior, and media and politics. His research interests also include Middle East democratization and human rights in the Organization of the Islamic Conference.

Tony E. Carey Jr. is an associate professor of political science at the University of North Texas. His research and teaching interests focus on identity politics, with an emphasis on racial and ethnic politics, gender politics, and social movements. His work has been published in the *American Journal of Political Science, Political Research Quarterly, Urban Affairs Review,* and *Politics, Groups and Identities.*

Youssef Chouhoud is an assistant professor at Christopher Newport University, where he is affiliated with the Reiff Center for Human Rights and Conflict Resolution. He researches comparative political attitudes and behavior and has conducted fieldwork in America, Sweden, and North Africa.

Karam Dana is an associate professor in the School of Interdisciplinary Arts and Sciences at the University of Washington, Bothell. He is the founding director of the American Muslim Research Institute and the co–principal investigator of the Muslim American Public Opinion Survey. His research examines the American Muslim community, their racialization, and their political participation in the United States. He also studies Palestinian political identity and the impact of Israeli occupation on Palestinian society.

Oguzhan (Oz) Dincer is an associate professor of economics and the director of the Institute for Corruption Studies at Illinois State University. His research interests lie in the intersection between public economics, institutional economics, and development economics, with a focus on corruption. He received his Ph.D. in economics from the University of Oregon in 2004.

Rachel M. Gillum is an affiliate of Stanford University's Immigration Policy Lab. She is the author of *Muslims in a Post-9/11 America: A Survey of Attitudes and Beliefs and Their Implications for U.S. National Security Policy* (2018) and the principal investigator of the Muslim American National Opinion Survey (MANOS). She is also an advisor to the Institute for Social Policy and Understanding.

Kerem Ozan Kalkan is an assistant professor of political science at Eastern Kentucky University. His research interests include prejudice toward Muslims in the United States and Western Europe, Muslims' integration into Western societies, religion and politics, Turkish politics, and advanced quantitative methods. His work appears in journals such as *American Journal of Political Science, Journal of Politics, Journal for the Scientific Study of Religion, Politics and Religion,* and *Turkish Politics.* He is currently finishing a book project that examines psychological foundations of prejudice toward Muslims and its electoral implications.

Nazita Lajevardi is a political scientist and attorney. She is an assistant professor in the Department of Political Science at Michigan State University. Her work centers on issues related to race and ethnic politics, political behavior, and voting rights. Her research has appeared in the *Journal of Politics, American Political Science Review, Political Behavior, Journal of Race and Ethnic Politics, Politics and Religion,* and *Politics, Groups, and Identities.* She is an affiliated researcher with the CONPOL (Contexts, Networks, and Participation: The Social Logic of Political Engagement) project at Uppsala University.

Valerie Martinez-Ebers is a University Distinguished Research Professor and the director of Latino and Mexican American studies at the University of North Texas, as well as a former editor of the *American Political Science Review.* She specializes in the politics of race and ethnicity, especially Latino politics, and has published in all the top-ranked general interest journals in political science. Her book publications include *Latina Public Officials in Texas*; *Latino Lives in America: Making It Home*; *Latinos in the New Millennium: An Almanac of Opinion, Behavior and Policy Preferences*; and *Perspectives on Race, Ethnicity and Religion: Identity Politics in America.*

Danielle M. McLaughlin is a doctoral student in the Political Science Department at the University of Cincinnati. She is particularly interested in decision making, group behavior, and complex governance systems.

Anwar Mhajne is a postdoctoral teaching fellow at Stonehill College. She received her Ph.D. in political science from the University of Cincinnati, specializing in international relations and comparative politics with a focus on gender, politics, and religion. Her other research interests include feminist security studies, feminist international relations, democratization, governance and institutions, civil society, political Islam, the Middle East, and social movements.

Melissa R. Michelson (Ph.D.) is a professor of political science at Menlo College. She is coauthor of *Mobilizing Inclusion: Redefining Citizenship through Get-Out-the-Vote Campaigns* (2012), *Living the Dream: New Immigration Policies and the Lives of Undocumented Latino Youth* (2014), *Listen, We Need to Talk: How to Change Attitudes about LGBT Rights* (2017), and *A Matter of Discretion: The Politics of Catholic Priests in the United States and Ireland* (2017). She has published dozens of articles in peer-reviewed academic journals, including the *American Political Science Review, Journal of Politics,* and *International Migration Review.*

Yusuf Sarfati is an associate professor of politics and government at Illinois State University, where he teaches comparative politics of the Middle East. Sarfati's research interests revolve around religious politics, social movements, politics of culture and identity, and democratization. Sarfati's research appeared in various books, edited volumes, and journals, including *Turkish Studies, Journal of Language and Politics, Language Policy, and Critical Muslim.*

Ahmet Selim Tekelioglu is the editor of digital scholarship initiative the Maydan (https://www.themaydan.com) and an instructor at the Ali Vural Ak Center for Global Islamic Studies at George Mason University. He received his Ph.D. in political science from Boston University, where his dissertation focused on conversations about national and religious identity among American Muslim communities in Boston, the San Francisco Bay Area, and Los Angeles.

Marianne Marar Yacobian (Ed.D.) is a transnational educator-scholar. Her research interests include diaspora studies (particularly refugee human rights education), genocide recognition, social movements/revolution, and tribal collectivism. Yacobian is currently an associate professor of global studies at Menlo College.

Index

www.ingramcontent.com/pod-product-compliance
Lightning Source LLC
Chambersburg PA
CBHW050808270326
41926CB00026B/4633